D0908231

THE BRITISH DOCUMENTARY FILM MOVEMENT, 1926–1946

**CAMBRIDGE
STUDIES
IN FILM**

GENERAL EDITORS

Henry Breitrose, *Stanford University*
William Rothman

ADVISORY BOARD

Dudley Andrew, *University of Iowa*
Garth Jowett, *University of Texas at Houston*
Anthony Smith, *British Film Institute*
Colin Young, *National Film School*

OTHER BOOKS IN THE SERIES

Paul Clark, *Chinese Cinema: Culture and Politics since 1949*
Sergei Eisenstein, *Nonindifferent Nature: Film and the Structure of Things*
(trans. Herbert Marshall)
Vlada Petrić, *Constructivism in Film: The Man with the Movie Camera –
A Cinematic Analysis*
William Rothman, *The "I" of the Camera*

THE BRITISH DOCUMENTARY FILM MOVEMENT, 1926–1946

PAUL SWANN

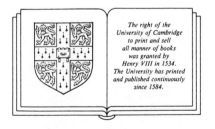

The right of the
University of Cambridge
to print and sell
all manner of books
was granted by
Henry VIII in 1534.
The University has printed
and published continuously
since 1584.

CAMBRIDGE UNIVERSITY PRESS
CAMBRIDGE
NEW YORK   NEW ROCHELLE   MELBOURNE   SYDNEY

Published by the Press Syndicate of the University of Cambridge
The Pitt Building, Trumpington Street, Cambridge CB2 1RP
32 East 57th Street, New York, NY 10022, USA
10 Stamford Road, Oakleigh, Melbourne 3166, Australia

First published in 1989

Printed in the United States of America

Library of Congress Cataloging-in-Publication Data

Swann, Paul.
The British documentary film movement, 1926–1946 / Paul Swann.
   p.   cm. – (Cambridge studies in film)
Bibliography: p.
Includes index.
ISBN 0-521-33479-9
1. Documentary films – Great Britain – History and criticism.
I. Title.   II. Series.
PN1995.9.D6S88   1989
791.43'53'0941 – dc19   88–25693

British Library Cataloguing-in-Publication Data
Swann, Paul
The British documentary film movement,
1926–1946. – (Cambridge studies in film).
1. British documentary films. 1926–1946
I. title
791.43'53

ISBN 0-521-33479-9

Contents

Preface

This book is a political and social history of the British documentary film movement. It investigates the development by John Grierson and his followers of the actuality-based film as a means of public education and as an art form. The activities of Grierson and his colleagues are the focus of this book, which is not a comprehensive history of British nonfiction film. This is not intended as an extended piece of formal film analysis, although inevitably a discussion of mode of production demands some explanation of style in specific films. Primarily this is an examination of how and why documentary films were made by the British government in the 1920s and 1930s, and how and why it went into the filmmaking business.

The production and distribution of these documentary films developed outside the commercial film industry. Politically, documentary filmmaking was tied to the civil servants in Whitehall rather than the politicians in Westminster. John Grierson's dealings with senior civil servants often figure more prominently in this narrative than the policies of whichever party was in power. Films were commissioned by government departments, semipublic bodies, and private enterprise concerns as direct or indirect publicity. Commercial renters and exhibitors generally declined to display these films, which they thought propaganda or unpaid advertisements, disliked by themselves and their audiences.

The question of audiences for documentary films in Britain is one I attempt to address. The state became involved in film production largely because of a belief that motion pictures could have an impact on a mass audience thought to be immune to other types of appeal. Recently, there has been some good work on the experience of the commercial cinema audiences in prewar Britain; however, there has been less interest in audiences for documentary films. Initially, officially sponsored documentary films were primarily targeted at commercial audiences, and when this policy produced mixed results, the emphasis shifted to nontheatrical audiences. It is difficult to gauge the numbers of people who saw officially sponsored documentary films in the interwar years and perhaps even harder to assess the effect these films may have had.

This history begins with the founding of the Empire Marketing Board in 1926. The Board took an immediate interest in film, which was then widely believed to be the most potent means of mass persuasion. There, Grierson gathered together the first recruits for his school of purposive filmmaking, which was subsequently called the "documentary movement."

The publicity methods developed by the Board, among which the use of documentary film was prominent, spread to many other government departments and outside bodies. The documentarists moved into independent production when Treasury sanctions threatened to limit severely the activities of documentary filmmakers directly employed by government departments.

During World War II, documentary filmmaking was centralized under official control at the Films Division of the Ministry of Information. The war led to a massive expansion of the opportunities and activities of the documentarists. My brief concludes with the abolition of the Ministry of Information in 1946.

This book is based upon a range of unpublished government documents, the Grierson papers at the University of Stirling, the Paul Rotha papers at the University of California, the cinema periodicals, and the film trade and lay press of the period.

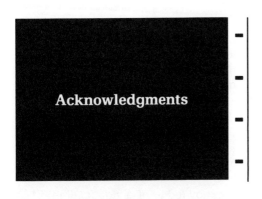

Acknowledgments

This book could not have been written without the constant encouragement and support of my former dissertation supervisor, Mr. Nicholas Pronay, senior reader in the University of Leeds. I will always be grateful to him for guiding my research and for his helpful comments during successive drafts of the manuscript. In addition, I must thank several of my colleagues at Temple University, specifically Calvin Pryluck and Jeanne Allen, both of whom went far beyond the reasonable limits of collegiality in responding to my requests for their reaction to the book in its various stages.

I am also indebted to Dr. Stephen Mamber of the University of California at Los Angeles and Dr. Philip Taylor of the University of Leeds. Both were very willing to share their knowledge of film and the history of the interwar years with me. Lady Margaret Elton kindly shared with me her personal recollections of John Grierson and the other documentarists. She also granted me access to the papers relating to the British documentary film kept at Clevedon Court. Mr. Godfrey Jennison, Films Officer for Shell-Mex and B.P., was most helpful in explaining the complex history of his company's sponsorship of documentary films.

I would like to thank the staff of the following institutions: the Paley Library, Temple University, the Public Records Office, the General Post Office Records Department, the British Film Institute, the National Film Archive, the Free Library (Philadelphia), the Brotherton Library at the University of Leeds, and the Research Library and Film Archive at the University of California at Los Angeles. They have been very helpful, courteous, and unstinting with their time and knowledge during my research. The staff of the Grierson Archive at the University of Stirling, the Lincoln Center for the Performing Arts, New York, and Hammersmith Public Library, London, also rendered me invaluable assistance.

All photographs are courtesy of the National Film Archive and reproduced with the permission of the British Post Office, British Gas, and the Central Office of Information.

Temple University generously awarded me a summer fellowship and grant in aid funds in 1984, which made it possible to complete the book. I am grateful for this financial support.

I would also like to thank Professor Henry Breitrose at Stanford University and Liz Maguire at Cambridge University Press for their unfailing support and encouragement during the later stages of this book. Michael Gnat, Joanne Burke, Lois Driver, and Ernestine Franco are also thanked for helping to edit the text.

I take full responsibility for any of the opinions and errors expressed in this book.

There are other debts I wish to acknowledge of a nonacademic but undoubtedly even more vital and instrumental nature. I must thank my mother for her constant moral support, and I wish she were still alive to see this thanks being expressed in print. My wife, Lisa Manheim, during the past decade has shown more understanding and given me more encouragement than I have had any right to expect. This book is dedicated to her and to our newborn son, Noah.

Paul Swann
Associate Professor, Communications

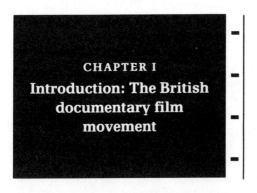

CHAPTER I

Introduction: The British documentary film movement

British filmmaking has been inextricably bound with actuality for almost as long as Hollywood has been associated with the fiction film. "Actuality" and "documentary" are terms as synonymous with Britain as neorealism is with Italy and the New Wave with France. Interestingly, all these trends were attempts to respond to the colonial control of the American film in their respective countries. Each, to coin a phrase that will be used extensively in the course of this book, was an exercise in national projection. The cinematic metaphor is an apt one. Filmmakers in each of these countries rejected the forms and content of American narrative film; yet at the same time they were very indebted to the American example and ensnared by American financial control. All this had to be jettisoned when these filmmakers aspired to build their own national film cultures and national film industries.

Many assessments of the British documentary film have been at great pains to explain the work of John Grierson and his protégés and rivals as a uniquely *British* accomplishment, one that paralleled similar work in journalism, painting, and photography in the 1930s. More recently, some cultural critics have sought to critique work in all of these areas, arguing that this effectively appropriated these forms for a fairly narrow, not to say élite, point of view.[1]

My concern in this book, under which I feel all this contemporary criticism can safely be subsumed, is in a series of relationships – administrative, ideological, and intellectual – between the state in Britain and the British documentary film. The United States is perhaps unique in the extent to which its film industry has been and remains controlled by private enterprise. Whatever forms private enterprise has assumed in the last century – and every type has been found in the film industry – it is safe to say that Hollywood is the only major film industry in the world not dependent on public funding. As I have argued elsewhere, the American government and Hollywood – a name that, following common practice, I see to stand for a whole host of technical accomplishments, a worldview, and an approach to narrative film form – have

1

invariably worked closely together.[2] They have never, however, had a relationship akin to that between the British film industry and the British government. This relationship has recently been the basis for an extended study of the British government's film policy, particularly with regards to financial affairs and an examination of the British government's attempts to protect and nurture a domestic film industry.[3]

The time frame for this study extends from the early 1920s until the conclusion of World War II. A central proposition will be the significance of intellectual links between British documentary theory and practice and American work in the areas not only of filmmaking but also public relations and commercial advertising praxis.

After World War I, the very nature of domestic politics in Britain was permanently changed. The state did not just govern – it also felt an obligation to consult and inform the people it governed. This conception of the work of the state as a two-way street between citizens and authority was very alien to British politics. As R. S. Lambert noted in his 1938 book on propaganda:

The change-over from the strictly limited function of nineteenth century government to the ubiquitous activities of twentieth century government has brought the Administration charged with these services face to face with problems of publicity which are wholly novel to it . . . the old policy of saying as little as possible to the public has proved inapplicable in the case of the newer, wider government and public utility enterprises, which have to make direct contact with the voter.[4]

During the 1920s, as a consequence of the arrival of universal suffrage and the growing extent to which government departments intervened in the lives of the general public, politicians, especially those on the right, were compelled to pay much greater attention to public opinion in Britain than they had previously. During World War I, the British government assumed control over new and wide-ranging areas of social and economic policy. The government's brief was no longer restricted primarily to foreign policy, which was traditionally of little interest to the majority of Britain's population. The vocabulary of democracy itself was new to British politics. Terms such as "general public" and "public opinion" implied a regard for the feelings of the general population very much at odds with the traditionally hierarchic nature of British politics. As Sir Stephen Tallents noted:

Today the state is always being called upon by Parliament to undertake new tasks of organization and to provide new services. At the same time Government has to win consent for its actions, and to secure assistance in carrying them out from a much greater electorate than even twenty years ago.[5]

Some politicians and many civil servants were quick to grasp the importance of modern methods of public relations for official ends. They were very impressed by the developments in this field in the United States, and were introduced to these new ideas in Walter Lippmann's influential work on the subject, *Public Opinion,* which went into its first British edition in 1922. This book prepared the way for John Grierson and others who imported American propaganda and public relations expertise into Britain in the 1920s.

John Grierson went to the United States on a Rockefeller scholarship in 1924. There, he was one of a number of Scots who became keenly interested in the methods of mass persuasion that had been developed by big business and the United States government during the war. John Grierson, John Reith, and the advertising magnate, William Crawford, were all Scots of Presbyterian upbringing who noted the manner in which public opinion functioned in the United States. It would be misleading to draw too many parallels between Reith and Grierson. The American influence was by no means as vital for Reith's work in the mass media as it was for Grierson. Reith went to the United States to supervise armaments production in the Remington works. There, he was soon drawn into the extensive public speaking circuit, which, as Charles Stuart has noted, "afforded him opportunities to exercise his powers of moral leadership."[6]

This was an experience curiously similar to Grierson's own background. As a university student pursuing a degree in moral philosophy, Grierson took the opportunity to preach in nearby churches on a regular basis. Some of the lessons he read there are preserved in the Grierson Archive at Stirling University. Reith's visit preceded the massive use of publicity by the American government during the war, however, and he therefore was denied the opportunity to become familiar with these developments. Grierson and Reith were both drawn by missionary zeal to the mass media, which they anticipated employing in an inspirational manner.

Many more comparisons can be made between John Grierson and William Crawford. Crawford headed one of the largest and most progressive advertising agencies in Great Britain. Significantly, during the interwar years, he was frequently called upon to serve on advisory bodies relating to official publicity and public relations in Great Britain. Although they served in different capacities and at very different levels, the paths of Grierson and Crawford crossed fairly often. They were just two of the many Scots and Scots Canadians who exercised an inordinate amount of control over the British mass media in the interwar years.

The religious background of both men affected their experience in the United States. Commentaries on the two men often employed strikingly similar language. It was noted of Crawford, for example:

He allies the zeal of a covenantor with the faith of the prophet, and, with Scottish fanaticism tempered with Glaswegian common sense, he preaches the educational mission of the advertiser and the necessity for modernism in publicity.[7]

Gervas Huxley commented on Crawford's work as a member of the Empire Marketing Board that "his approach to advertising was inspirational rather than logical."[8] Similar charges were frequently leveled at Grierson throughout his career. In the field of advertising, Crawford introduced many American publicity and public relations techniques. He strongly believed in market research and in "scientific" advertising, which was based on "the engineering of consent."[9] He maintained that public education was the basis of good public relations and as he once commented, "advertising is education. It makes people think. And thinking leads to action."[10]

Roland Marchand has noted that American advertising men in the 1920s wanted responsibility and respectability and to dissociate their profession's ties from its origins in promoting snake oil and patent medicines. Consequently, American advertising agencies were inclined in one of two philosophical directions: They emphasized either their professionalism and commitment to the client or their public service work and their representation of the interests of the consumer. In many respects, as Marchand notes, these positions were mutually exclusive. Public service became part of the domain of the advertising agencies in the United States, and to a much lesser extent, in Great Britain, during World War I. Then, as Daniel Pope has argued, the advertising profession illustrated that it could be used responsibly and for patriotic goals.[11]

In the course of World War I, the advertising profession developed a belief that it had a special responsibility to the American public. As Marchand puts it:

Advertising agents constantly spoke of the consuming public as a constituency. They shouldered a dual responsibility: to determine the wants of their constituents, and then to propose new or improved products to the manufacturer who could satisfy those wants.[12]

The American advertising agencies were very prompt in pressing modern art into service. All the modernist art movements of the interwar period were quickly appropriated and incorporated into commercial advertising copy. In this respect, Crawford was no different than his American contemporaries. He also believed that the artist had a key part to play as the translator of advertisers' ideas to the general public.

Crawford was instrumental in spreading thoroughly modern ideas about publicity and public relations within official circles in Great Britain. He was an important member of both the Empire Marketing Board and the Post Office Publicity Committee and acted as publicity advisor to the Ministry of Agriculture, the Ministry of Health, and the National Savings Movement. He was also a member of the Art in Industry Council. Everywhere he played a part in obtaining acceptance for the idea of using documentary films as publicity. Crawford's career evidenced the manner

Figure 1. The young John Grierson.

in which Scots passion for proselytizing found expression through the
new techniques of mass persuasion. In the case of John Grierson, it is
equally clear that ideas and an outlook forged within the Scottish intellectual and religious tradition were reshaped by first hand experience of
developments in publicity and public relations in the United States.

John Grierson believed in the individual fulfilling his or her social
obligations. He thought, very much in a nineteenth-century liberal way,
that ruling élites had a commitment to inform and educate those over
whom they held "stewardship." Yet at the same time, this idea was analo-
gous to the philosophy evolving 3,000 miles away, across the Atlantic.
For Grierson, this notion was bedded in his upbringing as deeply as in
his own intellectual position. Grierson was an élitist with populist incli-

nations throughout his life. He was able to articulate his perspective long before any involvement with government departments or film production. As a young university student he was given the opportunity to preach before the congregations of local kirks. In one early sermon delivered in 1920, which addressed some of the themes he would return to again and again during his career – the problems of making large-scale democracy work – he had noted:

Perfecting the world is not an easy thing but it demands all the hardness of hard thinking . . . and it is not the thinking of the few but the thinking of everyone that is needed. And that is because everyone of us have to make decisions and judgments and to get anywhere we have to make them right judgments. When you think of it the whole well-being of the country depends on how each one of us votes.[13]

He recognized the difficulties facing anyone who attempted to undertake the education necessary to enable everyone to take part in decision making. In the United States, Grierson found theorists and practitioners who formulated the same question in political terms. There, as Forsyth Hardy noted:

Men like Walter Lippmann were saying at the time that the older expectations of democratic education were impossible since they appeared to require that the ordinary citizen should know every detail of public affairs as they developed from moment to moment.[14]

Grierson and Crawford had both been grounded in an intellectual tradition in which art and cultural production could only be conceived as purposive and functional, not ends in themselves. Grierson's fellow countryman, Thomas Baird, once noted that Scotland had never had the same division between bourgeois "bookish" culture and the popular culture of the masses that existed in England. He noted that there was "less gulf between the culture of the gentleman and the leisure of the worker" in Scotland.[15] Art and culture could therefore be thought of as communication between classes. This was completely outside the English intellectual tradition. In England "culture" was jealously guarded by the intellectuals who anxiously watched the development of mass "Woolworth" culture among the ordinary vulgar people during the 1920s and 1930s. As a prominent representative of this English intellectual tradition, Frank Leavis felt compelled to comment, on the advance of what was, for him, an abhorrent mass culture, that "civilization and culture are coming to be antithetical terms."[16] One of the many contradictions about John Grierson was that although he believed art and culture were potentially a means of universal communication, he remained a devotee of the "high" art that gave rise to Leavis's lament.

Grierson and his biographer gave credit to Walter Lippmann for the inspiration that the cinema might prove to be the art form and mass medium capable of undertaking the mass education they both advocated. Before he became familiar with Lippmann, however, Grierson was almost certainly alerted to the political possibilities of the cinema by his study of Lenin. Lenin had been very conscious of the persuasive power of the cinema, so much so that in 1922 he noted that, "of all the arts, for us the cinema is the most important."[17] In his early reports for the Empire Marketing Board and the Inter-Departmental Committee on Trade Propaganda and Advertisement, Grierson was prompt to note Lenin's belief in "the power of film for ideological propaganda."[18] Grierson's great innovation was to adapt this revolutionary dictum to the purposes of social democracy.

In America, Grierson was very impressed by the power exercised by two of the mass media, the yellow press and the cinema. He noted that both reached out to precisely those social groups immune to traditional forms of exhortation. Tabloid newspapers and motion pictures were both forms of expression unabashedly aimed at a mass audience. They were anathema to the traditional intellectual aristocracies in both Great Britain and the United States. In Europe they were regarded as primarily American phenomena. Yet Grierson was by no means alone in believing that both could be utilized for serious ends. Cinema, he wrote for an American film trade magazine in 1926, had a unique capacity for uplift:

The modern multitude craves a release from the everyday as all other multitudes before it. It craves participation in a world where dreams come true, where life is more free, more powerful, more pungent, more obviously dramatic . . . In the meanwhile, the old folk worlds, the worlds of established heroes and familiar heroes are so dead and so distant that the multitude have lost touch with them and the imagination of the average people are [sic] without a sticking point.[19]

Grierson was appalled, however, at the manner in which Hollywood and the fiction feature film met this demand. As he noted elsewhere:

In an age when the faiths, the loyalties and the purposes have been more than usually undermined, mental fatigue – or is it spiritual fatigue – represents a large factor in everyday experience. Our cinema magnate does no more than exploit the occasion. He also, more or less frankly, is a dope pedlar.[20]

Grierson believed that Hollywood's imperatives were purely commercial, not moral or artistic. He always argued that this had a detrimental effect on the way films were made there:

There are too many cooks and they spoil the broth . . . They don't pull together. A picture has to be a composite effort granted, but the spirit of co-operation is not developed to the point of producing consistently good things. Then again, people are too haphazard in the making of pictures, too scrappy. Above all, they are not serious enough. They are energetic enough, but in the real sense of the term they are not serious enough.[21]

Grierson, in common with all those who hoped to appropriate motion pictures for moral and spiritual uplift, was gravely disappointed with the fiction film. He retained his conviction, however, that "it is the destiny of cinema to be the source of imaginative release and everyday inspiration for the common people of the world."[22] In this he was joined by many social and cultural critics who believed that the film was untainted by association with highbrow culture. The cinéaste movement and other attempts to intellectualize the motion picture argued that occasionally great artists such as Flaherty, Chaplin, and Von Sternberg were able to produce films that yielded these qualities within the Hollywood system. Generally, however, Grierson believed, the purposive and inspirational film had to come from outside the commercial film industry.

Russian cinema in the 1920s and the early work of Robert Flaherty suggested alternatives to Hollywood for Grierson. Russian cinema was remarkable in many ways in the 1920s. It was a unique fusion of theory and practice in stark contrast to the American commercial cinema, where theory and practice in film almost never mixed. Soviet filmmakers had also dedicated themselves to political education rather than to entertainment. Furthermore, they were civil servants working for the state, not for commercial studios. Lev Kuleshov's unique state film school, Dziga Vertov's experiments with restructuring actuality, Eisenstein's attempts to dramatize actuality, and the nationalization of the film industry in Russia all had a profound influence upon the evolution of the ideology and organization of the British documentary film.

Robert Flaherty's work in ethnographic film was equally important to Grierson, but for very different reasons. Flaherty's romanticization of third-world cultures in films like *Nanook of the North* (1922) and *Moana* (1925) was very different from the Russian attempts to blend modernistic art and contemporary social and political change. Grierson was impressed by Flaherty's use of actuality for his films rather than scripted fiction. He was also intrigued by the manner in which Flaherty financed his first film, *Nanook of the North,* outside the commercial industry. Flaherty had obtained funding from the furriers, Revillon Frères. Furthermore, the film had actually done fairly well in commercial exhibition and in international release. As Grierson noted, *Nanook* "was in the first place an advertisement for furs, though it appeared in theaters all over the world as a straightforward epic of Eskimo life."[23]

Subsequently, Grierson often noted how Flaherty's artistry was compromised when he attempted to work with the commercial film industry. He felt Flaherty's *Moana* and *Man of Aran* (1934) were both debased when the film industry attempted to sell them as ordinary commercial feature films. As Grierson noted about Flaherty's films and Hollywood: "They have been all too novel for a showmanship built on garish spectacle and a red-hot presentation of the latest curves."[24] Ultimately, Grierson found Flaherty's idylls of "the noble savage" as escapist as fiction film make-believe. Initially, however, Flaherty's films served to suggest to Grierson that the creative and dramatic interpretation of actuality was an alternative form of cinematic expression to commercial feature film.

Grierson found actuality wedded to purposive filmmaking in the work of Sergei Eisenstein and some of the other leading Russian filmmakers. In New York, for example, he prepared the subtitles of the English edition of Eisenstein's *Battleship Potemkin* (1925). The film had perhaps a greater impact upon Grierson's work than any other film; certainly it is the one upon which his own *Drifters* (1929) was most dependent. He wrote one of the first analyses in English of the use of montage in *Potemkin* for the film trade press in the United States.[25] The Russian filmmakers' approach to their material, and in particular, their use of editing to "dramatize" were a profound influence upon the early Griersonian documentary film. Grierson owed a great theoretical and artistic debt to Russian cinema, which he never denied.

Grierson was enthralled by the manner in which the state in Russia controlled the mechanism of film production. Russian filmmaking in the 1920s was an exciting mixture of formal experiment and dedicated political activism. Films were intended to raise the consciousness of their viewers – not to lull them into escapist fantasies. Furthermore, filmmakers worked directly for the state, which, Grierson noted, was radically different from how the film industry operated in the United States. He constantly drew official attention to this instance of how both cinema and the state benefited from government control of the means of film production:

The secret of Russian success in this field is due to the constant governmental drive (in state controlled production units) in favour of propaganda and to a certain freshness of technical approach which this limitation of genre forced on the film artists. By new-found devices of editing and photography they have been able to add dramatic emphasis to what might seem intractable and dull everyday material.[26]

Drawing upon the Russian example, Grierson always subsequently looked to the state rather than the film industry for support and finance for his work. The early style of the documentary film in Britain also owed much to the Russian example. Many of the first British documentary films, those made in the late 1920s and early 1930s, essentially mimicked the forms and content of Russian montage and heroic worker stereotypes. In many ways Grierson's own *Drifters* did this.

Grierson returned from North America to Britain in January 1927. He had gathered together, from his upbringing in Scotland, his experiences in the United States, and his reading of writers as diverse as Lenin and Lippmann, Kant and John Stuart Mill, the intellectual basis for his life's work in communications and public service. He returned to a country already keenly aware of the persuasive possibilities of film. Michael Biddiss has commented of the Europe of the 1920s and 1930s that, "the political relevance of the cinema was most urgently clear to those who supervised cinematic activity in totalitarian settings."[27] It is true that the Soviet and Nazi governments were both very prompt to engage the film industry in their countries. In Britain in the 1920s, many groups were as conscious of the political relevance of film as the governments in these totalitarian countries. This awareness sprang from the fact that the British film industry, unlike that of Russia and Germany, was completely dominated by the film industry of another country.

By the mid-1920s the British feature film industry had yielded completely to American domination. The United States achieved ascendancy over the indigenous film industries of virtually every country during World War I. In Britain this became a chronic condition that has persisted until the present day. American film companies had a major stake in British renting interests. Britain was the single biggest source of overseas revenue for the American film industry, accounting for 35 percent of its overseas earnings. In fact, 95 percent of all films shown in Britain at that time were American. Widespread concern about the adverse effects of American films on British and Empire cinema screens produced a prolonged public debate and led ultimately to the 1927 Cinematograph Films Act. The system of quotas that the Act introduced had a slight effect. The British film industry did revive somewhat in the 1930s. Even so, during the supposed revival of the British film industry, attributed to Michael Balcon, Alexander Korda, Max Schach, and others in the 1930s, American films still accounted for over 70 percent of the films shown in British cinemas.[28] This figure exaggerates the British recovery. Many of the British films were "quota quickies": films made as cheaply as the law would allow, to be displayed so that renters and exhibitors could fulfill their legal obligations to show British films. These films were often shown when the cinemas were empty; when full, they would be given programs consisting of American feature films.[29]

The 1927 Cinematograph Films Act was the result of the furor during the previous five years about the American domination of British and Empire cinema screens. In addition to agitation from the British film industry, commercial trade interests feared the effect upon their business of the indirect propaganda carried in these films.[30] After its use in a speech by the Prince of Wales in 1923, the phrase "trade follows the film" became a common one in public debate throughout the 1920s. There was also widespread concern over the submergence of national habits and culture beneath those of another country. These interests demanded that something be done to wrest control of the British cinema from the United States because "one of the most powerful instruments of national publicity and propaganda can no longer be left in Alien hands."[31] The campaign for protection for the British film industry alerted the ruling élites to the influence of film. Its great power was believed to reside in reaching and affecting those people not touched by the traditional forms of political communication. Motion pictures were widely thought to be a universal form of language. R. S. Lambert expressed this position:

The moving picture is a far more powerful instrument for influencing thought than the printed word or the spoken word. For even a backward mind can grasp a picture, where it could not comprehend a newspaper article or remember a spoken message clearly.[32]

The Conservative party quickly acted upon its newfound conviction about the effectiveness of film as publicity. Conservative politicians found that although exhibitors tended to be sympathetic toward their views, they were not prepared to lend their cinema screens to partisan propaganda of an explicit nature. It was considered sound commercial sense not to alienate any part of the audience that might be offended by publicity of this type. It was also thought that audiences paid for entertainment, not propaganda. As *Kine Weekly* commented:

Exhibitors of this country have a very well-understood rule that politics on the screen should be absolutely taboo . . . while the public pays for entertainment the man who lends his aid to any political propaganda is committing a direct breach of faith.[33]

The Conservative party therefore had to approach the public outside the cinemas. In April 1926, the National Unionist Association began experiments with a small fleet of cinema vans, showing specially made films in conjunction with public speakers. *The Times* watched this development with much interest:

The Conservative Party are now making use of the cinematograph regularly in propaganda work. Political propaganda seems to be the thin end of the wedge, the other end of which may be national propaganda.[34]

From this time onward, the Conservative party remained acutely aware of the political influence of films.[35]

Direct government intervention into the affairs of the film industry in Britain during the interwar years consisted primarily of the 1927 and 1938 Cinematograph Film Acts. The intention of both these pieces of legislation was to build a strong and independent film industry, which was the very antithesis of the direct state control of the industry employed in the totalitarian countries. Successive British governments steadfastly rejected the idea of a state-run film industry. For example, the possibility of state control arose when Isidore Ostrer offered his controlling interest in the Gaumont–British Picture Corporation to the government in 1931, but the Board of Trade rejected the suggestion.[36] Instead of conspicuous links between the film industry and the government, there were many discreet connections between senior political figures and the leaders of the British film industry. The Conservative party had very extensive contacts of this type. Figures like Alexander Korda also went to great lengths to be accepted into the circles of men like Churchill and Lord Vansittart.[37]

National film publicity was generally recognized as being important in the mid-1920s, yet there were no attempts to erect government control of film production or exhibition. Some government departments therefore began to pay attention to the question of film publicity themselves. Within some departments, there was an initial prejudice against the practice of publicity. There was a belief, as Sir Stephen Tallents himself once put it, that

there is something a little discreditable in government publicity – that it is apt, for example, to be pursued as a substitute for efficient work, or that it must always be mixed up with personal advertisement.[38]

The first departments to overcome this prejudice were those with an interest in trade and industry. Agencies such as the Department of Overseas Trade, and its offspring, the Empire Marketing Board and the Travel and Industrial Development Association, were all early devotees of film publicity. They provided the original source of patronage and support for John Grierson and the British documentary film. The inroads being made into British and Empire trade as a result of the indirect propaganda of American films led to discussion of the subject at successive Imperial Conferences. This examination of film as trade propaganda soon led to discussion about the persuasive power of film in general. As the 1926 Imperial Conference General Economic Sub-Committee on Films noted:

The importance and far-reaching influence of the cinema are now generally recognized. The cinema is not merely a form of entertainment but, in addition, a powerful instrument of education in the widest sense of that term, and, even where it is not used avowedly for purposes of instruction, advertisement or propaganda, it exercises indirectly a great influence in shaping the ideas of the very large numbers to whom it appeals. Its potentialities in this respect are almost unlimited.[39]

From the initial and very specific concerns with trade publicity, there developed the belief that film could be utilized for other publicity purposes. It was used by several of the government departments that had extensive dealings with the public, in particular, the Post Office and the Ministries of Labour and Health. Sir Stephen Tallents provided the first opportunity for Grierson and the documentary film at the Empire Marketing Board, which was the first official body to take up many of the imported publicity and public relations practices. When the Board was abolished in 1933, its public relations expertise was dispersed among a number of public, semipublic, and private concerns. Tallents went to the Post Office, where he became its first public relations officer. The Post Office subsequently became the unlikely official authority on public relations, and particularly the use of film publicity. His colleagues took their expertise elsewhere. Gervas Huxley went to the Ceylon Tea Propaganda Board, and A. P. Ryan was recruited by the Gas, Light and Coke Company to set up a public relations department. Significantly, both men went on to enjoy long careers in public relations and official publicity. After the Tea Board, Huxley was appointed as adviser on Empire publicity and had special responsibility for relations with the American forces in Britain at the Ministry of Information. Ryan had an equally distinguished career with the British Broadcasting Corporation and the Ministry of Information.

John Grierson founded a school of filmmaking within an apparently very fertile atmosphere. British officials, politicians, and many industrialists were already convinced that, as Philip Cunliffe-Lister, the President of the Board of Trade put it, "the cinema is today the most universal means through which national ideas and national atmosphere can be spread."[40] When he began his association with the Empire Marketing Board, Grierson initially had some very powerful supporters. Cunliffe-Lister, who was then in the process of framing the 1927 Cinematograph Films Act, thought Grierson's first reports on film propaganda for the Empire Marketing Board "really very interesting indeed."[41] Leo Amery, John Buchan, and many others concerned about national publicity were equally impressed with Grierson's early work for the Empire Marketing Board.[42] Grierson's patrons tended to come from the ranks of the civil service, rather than the political parties. Many other public servants joined Tallents in supporting Grierson's work. Sir Arnold Wilson, chairman of the Board of Trade Advisory Committee on Film in the 1930s for example, compared British documentary films favorably with the commercially made fiction film.[43] Rowland Kenney, a member of the staff of the News Department of the Foreign Office, made certain that there was always an interest there in the use of documentary films as overseas publicity.

Private enterprise generally remained faithful to the tried and trusted methods of commercial advertising. Many of the major companies manufacturing consumer items such as liquor, tobacco, and candy spent heavily upon motion picture commercials, which were shown in regular theatrical screenings. This form of advertising was pioneered in Great Britain, because British film exhibitors were generally willing to show paid commercial advertising, whereas their American counterparts rarely did.

However, there were also many large concerns that were difficult to market in the same way as candy and cigarettes. Public utility companies, for example, were in general more preoccupied with corporate image building rather than expanding the market for their product. One way of doing this was to associate corporate policy with public education and benevolent public planning. There were some publicly owned concerns that found it necessary to engage in the new public relations methods. Under the guidance of A. P. Ryan, for example, the gas industry began sponsoring a series of films addressing a wide variety of social issues including poor housing, pollution, malnutrition, and education. In all these films, the gas industry was linked to liberal solutions to improve housing, education, and the general level of nutrition. The intention was to associate the industry with a modern, socially progressive image. As Sir David Milne-Watson, Governor of the Gas, Light and Coke Company explained, the industry had

produced a programme of films, designed not primarily to achieve commercial ends, but rather to awaken in the public mind a more enlightened consciousness of the social significance of our work in providing a vital necessity.[44]

Production and distribution of the British documentary film relied upon support from government departments and agencies such as the gas industry. It developed in almost complete independence from the commercial film industry. Grierson definitely wanted production to take place in officially controlled units. He was less certain about distribution and exhibition and at first was optimistic about the prospects of officially produced documentary films in regular commercial release. Throughout this period, Grierson's productions were only rarely taken up by the commercial renters and exhibitors. Ironically, the British actuality film was one of the few profitable parts of the film industry. In the 1920s, H. Bruce Woolfe's British Instructional Films Company was responsible for many types of commercially successful actuality films. Perhaps the company's greatest success was the excellent cine-biology series, *The Secrets of Nature.* Andrew Buchanan's pioneering efforts with the compilation of actuality material in magazine form in his long-running *Ideal Cinemagazine* had a comparable commercial success. Grierson gave fulsome praise to the popular manner in which Buchanan handled his films:

Mr. Buchanan, whatever his ultimate ambition, must impose the flash of entertainment on everything he touches. Working with very similar matter, he must be amusing or exciting or novel in his treatment. He is, in fact, the one member of our documentary school who has translated industry and commerce and community into the widest terms of public circulation and public appreciation.[45]

Exhibitors and renters developed an entrenched hostility toward the Griersonian documentary film. For a number of reasons, it was generally felt within the film trade that cinema audiences did not want serious information films when they went to the cinema. The trade was protecting its own interests when it decided not to book films of this type. For example, *BBC: The Voice of Britain* (Legg, 1935) was the most expensive and lavish documentary film made in Britain before World War II. It was made with a deliberately popular approach to make it acceptable to commercial audiences. T. H. Fligelstone, President of the Cinematograph Exhibitors Association, commented to the Moyne Committee, however, that he was pleased that a rival company had had the misfortune to book the film, which did very poorly in the cinemas.[46] The few documentaries that did receive great popular success, such as *Night Mail* (Watt and Wright, 1936) and *North Sea* (Watt, 1938), were not, significantly, of the straightforward pedagogical type of film, but were much more humanistic, and most important perhaps, employed narrative devices such as scripted dialogue, studio sets, and conventional dramatic development and resolution, which engaged viewers like regular commercial motion pictures.

The predicament of short films in general, and of documentary films in particular, was exacerbated by changes in film booking and display practices in the 1930s. Competition between the major film renters and cinema circuits led to the introduction of the double-feature program. The display of two feature length films in the same cinema program left little room for anything other than a newsreel. The Short Films Committee of the Cinematograph Films Council discovered that by 1939, only one-third of the country's cinemas still carried single-feature programs. It also found that cinemas that carried double features devoted only 2.25 percent of their screen time to short films.[47] The market for short films in the commercial cinema disappeared during the 1930s. Sponsored documentary production was affected by this disappearance less than the commercial production of short films, which had flourished in the 1920s. As Bruce Woolfe commented:

The production of high quality British shorts has only been made possible by the existence of sponsors, who finance films wholly or in part. Both industrial, commercial or official bodies commission a film and the producer has no financial dependence on its distribution.[48]

This did not alter the fact, however, that the market for short films was steadily shrinking during the 1930s. Exhibitors had never had much respect for short films, which were regarded as mere "fill ups" for their programs. As Grierson noted for the Moyne Committee:

The exhibitor is mostly interested in what pulls his audience, and shorts do not, in any theatres, except in very special circumstances, pull on the audience . . . I might cite the notorious case . . . from Birmingham, of a man who ordered 24 of the worst shorts because he maintained they cleared his audiences quickly![49]

The double-feature policy meant that exhibitors had even less interest in and time for short films than previously.

Documentary films were also at a disadvantage under the terms of the 1927 Cinematograph Films Act, which gave them no protection, for documentary films generally did not count for quota purposes. If an exhibitor showed such films, he took up time in his program that could more profitably be used to display films that could be counted against American films to fulfill quota commitments. The 1938 Cinematograph Films Act introduced separate quotas for short films, for which documentary films were eligible. The onset of the war, however, makes it impossible to assess what the impact of this legislation would have been in peacetime. Given the continuing popularity of the double feature, it would most likely not have made a great difference to the position of the documentary film in the commercial cinema.

The failure of the documentary film in commercial release led Grierson and his colleagues to emphasize the advances they were making in nontheatrical distribution. Grierson maintained that a large and important audience was growing outside the commercial cinemas in the 1930s. By 1939, his colleague, Thomas Baird, was claiming annual nontheatrical audiences of ten million.[50] The impetus for this development again came from the United States and Canada. Grierson was very impressed by the extent of nontheatrical distribution in both these countries. This development in Britain was made possible by the introduction of relatively inexpensive and reliable 16mm sound projection equipment in the early 1930s.

Grierson surrounded himself with a small coterie whom he trained and tutored in the art of purposive filmmaking. This group came to call themselves, and remain known as the British documentary movement. At the heart of this movement were a small number of young middle- and upper-class people who fell under the spell of Grierson's personality and ideology. The most prominent members of this group were Basil Wright, Arthur Elton, Edgar Anstey, and Stuart Legg. Paul Rotha was an associate of this clique, but was not a member. He accepted wholeheartedly Grierson's ideology, and with the publication of the first edition of his *Documentary Film* in 1935 became widely recognized as the leading protagonist of documentary after Grierson himself. He was unable, however, to accept the absolute obedience and discipline that Grierson expected from his followers.

Another section within the movement consisted of filmmakers who were committed to Grierson's policies and ideas only while he exerted authority over them. The most important members of this group consisted of Alberto Cavalcanti and his protégés, Harry Watt and Humphrey Jennings. These filmmakers became important when they inherited control of the General Post Office Film Unit in the later 1930s. Cavalcanti then directed film production there toward different ends from those envisaged by Grierson.

This group of filmmakers, who constituted the documentary movement, were linked loosely by their varying degrees of allegiance to Grierson. They were joined much more tightly by the fact that they all worked outside the commercial film industry. Their time with Grierson was in many respects an experience similar to going to film school, combining on-the-job training, minimal pay, and an apprenticeship system. Like the New Wave filmmakers a quarter century later, Grierson's protégés tended to be drawn from the membership rolls of the fledgling cinéaste and film society groups. Similar groups provided recruits for a variety of surrealist and experimental efforts in France, Germany, and the United States. In Britain also, many of the documentarists' first efforts could be broadly characterized as avant-garde activity. However, nowhere else was there an individual like Grierson capable of educating and pushing filmmakers and civil servants alike. Yet in many ways, Grierson's development of film as a tool of persuasion and education used, in the first instance, by the state, paralleled developments in other countries. Russia led the way in state-controlled purposive filmmaking. Grierson and Britain were not the only ones to follow. As Erik Barnouw notes: "The politicizing of documentary was not a Grierson innovation but a world phenomenon, a product of the times."[51] In many parts of the world, the development of the actuality film in the 1920s and 1930s took place under government auspices. In some countries, development was closely related to central government policy, as in Russia and Germany; in others, it took place as a result of the initiative of individual government departments.

Internationally, the use of actuality film for ideological ends was linked to a general and growing awareness among governments of the potential power of film. For filmmakers, the decision to participate in this type of work was the result of the urgency that permeated virtually all cultural endeavor during the 1920s and 1930s. M. D. Biddiss has noted how Walter Benjamin distinguished between the efforts of the fascists to render politics aesthetic and the communists' intention of politicizing art. Biddess goes on to point out that the extremists were not alone in recruiting culture for political causes:

Those who were not sympathetic towards either camp tended to see less crucial difference between these two aims than he; but even they were having to treat as redundant luxury any form of cultural activity that was not somehow engaged in promoting political values, albeit of a more moderate kind.[52]

The development of the British documentary film was part of this growing ideological use of film in general and actuality film in particular. Only in Britain, however, did the filmmakers envisage their efforts as being part of a movement. They conceived of themselves as a clearly defined school, working within a particular art form, working toward common ends, and, initially at least, with a common leader. This notion of a movement was also an aspect of the elaborate publicity strategy that the group employed to ensure its own survival. Discussing and publicizing the work of filmmakers as part of something greater than the efforts of individual artists gave it added stature. The idea of a documentary movement has influenced subsequent efforts to provide a history of the documentary film in Britain in the 1930s and the 1940s.

The members of this movement and the ideals they associated with it were, with the exception of heretics like Alberto Cavalcanti and Harry Watt, fiercely loyal to their leader, to each other, and to their cause. They manufactured an image for the movement that has gone largely unchallenged. A number of accounts of the documentary film in Britain have been produced by members of the documentary movement, including Rotha's *Documentary Film* and The Arts Enquiry's *The Factual Film*.[53] These works were not intended as straightforward accounts of the development of the documentary film in Britain. *The Factual Film,* particularly, was intended, by the manner in which it lauded the accomplishments of documentary filmmakers during the war, to add to the prestige of the documentary movement.

In more recent accounts, survivors of the documentary movement have remained faithful to their colleagues and their cause. In their reminiscences, Basil Wright, Paul Rotha, and Harry Watt reiterated the image of the documentary movement they created in the 1920s.[54] They present a picture of a group of dedicated and idealistic filmmakers subjected to "hard work and intense application . . . long hours and low wages."[55] Grierson is portrayed as a messianic figure, constantly at war with the civil service's "gruesome gnomes,"[56] who had to be made, much against their wishes, to provide the necessary wherewithal for filmmaking. Forsyth Hardy presents an equally heroic account of their leader in his biography of Grierson.

Hardy has continued to play Grierson's Boswell. His biography of Grierson is a very useful contribution to the literature. Accompanying this biography was a new edition of *Grierson on Documentary*, a selection of Grierson's own writings edited by Hardy. It is interesting that this is the nearest thing we have to a volume written by Grierson himself. Although a prodigious writer, he never produced a book-length synthesis of his own thoughts. This was partly because of the way in which Grierson's many articles, written for the film trade press, for highbrow and specialist journals of all kinds, and for newspapers, were often 'stimulated by the heat of specific campaigns, so it is difficult to visualize them as the systematic laying out and articulation of Grierson's own position. We badly need a full bibliography of Grierson's writings.

Several writers coming from outside the documentary clique have also produced accounts of the documentary movement. Both Elizabeth Sussex and Eva Orbanz have produced works that rely almost completely upon the edited reminiscences of the survivors of the documentary movement.[57] Of necessity, these accounts contain many of the shortcomings of the works produced by the survivors themselves. Many of the assumptions of the survivors of the movement are allowed to go unchallenged.

Perhaps the gravest fault has been to continue to emphasize the role of Grierson at the expense of others. Paul Rotha has particularly suffered from neglect resulting from this tendency to concentrate upon the work of Grierson. Orbanz has gone some way to correcting this situation, but Rotha has still not been given full credit for his contribution. He was, after all, as Alan Lovell notes, "director and producer as well as critic, historian and theorist of the cinema, whose contribution was just as varied as Grierson's."[58]

Another group of writers have subjected the British documentary film to serious aesthetic analysis. Alan Lovell and Jim Hillier investigated the work of the documentary movement in relation to the development of film art. Andrew Tudor has produced a very interesting analysis of the film theory and aesthetics that he feels underlay the British documentary film.[59] Both these works have made useful contributions to an understanding of the ideology and aesthetics of the documentary movement. They have made no pretense to be comprehensive histories of the documentary movement. There have also been a number of close textual readings of specific films made by members of the documentary movement, especially those made by Humphrey Jennings. Less attention has been given to the historical and cultural context within which the British documentary film initially evolved.

Rachel Low has performed an important task in systematically tracing the major films produced by the companies that specialized in documentary and educational film production in pre-World War II Britain. Her two volumes, *Films of Comment and Persuasion of the 1930s* and *Documentary and Educational Films of the 1930s*, are the closest thing we have to an encyclopedic listing and assessment of the actuality films made in Britain in the interwar years.[60]

This account, based largely on unpublished government papers, examines the problems and issues surrounding state involvement in film production, publicity, and patronage of the arts that emerged with government sponsorship of documentary film. My brief is the state-funded actuality film made in peacetime, with some reference to commercially sponsored films and the effects of the state-funding tradition during World War II. In Britain, the links between the state and documentary film production were largely forged by one man – John Grierson, who spent over a decade during the interwar years in public service in this field. In many ways he dictated the terms for discussion of state film production and distribution. Traditionally, it has been argued that Grierson literally sold documentary to unwilling and uninterested civil servants who were ill-equipped to appreciate Grierson's position. The documents suggest a quite different story. Grierson encountered a wide range of reactions to his proposals for state filmmaking, but rarely outright hostility or antipathy. He was ambitious, in a hurry, and often unsympathetic to the needs and procedures of a bureaucracy, and this attitude and the actions it engendered found their way into the committee minutes, memoranda, and correspondence that survive in the official files.

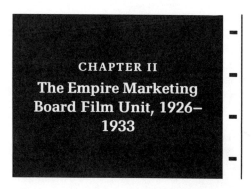

It was a department among departments, and part of a very much larger scheme of educational and propaganda services. Whatever its pretensions in purely cinematic terms, it was dedicated and devoted to the usual cold-blooded ends of government.[1]

The Empire Marketing Board (EMB) was set up under the auspices of the Dominions Office in May 1926. The creation of the Board was a result of the electorate's rejection of Conservative party proposals for preferential tariffs at the 1923 General Election. When Prime Minister Stanley Baldwin returned to power in 1924, he regarded himself as pledged not to introduce tariffs. Meanwhile, the continuing economic depression made the trade and industrial problems of the Empire all the more pressing. The Conservatives were determined to derive economic advantage from the Empire – so they wanted to institute the old panacea of Imperial Preference. Under this system, the United Kingdom would be the major market for the colonial and Dominion economies, and it in turn, would use them as the principal market for its own products. Therefore, instead of the introduction of tariffs, the Empire Marketing Fund was created. The Board was intended to administer this fund to improve Empire trade. It was particularly concerned with stimulating the sale of Dominion products in the United Kingdom.[2]

The Board's work fell into three main areas. It encouraged scientific research directed toward improving the quality of Empire products, it gathered information about national and international markets, and it engaged in publicity for Empire products. L. S. Amery was the Colonial and Dominions Secretary originally responsible for the EMB. He noted how from the very beginning there were differences of opinion concerning the Board's priorities. The Imperial Economic Committee met Amery and his colleagues to map out the functions of the new body prior to the 1926 Imperial Conference:

At this initial stage it suggested a general outline of policy for the apportionment of our expenditure, namely sixty-five percent to publicity, fifteen percent to research, twenty percent to various schemes such as the development of the trade in tropical fruits and the export of pedigree cattle. This was not however, the order in which we on the EMB viewed the task before us. Publicity for Empire produce would do little good unless the arrangements for the marketing of the goods from the producer to the consumer were working efficiently. These, in turn, depended for their success entirely upon the goods themselves holding their own in quality and being available in sufficient quantity. Our conclusion was that it was research that should have the sixty-five percent, marketing the twenty percent and direct publicity only fifteen percent. It is worth emphasising the point for the conspicuous success of our publicity schemes tended to impress the general public with the idea that they were the main point of our work.[3]

Amery's point is perfectly valid. The EMB consistently spent the greater part of its budget upon research activities and gathering market intelligence. This was especially the case after 1931, when the Board's publicity activities bore the brunt of the economy cuts imposed by the May Committee.[4] Yet despite this allocation of resources, the Board became best known for its publicity activities.

The EMB was in many ways without precedent. Never before had such an elaborate domestic publicity machine been operated by a British government department in peacetime. All the mass media and the arts were used extensively and innovatively in the pursuit of this publicity. As Grierson himself commented years later:

In creating its machinery of interpretation it enlisted the services of the best artists to paint its posters, it brought in the best architects to design its public exhibitions and it sought the help of writers, speakers, journalists and film producers.[5]

The greatest innovation was the Board's basic approach to the question of publicity. The EMB was the point of entry into Britain for many ideas about publicity and public relations imported from the United States by men like Grierson and Sir William Crawford. This approach to public relations stressed the importance of public education as the basis for publicity undertaken by government departments and commercial concerns. The newest of the mass media were understood to be the vital manipulators of public opinion. For a variety of reasons, film was considered to be the most potent of all the media. The American feature film at home and overseas was believed to dramatize the world in a way that no other form could. As Edward L. Bernays, the father of American public relations commented: "The American motion picture is the greatest unconscious carrier of propaganda in the world today. It is a great distributor for ideas and opinions."[6] Bernays might have added, as the trade interests in Britain noted in the mid-1920s, that American films were excellent advertisements for American goods and services. The widespread awareness of the importance of incidental publicity in films made it inevitable that any official organization involved in trade publicity would give some attention to films.

The EMB's secretary was Stephen Tallents. From the very beginning and sporadically throughout the next decade, the documentary movement was tied to the career of this unusual civil servant. Gervas Huxley, who was appointed by Tallents as secretary of the EMB Publicity Committee, thought that

where Tallents was exceptional was that he was a civil servant with an imagination completely unfettered by red tape . . . outward reticence hid, however, a highly romantic side to his complex nature, which had found expression in writing over-stylized prose articles for the back page of the *Manchester Guardian*.[7]

In addition to his poetic traits, Tallents had been alerted to the significance of official public relations by prior experience in several politically sensitive areas. During World War I, Tallents worked on organizing food rationing in Britain. Administering national food rationing demanded extensive advertising expertise, and it was unquestionably one of the areas where the war had its greatest immediate impact on Britain's civilian population. Subsequently, he had been British Commissioner for the Baltic Provinces and then the Imperial Secretary for Irish Affairs. Tallents also acted as secretary to the Cabinet Committee set up to deal with the General Strike.[8] All of Tallents's appointments placed him in positions where he was required to work with public opinion, either in Great Britain or overseas.

Tallents recruited individuals with a press background, like Gervas Huxley and A. P. Ryan to run the secretariat responsible for publicity at the EMB. Huxley served with the Publicity and Film Committees; Ryan, an Australian who had come to Britain as an aide to the Australian Prime Minister at the 1926 Imperial Conference, was appointed as secretary to the Press Committee. They gave order to the committee meetings at which Sir William Crawford, Frank Pick, and Sir Woodman Burbridge introduced ideas about public relations and the extensive use of art and the mass media for the Board's publicity. Pick had pioneered the use of artistic patronage at the London Passenger Transport Board where a systematic yet imaginative approach to corporate design and public image building had played a vital role in transforming a diversity of transportation concerns into the London Passenger Transport Board. He had been responsible, for example, for the Board's support of the avant-garde sculptor, Jacob Epstein. He argued that the art patron's image took on the traits of its protégés:

The public regard Epstein as avant-garde in art. If the Underground uses him as a matter of course in its architecture, the implication is how up-to-date must be its transport system.[9]

Patronage of the arts, as Pick and Crawford believed, was wedded to the notion of background publicity. The EMB, under the guidance of Pick, Crawford, and Tallents, pursued a policy of providing the background against which merchants and their trade associations could provide advertisement for specific commodities, or foreground publicity.

EMB publicists could not rely upon the example of most contemporary commercial advertising or the work of the first Ministry of Information, because their brief was quite different from that of both these enterprises. As Gervas Huxley noted: "No British Government in peacetime had ever embarked on so large a publicity campaign and its aims were such that ordinary commercial advertising afforded us little guidance."[10] It is hard to convey to a contemporary reader the extent to which commercial advertising in the 1920s was generally regarded as disreputable and tainted by its associations with the fake claims and malpractices of late-nineteenth-century commercial advertising. The first Ministry of Information was an altogether different and much more respectable model. However, it had been regarded as only appropriate during the exigencies of war, so it had been rapidly dismantled and its personnel scattered with the return of peace. The EMB's poster and film publicity work proved to be the areas where it diverged most clearly and dramatically from commercial practitioners' methods. For example, the Board set up a nationwide system of specially made poster frames upon which original posters, often by renowned artists, were exhibited. The commercial poster trade complained about the EMB's posters on the grounds that they were unfair competition, and they also questioned the efficacy of the posters. The British Poster Association, the official trade organization, condemned the Board's designs because they were "unpractical critically judged in the light of the purpose to be fulfilled. They betray a lack of study of the mass-mind."[11]

There are many parallels between the commercial trade's reaction to the Board's poster publicity and its film publicity. Both were constantly praised for their artistic merit and chastised for their lack of popular appeal. For example, Sir Gordon Craig, a commercial film producer, echoed the Poster Association's criticisms of the EMB posters when he declared that the titling on Grierson's *Drifters* was "over the head of the ordinary man in the street."[12] There was also, as in the case of EMB poster publicity, a great deal of trade antagonism toward the idea of government competition with legitimate commercial business. Furthermore, the commercial advertising and motion picture industries complained regularly that the EMB lacked the "common touch" so necessary if one was to create mass appeal.

The poster and film lobbies both failed to appreciate the EMB's new approach to publicity. Frank Pick stated that the purpose of this publicity was to "establish a background and to develop gradually a permanent

Empire consciousness rather than to try and create an immediate demand for goods."[13] This was very alien to the commercial practitioners who replied that "advertising in the commercial sense, advertising to gain and hold markets, must be in the highest degree, specific."[14] The Board's interest in artistic patronage and background publicity, together with its refusal to be bound by the old commercial formulas, made it a fertile ground for the cultivation of notions about art in the public service. As a result, it was receptive to new ideas to an extent that was rare in contemporary commercial advertising houses, and without parallel in the commercial film studios.

The EMB was born at a time of growing awareness of the publicity value of films. Most of this attention related to the desire to increase the number of British films within the Empire as a means of advertising British and Empire products. Only weeks before the creation of the EMB, Conservative Party Central Office established a Film Department. Central Office also anticipated the EMB's subsequent development of nontheatrical film distribution when it began using a fleet of mobile film units. Significantly, the ancilliary role of the units, after displaying party propaganda films, was to advertise Empire products.[15] In the same month, an Empire Film Institute was established by the British film industry. This body intended to combat the pernicious effects of the American feature films that then completely dominated British and Empire cinema screens. Significantly, Lord Askwith, a leading founding member of the Institute, was also President of the National Association of Trade Protection Societies and Vice-President of the Federation of British Industries. He was typical of a class forced to take an interest in cinema, that most vulgar of the mass media, largely because of the threat they felt was posed to their commercial interests by American motion pictures.

During 1926 there was a concerted campaign to get the whole question of films on the agenda of the forthcoming Imperial Conference. *The Times* was prompted to comment in its special Empire issue:

It is probable that more has been said and written during the last year about the connexion between British films and the British Empire than ever before. It is certain that less has been done . . . Everybody realises what wonderful propaganda the film may provide. Countless people write and talk about it, but no one does anything.[16]

Rudyard Kipling, champion of Empire and the Conservative party and perhaps the most popular living British novelist and poet, gave the initial impetus to the Board's inevitable interest in film publicity. Kipling suggested to Tallents that the Board should undertake the production of a major feature film, which would contain a strong element of Empire propaganda. He suggested Walter Creighton, with whom he had helped produce the Wembley Tattoo two years earlier as a suitable person to direct such a venture for the Board. Tallents was encouraged to pursue the project by Amery, who was then being pressed to do something for the British film industry at the Imperial Conference.

Tallents called together the first film caucus at the EMB in February 1927. He presented it a scenario written by Kipling and Creighton for a feature-length fiction film that, it was hoped, would be "suitable at its finished stage for distribution on its merits in the ordinary commercial way."[17] Tallents's colleagues were very eager to associate the venture with Kipling's prestige and reputation, which helps explain the otherwise inexplicable choice of Creighton, a man who knew nothing about filmmaking, as the EMB's first film officer. The EMB's Publicity Committee thought that

the collaboration of Mr. Kipling, would, it was felt, prove of the greatest value to the film as a commercial asset, and the Conference considered that Major Creighton, with whom there was reason to believe Mr. Kipling would freely collaborate, was particularly well qualified to assist the Board in the production of a suitable film, though he was admittedly unacquainted with film technique.[18]

The Conference was also pushed into the hasty appointment of Creighton, which it had much cause to regret later, by recent comments about films at the Imperial Conference. An economic subcommittee had recommended the production of films illustrating the Empire's resources. It noted the success films of this type had had at the recent Empire Exhibition.[19] The Imperial Conference as a whole had itself concluded that, "it is of the greatest importance that a larger and increasing proportion of the films exhibited throughout the Empire should be of Empire production."[20] The EMB's members soon concluded that there was not a commercial film production company in Britain capable of undertaking work of sufficient quality for the Board. Its film officer therefore was immediately made directly responsible for the direction and production of the Board's first film. Since Creighton knew practically nothing about filmmaking, it was agreed that he would first make a tour of film production centers in Europe and the United States before officially being appointed.

Grierson met Tallents only weeks after the decision to employ Creighton had been made. Tallents was very impressed with the young Scotsman, who, in contrast to Creighton, apparently had extensive experience with film and most importantly perhaps, seemed very familiar with developments in both Hollywood and New York. Although Tallents was committed to hiring Creighton, he did not wish to lose Grierson's services, so he arranged for Grierson to produce a series of reports on film production for the EMB Film Committee. Grierson immediately became the resident film expert at the EMB, although he did not officially receive an appointment as film officer until 1930. This usurpation was made easier by Creighton's prolonged absence while on his study tour.

Grierson's first employment with the EMB consisted of writing an elaborate memorandum for the EMB Film Committee, dealing with the two issues then most interesting to the Committee: how to undertake film propaganda and how to compete with the American film industry. This memorandum, "Notes for English Producers," was a synthesis of Grierson's American writings. It owed a great deal to the American public opinion theorists, particularly Bernays, Lippmann, and Harold Lasswell, with whom Grierson had become familiar in the United States. Lippmann spelled out his belief in the potency of films when he maintained that "on the screen the whole process of observing, describing, reporting and then imagining, has been accomplished for you. Without more trouble than is needed to stay awake the result which your imagination is always aiming at is reeled off on the screen. The shadowy idea becomes vivid."[21] The sense that motion pictures were a new and dynamic force capable of doing a great deal of good was widespread in the United States. Hollywood's film czar, Will Hays, spoke of film as "possibly the most potent instrument in the world for moral influence and education, and certainly one of the most universal mediums of artistic expression."[22] In this insightful memorandum, which was really the first systematic attempt to suggest what British filmmakers could do to compete with the American studio system, Grierson was equally fervent in his belief in the efficacy of cinema as a mover of men's minds. He noted films had

a practical monopoly over the dramatic strata of the common mind in which preferences, sympathies, affections and loyalties, if not actually created are at least crystallised and coloured . . . Cinema is recognised as having a peculiar influence on the ideological centres to which advertisement endeavours to make its appeal; this is not only because of the widespread and continuous march of the cinema, but because it is an ideal medium for all manner of suggestion . . . It seems that what people want more than anything of cinema is practical example and a renewal of vitality.[23]

In the memorandum Grierson made some practical suggestions as to how the British Empire could make films that would compete with American motion pictures. He argued that the far reaches of the Empire were just as exotic and mythic as say, the American West, and that "the progress of industry, the story of invention, the pioneering and developing of new lands and the exploration of lost ones, the widening horizons of commerce, the complexities of manufacture" were all subjects that awaited an adequate film treatment. Such a treatment was unlikely to come from the feature film industry, he believed, but rather from the makers of short films, who did not exist by attempting to copy the efforts of the Americans. Makers of short films had to appreciate that it was possible to dramatize natural material through a cinematic technique that did not rely on straightforward narrative. As Grierson noted, "even where there is no story, the visual aspects of a seemingly prosaic subject can be orchestrated into a cinematic sequence of enormous vitality."

Even in this very first report, Grierson stated his firm belief that the EMB should operate its own film unit. He argued that the commercial film industry could contribute little to the type of film production he envisaged the Board undertaking. Again, he was clearly influenced by American speculations on the possibilities of what could be accomplished if the media were not run on a simple for-profit basis. As Lippmann argued:

If the financial investment in each film and in popular magazines were not so exorbitant as to require instant and widespread popularity, men of spirit and imagination would be able to use the screen and the periodical, as one might dream of their being used to enlarge and refine, to verify and criticize the repertory images with which our imaginations work.[24]

"Men of spirit and imagination" would be an apt way of describing the group Grierson assembled at the Empire Marketing Board. Grierson did not believe the moribund British film industry was likely to adopt the new cinematic forms and treatments he proposed. He was determined to start afresh outside the commercial film industry.

Grierson's first report was very favorably received. Outside the EMB Film Committee it circulated widely within those circles who had followed the earlier debate about the British Empire and films. It was distributed precisely during the period when the first Cinematograph Films Act was going through Parliament, which gave it an immediate relevance. Cunliffe-Lister, President of the Board of Trade, and the man most responsible for the first Films Act, was very impressed with the report. So too was the novelist and former information minister, John Buchan. He thought, like Grierson, that effective propaganda films "must appeal not by psychological subtleties to the intellect, but must, to refer to Aristotle, 'follow the main march of human affection.' They must deal with common virtues at a high power."[25]

Grierson's next report for the EMB Film Committee dealt with the subject of film distribution. He examined both commercial and nontheatrical distribution. The concept of nontheatrical distribution was in fact ill-defined, but Grierson used the term to describe the loose-knit network of schools, film societies, and self-improvement organizations that occasionally showed films to audiences, usually on a free admission basis. This type of development had gone much further in the United States than in Britain, and this remained true through the 1930s. The emergence of nontheatrical screenings on a wide scale was held back everywhere by the expense of 35mm projection equipment and awaited the arrival of cheap and efficient 16mm apparatus. Perhaps the real model for Grierson's ideas concerning nontheatrical distribution and exhibition – although this is not mentioned in his memorandum – was the Soviet Union, which as a matter of course arranged regular screenings in noncommercial settings and did not make a distinction between theatrical and nontheatrical exhibition. Grierson believed nontheatrical distribution in Britain to be extremely casual and poorly organized. This, he wrote, was symptomatic of the films themselves, which were made for this type of distribution: "Privacy is in fact written all over these films, and the lack of discipline which comes with the consciousness of a definite world of release, prevents them from being really effective."[26] Even at this early date, Grierson believed the nontheatrical audiences should be cultivated. He saw them as an important outlet for nonfiction films, which he thought should constitute most of the EMB's film activities. He did, however, believe that the commercial cinema would continue to be the most important means of reaching the general public.

Creighton's departure for the United States in July 1927 enabled Grierson to expand his work for the EMB beyond reports for the Film Committee. During the autumn, for example, Grierson organized a series of film shows at the Imperial Institute cinema for representatives of government departments. Twice a week, civil servants were invited to watch strange polyglot programs consisting typically of westerns, the latest offerings from the Russian filmmakers, and some of the rare but very successful excursions of some British filmmakers into the area of the actuality film, such as British Instructional's *Secrets of Nature* series. Grierson admired the westerns for their location film work, which in a sense made them a genre that escaped the synthetic forms of Hollywood studio production. He also admired their idealizing "epic" quality. The Russian films were admired particularly for the manner in which they linked radical technique to politial purpose and social change. The *Secrets of Nature* series was representative of the best work of the British film industry. He found it significant that this success resulted from the rejection of the fiction film form. The films shown that autumn ranged between "the dramatic forms affecting the imagination and crystallising the sentiments of large audiences to the documentary forms recording the processes of industry and commerce."[27] Sadly, the screenings were not as well attended as Grierson and Tallents had hoped.[28]

Grierson simultaneously began a number of other projects. He compiled an index of films he thought would be valuable for Empire publicity. Indicative of Grierson's talent as publicist, he also arranged a film display to take place on the train carrying members of the Imperial Agricultural Committee from Edinburgh to London in October 1927. The event attracted a great deal of favorable press attention. Grierson also attracted attention within the Board. Gervas Huxley, returning from a tour of the Dominions in 1928 noticed the manner in which Grierson, who had been appointed in his absence, had come to dominate the EMB's publicity with his plans for using film. Tallents particularly seemed to have been mesmerized by the young Scot. Huxley's first impression of the Board's new recruit was of

John Grierson, a thirty year old Scot with the air of a tough little terrier, under whose dynamic spell Tallents had so completely fallen that it seemed that films should form the most valuable single medium for the attainment of the Board's objects.[29]

However, Grierson wanted to be more than the EMB film consultant. He wanted to become a director, but the Board was already committed to employing Walter Creighton as its first director. Years later, speaking with hindsight, Tallents claimed that he had doubts about the Creighton–Kipling venture from a very early date, but that he "had no qualifications to assess or criticize a popular film in the making. I had views, too about letting artists have their heads and a fear of fettering imaginative work in official shackles."[30]

In March 1928, Grierson presented proposals to the EMB Film Committee for direct production of films by the Board, quite independently of the Creighton feature film project. He suggested that the Board produce two films made from wholly new material and a series of films to be assembled from existing archival footage. As subjects for two new films, Grierson suggested a film about the pedigree cattle trade, advertising the Board's "assisted passage" bloodstock export scheme, and a film dealing with the herring industry.[31] Grierson claimed that the herring film was intended as a response to recent criticisms that the Board was not doing enough to advertise the herring industry. Apocryphally, there was also a tactical motive for choosing this particular subject. The Board required Treasury authority to commence film work, and Arthur Samuel, the Financial Secretary to the Treasury was the country's authority on the herring industry. As Tallents later noted:

At this point a justly cautious Treasury had to be wooed and won over. We noted with a strategic eye a fortunate combination of circumstances. The Financial Secretary of the day was the greatest living authority on the fascinating records of the British herring industry. Grierson had served a tough apprenticeship to the sea in mine-sweepers during the war. We baited our hook with the project of a film to illustrate the North Sea herring fisheries. The Treasury swallowed it, and Grierson set out to make his first film.[32]

Drifters was shot during the summer of 1928. Grierson was the director but was very careful to defer to technical expertise of others. The film was produced by the New Era Film Company, a fairly prominent production company that specialized in the production of short films. Its name made the company appear perhaps more progressive and radical than it actually was. The film was shot by Basil Emmott, one of Britain's foremost cameramen. Grierson appreciated that his own skills were theoretical and analytical, rather than technical. This use of proven talent was an example that was not followed up in many of the later films because Grierson's recruits tended to be enthusiastic amateurs not professional filmmakers. Later EMB films were generally made by youngsters without professional experience. This goes far in explaining why the early success of *Drifters* was not repeated in later EMB productions.

While making preparations to begin the herring film, Grierson simultaneously produced a series of memoranda on the film production activities of governments overseas. He was anxious to put film production at the EMB on a regular and permanent footing. His case was greatly strengthened by a visit from F. C. Badgeley, head of the Canadian Motion Picture Bureau. The Committee listened eagerly to Badgeley's report on what he claimed was the most extensive government film organization outside the Soviet Union.[33] Badgeley's opinion was valued because his bureau seemed to have had some success competing with the American film industry on its own ground. He noted how each year the Bureau reached twenty-five million Americans through nontheatrical distribution of its films. His comments regarding the generosity of the Canadian government and the effectiveness of nontheatrical distribution in North America were the basis for Grierson's own ambitions for nontheatrical distribution.

It was inevitable, perhaps, that there would be some opposition to the growth of centralized official publicity and public relations. Grierson had barely started the production of his first film, and was also attempting to induce the EMB to extend its film operations with his memoranda on the publicity activities of other government departments, when the Board's activities fell under the scrutiny of the Select Committee on Estimates. This was the first of many clashes between those who favored government publicity, and thought films a particularly valuable form of publicity, and those who thought publicity and films were expensive luxuries. The Committee was very perturbed to learn of the Creighton appointment, while Tallents, anxious not to arouse the Committee with news that the Board had in fact two full-time employees dedicated to film production and analysis, did not reveal Grierson's existence at all. The Committee's findings on film publicity were very discouraging, and it stated in its report that

after hearing the evidence your Committee doubt if the Board has at its disposal at present or could obtain at a reasonable cost the necessary technical skill to warrant it as a government department embarking upon this difficult and speculative enterprise and they recommend that the matter be reconsidered.[34]

Work on *Drifters* progressed regardless of the recommendations of the Select Committee. The speed with which Grierson worked contrasted

Figure 2. *Drifters* (John Grierson, 1929). "The visual aspects of a seemingly prosaic subject can be orchestrated into a cinematic sequence of enormous vitality."

with the failures that beset the Board's feature film project. Grierson had finished shooting his film before Creighton had even commenced work on his.[35] While Grierson began cutting his film, a subcommittee of the Film Committee met to discuss whether the entire Creighton project should be abandoned.[36]

The intricate Russian-style cutting of *Drifters* took a great deal of time. This was one area where Grierson could not be guided by expertise from the British film industry. While this work was in progress, the Board expanded the range of its other film activities. In particular, the Board began to erect an extensive nontheatrical distribution system. Film shows were arranged for the Ministry of Agriculture and the Scottish Board of Agriculture. In addition, elaborate film distribution plans were made for the forthcoming North East Coast Exhibition. The Board hoped to stage a series of film displays for schools, and eventually, it decided to cooperate with British Instructional Films in producing a series of films for display in Tyneside schools. British Instructional's success in this venture subsequently led the company to branch out into national distribution of specially made films to schools.[37]

Drifters was finished in the summer of 1929. It was very different from

Figure 3. *Drifters.*

anything being made by the British film industry at that time. It was neither a feature nor a short in the commercial sense. Its length, just fifty minutes, excluded it from either of these categories, as did its approach to its material. From the Russian cinema, Grierson had appropriated the notion of the workingman as hero and also the use of montage to dramatize realistic material. From Robert Flaherty, Grierson had learned the value of simple observational camerawork that could capture the essence of things in a gesture or a facial expression, and the possibility of finding romance in realistic material. Grierson wove through the film his own central theme of the interdependence of workingmen, the market place, and communications. The film cost a mere £2,948.[38] Grierson had rejected Hollywood-style illusionism and substituted for it a type of realism. It was one of the first attempts at national and oppositional cinema to embrace such an approach and to reject the Hollywood model. Like many later national schools of filmmaking, Grierson had opted to produce a type of film that bore little resemblance to the American rival.

The film premiered before the London Film Society, not in a commercial setting. It was typical of Grierson's flair as a publicist that he contrived to get *Drifters* on the same program as Eisenstein's *Battleship*

Potemkin, a film that always aroused controversy in public screenings in the 1920s and 1930s in Britain, then having its own English premiere. *Drifters* was very well received by the members of the film society, the critics, and, surprisingly, by the film trade. Sir Gordon Craig had revised his earlier opinion of the film, and he now commented:

Unquestionably the film is the most ambitious effort of its kind ever attempted in this country. The quality is first-rate, and compares very favorably with the better class of commercial film now being produced here.[39]

The trade press, which was unenthusiastic about *Potemkin,* was full of praise for *Drifters. Kine Weekly* thought the film "outstandingly good" and that "Basil Emmott's camerawork helped the clever direction of John Grierson."[40]

Commercial audiences liked *Drifters* too. The film was widely booked despite the disadvantages it suffered as a silent film when the cinemas were moving over to talkies at a very rapid clip and also because its unusual length was not easily accommodated in regular commercial cinema programs. *Drifters* immediately secured extensive theatrical bookings. Within a year, receipts from distribution had almost recouped the costs of production.[41] The film became well known in influential circles too. The Board was gratified to receive a request for a showing of *Drifters* at the House of Commons, and the subsequent viewing was well attended.[42]

The arrival of sound in the commercial cinemas presented more of a problem for the EMB's feature film. Creighton had shot his film during 1929. The picture, already four years in the making, was dogged by difficulties throughout its production. Now in postproduction, it had to be given a sound track or risked being refused any kind of commercial distribution. Exactly the same thing happened to Alfred Hitchcock's own first sound film *Blackmail* (1929). Originally intended as a silent film, Hitchcock had been forced to reshoot some of *Blackmail's* footage as sound sequences and to dub some of the silent footage to make the film commercially viable. The arrival of sound, and the hasty adding of a sound track to the film, was by no means solely responsible for the failure of Creighton's *One Family,* as his film was eventually titled. Creighton's film was a heavy-handed fantasy reminiscent of some of Kipling's own lighter pieces. It was a fable about the gathering of the ingredients for the royal Christmas pudding from all parts of the Empire as viewed through the eyes of a small boy, with society ladies personifying the Empire's colonies and the Dominions. The film had disaster written all over it even before its completion, and the fate of the film had been discussed with monotonous regularity at successive meetings of the EMB Film Committee. It committed the cardinal sin of not only attempting to compete with the commercial feature film but of doing so very badly. The film was premiered with a great deal of pageantry in July

Figure 4. *One Family* (Walter Creighton, 1930). "Lady Keele as Canada, Baroness Ravensdale as New Zealand . . ."

1930. It was berated by the critics and generally ignored by commercial exhibitors. As one critic wrote in the *Manchester Guardian:*

The minute I think of the story, and of a body of men solemnly thinking they can offer such a flippancy to the public, I get so angry that I lose all sense of proportion.[43]

One Family consumed most of the EMB's annual film budget for three years and cost £15,740; yet it secured commercial bookings worth only £334. This did not even pay for the cost of the band hired for the premiere of the film.[44]

The principal effect of *One Family* was to sour the EMB and its immediate successor in publicity matters, the Public Relations Department of the Post Office, against feature films. Grierson's advocacy of the documentary film as the appropriate vehicle for government propaganda was vindicated by the commercial success of his own film. The popular success of *Drifters* also greatly strengthened Grierson's case when he suggested that the EMB set up a permanent producing and editing unit. He wanted official recognition for a group he had already gathered together. This consisted of, as he described it, "several young beginners, employed at very small fees and working in the attic rooms hired by New Era."[45]

Basil Wright was Grierson's first recruit. He began work with Grierson in December 1929 after he had been impressed by a first viewing of *Drifters*. Wright and many of the first generation of filmmakers who worked under Grierson had much more in common with each other than they had with their mentor. He came into contact with Grierson through the young film society movement, which was an important gathering place for neophyte filmmakers, just as it was for Italian neorealists and the French New Wave in the 1940s and 1950s. Wright was not that much younger than Grierson – less than a decade separated the two – although to someone fresh out of Cambridge University, the distance between himself and the worldly Scot must have seemed great at the time. Grierson, as Harry Watt frequently remarks, went to great pains to keep this sense of distance between himself and the group he assembled. Furthermore, the emphasis was very much on the group rather than the individual, and the unit approach to film collaboration remained part of Grierson's philosophy throughout his life.

Under Grierson's supervision, Wright assembled *Conquest*, a compilation film largely constructed from footage from American westerns that Grierson had managed to borrow from Famous Players–Lasky, with whom he had been associated in the United States. Jay Leyda has written that *Conquest* was an experiment, intended to compare the compilation film based on archival material with films assembled from wholly new footage:

It was Grierson's test of two different kinds of film, a test in which price was measured against effectiveness. Grierson's large subsequent production schedule in Great Britain, establishing the British documentary film movement, shows no attempt to follow *Conquest*. One is led to assume that whatever advantages such a compilation showed Grierson, these could not compete in result with the greater control of *Drifters*.[46]

In fact, nearly all of the group of filmmakers, whom Grierson gradually assembled at the EMB, found they spent their early months with the unit assembling films out of existing footage. This course was dictated by the limited finances of the unit, which permitted only a very small amount of shooting of new film. Furthermore, like all beginning film students, Grierson's recruits were introduced to technique without the necessity of investing heavily in film stock and facilities. It was also a result of Grierson's conviction that editing was the key to film structure, based on his close scrutiny of the use of montage in Russian films.

These early efforts at compilation filmmaking were displayed in noncommercial settings. The Board developed a scheme employing daylight projectors erected at many major railway stations during EMB-sponsored "Empire Shopping Weeks," and at the EMB pavilions present at most agricultural shows and trade exhibitions in the early 1930s.

The EMB Film Unit was formally sanctioned in April 1930. From the outset it was always intended that some of its output should consist of films constructed out of entirely new footage. Initially, Grierson asked for and received £2,350 to produce these new films during the first six months of the life of the unit. The Film Committee was impressed with Grierson's suggestions for a unit that promised to be both economical and efficient.[47] With official approval, Grierson began to gather together at the EMB Film Unit those men and women who became the first generation of the documentary movement. Wright was soon joined by John Taylor, Paul Rotha, Donald Taylor, Arthur Elton, Edgar Anstey, Stuart Legg, J. N. G. Davidson, and several women, including Grierson's sisters, Ruby and Marion, Evelyn Spice, and Margaret Taylor, who eventually became Grierson's wife.[48] In fact the EMB Film Unit was one of the few places that offered employment behind the camera to women at this time.

During the first year of its operation, the unit was concerned exclusively with the production of poster films for display in the Board's network of daylight projectors and one-reel films for display at the Imperial Institute cinema. Films with titles as prosaic and straightforward as *Canadian Apples, Sheep Dipping, South African Fruit,* and many more advertising films poured out of the tiny unit's editing room. The unit was also able to assemble a film display for the delegates attending the 1930 Imperial Conference. As in 1926, the Conference was very conscious of the importance of films as trade propaganda, and so it was very impressed with the film display. The conferees also advocated closer cooperation between the different parts of the Empire on the question of films:

The Conference, recognising the value of films for propaganda purposes, whether direct or indirect, in connection with inter-Imperial trade, as well as for other purposes, and realizing that the present period is one of rapid development, and therefore, great opportunity, recommends that attention should be devoted to establishing and maintaining contact between the different parts of the Empire in relation to film production with a view to the sharing of experience and the promotion of the production of such films as will best serve the interests of the several parts of the Empire.[49]

Perhaps a more important result of the Conference's findings than its general conclusions about the nature of film production was a suggestion that the terms of reference of the EMB should be widened to handle publicity for trade throughout the Empire, not just the sale of Dominion goods within the United Kingdom.[50]

In January 1931, Grierson suggested expanding the work of the film unit. He believed that the unit should undertake a special series of films intended purely for nontheatrical distribution. He was particularly anxious to develop the distribution of films to schools since this had proven so successful at the North East Coast Exhibition. As he noted:

It is felt that the opportunity exists for the Board to provide an inexpensive, and, in time, extensive, distribution service for film displays organised independently by educational and social organisations, as part of their programmes.[51]

The unit increased its output of films for schools, and distribution was centralized with the creation in October 1931 of the Empire Film Library. The Empire Film Library maintained a growing library of films for screenings at schools and in other nontheatrical venues, making the EMB a pioneer of this type of educational use of film in the United Kingdom. This scheme was initially on a very small scale since it predated the development of portable 16mm sound projectors and 35mm equipment was prohibitively expensive. Within five years, however, the Empire Film Library grew into the largest film distributor catering to schools in Britain.

Grierson also proposed developing the distribution of films overseas through the Department of Overseas Trade. He believed that the Imperial Conference's decision to widen the Board's brief justified expanding the activities of the film unit, and so proposed a whole range of film productions, albeit on a limited budget. Grierson asked for an additional £3,000 to make two three-reelers dealing with the subject of British industry. He also asked for £1,800 for the production of six one-reelers to be made by reediting existing material, £2,500 for twenty short "interest" films, and £520 for the production of twenty-six poster films. Grierson emphasized that these films were all intended for nontheatrical distribution. He did not believe that the Board should turn its back totally on the commercial cinema but did stress that there should be no direct competition with the film trade:

Of films designed for commercial exploitation, probably second feature films (i.e. films of the *Drifters* type) offer better opportunities for the Board's purpose than films of greater length. First feature films are open to very keen competition from outside, as was apparent when *One Family* was presented to the trade, but with the second features, distribution is considerably easier, whilst production expenses are much smaller.[52]

This increased budget allowed the production of a series of films that progressed beyond simple editing exercises, poster films, and films for schools. These films – *O'er Hill and Dale* (Wright, 1931), *The Country Comes to Town* (Wright, 1931), *Lumber* (Wright, 1931), *Upstream* (Elton, 1931), and *Shadow on the Mountain* (Elton, 1931), together with a major film that Robert Flaherty began for the EMB, *Industrial Britain* (Flaherty, 1931) – comprised the films Grierson's team was able to make with its increased budget. At this time in Britain, short films were generally

Figure 5. *O'er Hill and Dale* (Basil Wright, 1931).

Figure 6. *Upstream* (Arthur Elton, 1931).

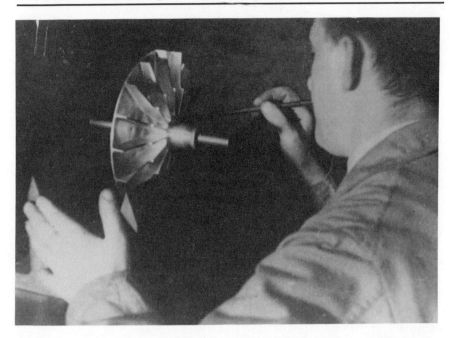

Figure 7. *Industrial Britain* (Robert Flaherty, 1931): the dignity of physical labor.

Figure 8. *Industrial Britain.*

booked in groups. Grierson's films were released as the *Imperial Six* group, but their distribution was impaired by the fact that they were silent films, facing a shrinking market in the commercial cinema. Meanwhile, Grierson paid another visit to North America and returned adamant about concentrating on nontheatrical distribution, rather than the commercial markets at which this group of films had been aimed.

On his second visit to North America Grierson focused on nontheatrical distribution in both Canada and the United States. In the United States he found that many government departments engaged in film publicity, but in what he perceived as a completely uncentralized and uncoordinated manner. He was freely critical of the bureaucratic mentality that he thought responsible for the chaos he found in the American civil service. He implicitly invited the British civil servants for whom his report was destined to draw their own conclusions about the limitations imposed by the bureaucratic mind, when he commented on the film activities of the U.S. Department of Agriculture:

The standard of film production and the standard of the educational value in the films is not very high. The old civil service atmosphere of the Bureau is probably responsible for this. It stops work every day at 4.30 with a half-day on Saturdays. It is out of touch with commercial production and whilst earnest in its intentions, is too secure from criticism and commercial comparison.[53]

Grierson was very impressed by the individual efforts of particular government departments, especially the Bureau of Mines. Grierson noted how this department cleverly relied upon sponsorship from industry to finance its own film activities. Grierson noted in some detail how this system worked, for it became the key to his later interest in industrial sponsorship:

A company undertakes to finance production at a cost to themselves varying between £2,000 and £15,000. The Bureau in its turn, agrees to supervise production, gives the company a general credit at the beginning of the film and looks after non-theatrical circulation. The agreement calls for the final O.K. by the Bureau and the absolute elimination of all material which could be construed as proprietory advertising in the body of the film. The industrial concern pays all the expenses of the Bureau officials engaged on the film.[54]

Grierson had come to believe that industrial sponsorship was a possible alternative to the direct funding of filmmaking by government departments. The EMB unit never adopted precisely the notion of looking to industrial concerns to provide the finance for films. Individual members of the unit, however, were able to find sponsorship for their work in this manner. For example, in the year of Grierson's second visit to North America, under the auspices of the New Era Company, Arthur Elton made *Voice of the World* (Elton, 1932) for the His Master's Voice Gramophone Company. Grierson saw industrial sponsorship as the logical alternative source of support for the documentary group. He noted the manner in which the so-called sponsored film operated: "Advertisers are content with the mere attachment of their name to the beginning of the film, the film in many cases having nothing to do with their own production."[55] This form of industrial patronage ultimately became the most important form of funding for the independent documentary production companies that sprang up in the mid-1930s.

The most productive period for the EMB Film Unit came during the years 1931 and 1932. During this time, the unit made many films for nontheatrical distribution. In fact, only one film made by the unit received commercial distribution, *Lumber*, a film compiled from footage Grierson had brought back from Canada. Ostensibly, the small number of films given commercial release was partially by design. Grierson was increasingly certain that entertainment films in general chose to waste their capacity for "crystallizing sentiments." The retreat from commercial exhibition was also a matter of necessity. The unit simply was not in a position to produce films of sufficient quality or quantity for regular commercial release. Actually some exhibitors, in fact, were very interested in the possibility of showing EMB films. After the trade showing of *Lumber*, for example, Arthur Jarratt, booking manager for the large Provincial Cinematograph Theatre chain was reported to have "expressed his desire to obtain more films of this type."[56] It was hard to generate a following among film distributors and renters as long as Grierson could not guarantee a steady flow of quality short films.

The EMB's failure to get films into general commercial release was not the result of trade hostility but a consequence of the advent of sound motion pictures. The unit had no facilities for recording sound, which would have been well beyond the means of the small unit. All the films made by the documentary group at the EMB were therefore silent, intended to have some form of musical accompaniment, and by 1932 it was very difficult indeed to obtain theatrical distribution of silent films. Grierson had to report to the Film Committee in December 1931 that the unit had seventeen films awaiting the addition of sound tracks. Admitting that sound was a necessity for the commercial distribution of the films, he asked for additional funds to create a sound studio.[57] The Board had recently fallen under the scrutiny of the economy-conscious May Committee and had been ordered to cut back expenditure. It found itself unable to comply with Grierson's request for sound equipment, although it acknowledged the commercial wisdom behind the proposal.[58]

Grierson was in a quandary. He wanted theatrical distribution for the Board's films, but there was money neither to acquire sound equipment for the unit nor to contract the work out to a professional audio studio. In any event, the films had been conceived as silent films. It would not be enough simply to add sound to films that had already been shot and edited. This situation continued through 1932 and effectively denied the EMB films access to any real commercial release. The solution to this problem came only in the last few months during the Board's life, when its financial affairs were actually being wound up. In late 1932, Tallents and Grierson entered into negotiations with a commercial production company, Ideal Films. This company already had considerable experience with films consisting of realistic material with its long-running *Ideal Cinemagazine.* Ideal agreed to buy the six best EMB films awaiting the addition of sound tracks. Tallents reported the sale of the films in January 1933.[59] Ideal's leading short film director and the producer of the *Cinemagazine,* Andrew Buchanan, added commentary and musical scores to the films of the *Imperial Six* group. This negated the effect that the documentarists had been trying to obtain. The *Imperial Six* became a strange mixture of Russian-style cutting and camera work very much influenced by Flaherty and a West End accent mouthing platitudes about the skilled English craftsman. Thus, the only group of films the EMB unit managed to get into commercial release were completely compromised and were shown in a form very different from what the documentarists had envisaged.

The documentary movement was much more successful in cultivating the nontheatrical distribution of its films than it was in obtaining their theatrical release. By late 1932, the unit had produced about 100 films for nontheatrical distribution. Most of this distribution consisted of displays arranged in schools. These films were mostly simple reediting exercises, and were essentially successors to the earlier *Conquest.* Nevertheless, there was a real demand for films of this type, which attempted to be history and geography lessons on film. Often, it is true, the EMB's efforts were not totally successful, and it was films of this type that had prompted film critic Ernest Betts to comment "there is no boredom in the world to be compared with that of sitting through a thoroughly bad film."[60]

Arrangements for centralizing film distribution had begun with the creation of the EMB Film Library, housed at the Imperial Institute in October 1931. Frequent accounts noted that the demands made on this library invariably exceeded the supply of films available. As one noted, there was a favorable response to the library and the films it supplied:

This service has clearly fulfilled a definite and important need. In a careful and detailed report recently drawn up by a Chesterfield school, it was stated in the preface to a list of various agencies from which schools could obtain films that "the EMB has the best of all film libraries."[61]

The EMB's nontheatrical efforts benefited greatly from the growing interest in the use of films for education, which was then being investigated by the Commission on Educational and Cultural Films, and also from the increasing concern in education as it related to the British Empire. The Commission was one of several bodies interested in breaking out of what was commonly known in the trade press as the "vicious circle" created by the lack of audio-visual equipment in schools, which meant a market for educational films that was too small to warrant developing. The circle was completed by the fact that schools would not buy projectors if they could not be assured of an extensive number of films of sufficient quality for their purposes. Equipment was also a problem. Filmmakers and schools both awaited the manufacture of a reliable and inexpensive 16mm sound film projector. Western Electric and Sound Services both finally began to market satisfactory versions of this type of equipment in 1933.[62] This meant that for two years the EMB had the educational film field to itself. It distributed its films in 35mm versions to a number of schools in a way that would have been impossible for a commercial concern. When Western Electric and Sound Services began producing equipment for the educational market, they found that the EMB was the biggest supplier of films to schools. Figures for the EMB's nontheatrical distribution of films are not very impressive. It was calculated that in the Empire Film Library's first year of operation, some 517,000 people saw EMB films. Fully three-quarters of these viewers were schoolchildren.[63] The figures become much more impressive when it is remembered that this was the first year of an entirely new venture. They were the humble beginnings of a much more extensive system of distribution that the documentary movement built during the next five years.

By 1933 the EMB unit had begun to resemble an official film service. It cooperated with other government departments and outside bodies on the production of films. The unit's biggest single client was the Ministry of Agriculture, with which there was a continuous record of cooperation dating from as early as 1928. In both 1931 and 1932, the unit produced a number of films to be shown in conjunction with the launching of the National Mark scheme for agricultural produce, then being jointly introduced by the Ministry of Agriculture and the Board. The unit also cooperated with the Post Office, making three films for the Telephone Advisory Service during 1932.[64] This early cooperation with the Post Office later proved vital for salvaging the unit when the EMB fell victim to the economy cuts of the May Committee. The EMB unit also made films for bodies outside the central government. In addition to Arthur Elton's film for His Master's Voice, Stuart Legg made *The New Generation* (Legg, 1932) for the Chesterfield Education Authority, and Grierson had begun negotiations to make films for the British Broadcasting Corporation and the Travel and Industrial Development Association.

The extent of the EMB's involvement with film publicity for other agencies indicated not only the considerable degree of interest in this type of propaganda that existed at the time but also the financial difficulties the Board and the unit were facing. Ironically, within months of the creation of the film unit, the Select Committee on Estimates had slated the Board for abolition. From its inception, the unit had to face shrinking budgets. In the first year of its life, the unit was given £25,000, which was more than it received in any subsequent year.[65] Much of this budget went to the ill-fated *One Family* and not the production of a coherent body of films. Grierson constantly had to fight for more money, and the work of the unit was always compromised by the lack of funds. The manner in which the unit's first series of films intended for commercial release was sabotaged by the lack of funds was typical of this state of affairs. Grierson had fought against the plan to sell the films outright. As he commented:

If the films are sold in silent form, synchronisation passes out of our control, and the final impression given by the film might not be the most useful for EMB purposes. In the interest of the unit as well as of the films themselves, synchronisation should be related to the editorial intention.[66]

Grierson employed many tactics to combat adverse financial circumstances. There is no doubt that one useful tactic that Grierson frequently employed was to simply leave his superiors, Tallents excepted, in complete ignorance of what the unit was actually doing. For example, the unit received £7,500 for the production of a film on the Port of London Authority. As Grierson later told Elizabeth Sussex:

I think I got £7,500 for a picture called *Port of London* and *Port of London* was merely used as an excuse to create the unit so we kept that running . . . I don't know how long, but there was always this mythical film that I kept on pretending was going to be made.[67]

Such measures might have seemed necessary at the time, but since they tended to occur with some frequency, they began to foster doubts within the civil service regarding Grierson's integrity. In the long run, Grierson's behavior was perhaps a disservice to the growth of the British documentary film. This incident was also indicative of the way in which Grierson was always prepared to do anything to obtain his ends. He was even prepared to exploit his young men. For example, he noted in a report for the EMB that when the unit was no longer able to pay the salaries of some members on its payroll, they were lent out to commercial companies. Their salaries were considerably higher than those received when working at the film unit, and so Grierson confiscated the difference between their salaries for the unit's own use. As he noted: "A percentage of these increased salaries was retained by the officers concerned but in all £17 profit to the EMB was realized from their loan."[68] This was a neglible amount perhaps, but the action reveals a lot about the discipline that Grierson exercised over the unit. It also reveals as much about the private incomes of the members of the documentary movement as it does about their commitment to their cause.

By 1931, or even earlier, if Gervas Huxley is to be believed, Grierson exercised a great deal of influence over Tallents. By that time, Tallents was fighting to keep the Board in existence.[69] The Board had acquired a number of enemies because, for all the publicity it had generated, its work seemed to have little or no effect on the worsening trade depression. Although it does seem that a combination of low prices for Empire products and EMB publicity had resulted in an increasing proportion of Britain's grocery bill spent within the British Empire.[70] Tallents was just beginning to formulate the ground rules for the conduct of national publicity in his influential pamphlet, *The Projection of England*. He had just received his knighthood for his work with the EMB, and now had to consider ways of preserving the Board's publicity activities in view of the abolition recommended by the May Committee. Under Grierson's influence, Tallents contrived to take the film unit with him to the Post Office, where he was appointed as its first Public Relations Officer. Tallents had come to accept the belief that film had an especially important role to play in public information services, and that public information was a necessary task for government departments. At the same time, Tallents agreed with Grierson that the British government and film industry would do well to learn from the Russian film industry. His tastes appear to have been completely dominated by Grierson's own. For example, both men thought Turin's *Turk-Sib* should be the prototype for similar work in Britain. Tallents noted:

It has no personal story, and no individual actors. Its hero is the slowly advancing railway, its villain the forces of drought and storm, of ice and rock and flood. I have seen its reception by a selected audience of English businessmen and labour representatives, and have heard them describe it as a finer film than any other they had viewed.[71]

Grierson's personal influence over Tallents, combined with Tallents's own belief in the efficacy of film publicity and his vision of himself as an official patron of the arts, led Tallents to make sure that the film unit was part of the publicity machinery he saved from the ruins of the Board.

Grierson and Tallents were both committed to the vision of developing a cadre of official information experts. Tallents had come to view the film unit as the nucleus of public relations experts, which he, like Walter Lippmann, believed should be placed in charge of national publicity. Tallents believed that such a group was urgently necessary. He elaborated on what he thought it should be like:

I see the members of this school as a small group, selected less on account of their existing affiliations than by reason of their diverse personal qualities. It must be their business to study professionally the art of national projection, and to draw for the materials of that art upon all the resources of English life. They must have something of the sense of responsibility, the prestige and the opportunities of government and entry to the fields of government activity, but they must be more free to make experiments, and like all experimenters, to make mistakes, than the ordinary government department dares to be.[72]

For Tallents, who was widely considered at the time to be "the first civil servant to make advertising his only particular subject," the future of good government public relations demanded the survival of the documentary unit.[73]

The film unit was also fortunate in that it had received a great deal of favorable publicity. It had, in fact, created much of this publicity itself. Grierson and his followers frequently wrote articles for the national press, the trade newspapers, and film and literary journals. Grierson himself gave the following eulogy to the unit in April 1932:

The Empire Marketing Board has a film unit, which is generally thought of by those who think about it at all, as a small organisation devoted to two principal purposes – the supply of classroom films to schools and the veiled advertising of Imperial products. To take this view of it is completely to misunderstand it. The project though restricted now by the limit of means at its disposal, is potentially of the highest importance to the film industry as a whole, and there is implied in its finer development, in association with the work being done by British Instructional, a possibility – the only hopeful possibility of which we are presently aware – of freeing British films from a slavish competition with American methods and of establishing for them a character of their own. This is looking far ahead: the EMB Film Unit is as yet in its youth; but there has not yet emerged from the dishonourable chaos of the films an enterprise more deserving of imaginative support.[74]

Grierson rallied support for the film unit during the summer of 1933. He was determined that it, at least, should survive the EMB's death. Many of Tallents's colleagues wrote to *The Times* and campaigned elsewhere for the continuation of the publicity machinery developed at the Board. Invariably, they were particularly anxious that the film unit should continue. Frank Pick, for example, believed that the Board was a "nucleus . . . [for] a complete publicity service for all departments."[75] William Crawford believed that the Board's work was "the greatest and most successful co-operative educational and advertising effort of recent times."[76] A number of other special pleas were made on behalf of the film unit. Robert Flaherty, for example, argued that "though we have many hundreds of pictures of industry and commerce in America, we have no production unit of anything like the same significance."[77]

While this salvage campaign continued in public, Tallents worked covertly on behalf of the unit. He made it a condition of his own appointment to the Public Relations Department of the Post Office that the film unit should be taken over intact by the Post Office. Tallents and Grierson had powerful friends at the Post Office; in particular, William Crawford, perhaps the most influential member of the EMB's publicity committee, was also a member of the Post Office Telephone Advancement Committee. The Post Office, like its American counterpart, was interested in developing domestic demand for telephones, which were perceived everywhere as essentially business equipment. Consequently, in this capacity, Crawford introduced the Post Office to the new methods of public relations and was able to convince them that Tallents was the leading civil service authority. The Post Office was anxious to secure Tallents's services and had been pleased with the films made on its behalf by Tallents's unit. Tallents went to the Post Office in September 1933 and the film unit went too.

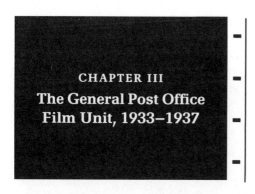

CHAPTER III

The General Post Office
Film Unit, 1933–1937

Is there a department of the Government which does not at one time or another need the services of a publicity section? One day it may be Imperial Trade, another day it may be milk marketing, another day it may be wise spending, still another day, slum clearance and rehousing, still another unemployment – and always there is something to be said to the people which only an efficient publicity organization can say in the right way so that the people both hear and see it.[1]

The Post Office Film Unit is not the only Government Film Unit. It is not an exception nor is it a freak. It is not even, as is sometimes suggested, a racket . . . The only distinction we have, if I may be allowed to say so, is that, outside Russia, we have probably the best Government Film Unit.[2]

Frank Pick gave this justification for government publicity machinery at the height of the struggle to keep the Empire Marketing Board's advertising and public relations expertise intact during the summer of 1933. Unknowingly, he charted the future that awaited one particular part of the Board's publicity wing, the film unit. During the next five years, Grierson's group of filmmakers made films about saving, housing, and unemployment – and they had already made a film about milk marketing.

The Empire Marketing Board's (EMB) popular support had begun to wane largely because its work seemed to have little effect upon the prevailing economic situation. Sir Edward Parry, for example, was not alone in welcoming the abolition of the Board as "a piece of national economy long overdue."[3] Its very existence was abhorrent to believers in freedom of the marketplace and small government. A rescue operation was possible, however, because there were some agencies willing to absorb the public relations expertise developed at the Board. The Board's publicists were dispersed into a number of semipublic and public utility concerns. Tallents himself went to work for the Post Office. The Post Office had actually set up its own Publicity Department in 1929. This had been the creation of A. G. Highet, a former commercial publicist, who like Tallents

Figure 9. *Song of Ceylon* (Basil Wright, 1934): publicity for the Ceylon Tea Propaganda Board.

himself subsequently went on to a distinguished career in official publicity at the Post Office and with Air Raid Precautions and the Ministry of Information during the war. Highet had organized Post Office publicity along the lines of commercial advertising, which meant a straightforward approach to the promotion of specific services. Tallents was invited to organize public relations at the Post Office, to work alongside the traditional type of appeal Highet employed. At the same time, Tallents's former assistants, Huxley and Ryan, were both appointed as public relations men for other semipublic concerns. Huxley went to the Ceylon Tea Propaganda Board, which immediately announced its intention of sponsoring films as a public relations exercise.[4] This Board cooperated with the Post Office Film Unit on several occasions, its most renowned film being Basil Wright's *Song of Ceylon* (1934). Ryan meanwhile was hired to create a public relations department for the Gas, Light and Coke Company, which ultimately was responsible for sponsoring a number of distinguished documentary films.

Initially, the commercial film trade lauded the actions of the Postmaster-General and Tallents for preserving the film unit. The film unit had gone over to the Post Office intact, and in the long run benefited materially from the transition. An editorial in *Kine Weekly* congratulated the Post Office for undertaking the rescue:

Government departments are at last awake to the value of films, both for educational work outside the departments and for the description of their working to the general public. The complexities of departmental work and its contacts with the public at a thousand points make the film activities increasingly necessary . . . what must be looked for now is a strengthening of their relations with the commercial distributors.[5]

Sadly, this benevolent attitude did not last. Two events crystallized trade hostility toward the newly named General Post Office (GPO) Film Unit and Film Library, both related to the trade's fear of unfair competition from the government.

The first significant change was the entry of the giant Gaumont–British group of film companies into the field of the educational, cultural, and interest film. In November 1933, it announced the creation of two new companies, Gaumont–British Instructional Ltd. and Gaumont–British Screen Services Ltd. This was the culmination of a scheme begun in the previous July, when Gaumont–British Equipment Ltd. had started manufacturing 16mm film projectors. Gaumont–British Instructional would make films that would be distributed by Gaumont–British Screen Services and shown on Gaumont–British Equipment's projectors. This new conglomerate was believed to be "the only organisation in the world at present which can handle adequately the vast non-theatrical educational and industrial market from production-to-projection, as one complete concern."[6] This new venture was intended to expand into the nontheatrical field pioneered by the Empire Marketing Board, particularly films for schools, and its owners expected to take over the distribution that had been built up by the EMB.

The film trade's hostility came out into the open after it was publicly announced that the GPO Film Unit would produce films for other agencies, including government departments and semipublic bodies, in addition to its original brief of making films for the Post Office. As the trade press commented:

It is difficult for an ordinary man to understand how a government department whose business is to handle telegraphs, telephones and postage has any warrant to engage in film production, and further, how it is to finance its production.[7]

M. Neville Kearney, Secretary of the Film Producers Group of the conservative Federation of British Industries, was prompt to complain about the unfair competition posed by the Post Office Film Unit. He believed that putting public expenditure into competition with his members' private enterprise concerns was "highly prejudicial to the interests of the tax-payer and to the development of an important and growing industry in which many millions of British capital have been invested."[8] The trade maintained that the Post Office's film production should be contracted out to private production companies. Kearney also thought that the new British Film Institute would prove a better base for the Empire Film Library than the Post Office, which he regarded as a very incongruous home for such a collection. The British Film Institute actually sent a deputation to the Postmaster-General to request custody of the Empire films, which it thought could become the nucleus of a national film library.[9] The Post Office's refusal to cooperate with the Institute on this subject became the basis for considerable hostility.

The film unit's transferral to the Post Office provoked a number of interesting reactions from various government departments. Edward Foxen-Cooper was the Government Cinematograph Adviser, and his primary responsibilities included preservation of official film and allocating the film contracts for the service departments to commercial firms. He advised the Treasury that this form of contracting out film production should be adopted by the Post Office.[10] A number of other government departments were less hostile to the notion of an official film service. Several departments already made extensive use of film publicity, particularly the Ministry of Agriculture, the Ministry of Labour, and the Ministry of Health. All had an obvious interest in reaching wide public audiences. These departments did not have facilities for film production themselves, and could only occasionally raise the funds for commercially produced films. Nevertheless, they shared a widespread belief that film was a very effective form of publicity. Officials at the Ministry of Health had perhaps a bigger interest in mass education than any other organization and saw film as a means of reaching those social classes who were relatively immune to traditional media. It was exactly these groups who were targeted by the Ministry in its campaigns against venereal and other social diseases. In the 1920s the Ministry regularly spent between £4,000 and £5,000 a year on the film propaganda activities of the British Social Hygiene Council.[11] The Ministry of Health supported developing an official film unit that might be able to produce such films on a regular basis. Real cooperation between the Ministry of Health and the Post Office only began when Kingsley Wood, who as Postmaster-General had played a vital part in rescuing the film unit, became Minister of Health. Initially, the Ministry relied upon commercial firms to produce its films, but at the end of the decade, the GPO film unit made several films for the Ministry, including Pat Jackson's *Men in Danger* (1939) and John Monck's *Health for the Nation* (1939). The Ministry of Labour had relied upon the film unit's advice while it was still at the Empire Marketing Board. Subsequently, Grierson acted as consultant to the Ministry when it was negotiating to have a film made by Gaumont–British Instructional. This cooperation eventually led to one of the members of the unit making a film for the Ministry.[12]

The Post Office's new public relations department and film unit were seen at a very early date as models for the public relations activities of other government departments. Tallents's appointment prompted *The Times* to comment:

The needs and opportunities for publicity differ as between different kinds of departments. Those which are largely removed from daily traffic with the public, such as the Foreign and Dominions Offices, and in some aspects of their work the departments which control the fighting services, need a less continuous and sympathetic contact with the public, such as the Ministries of Labour and of Health and the Post Office, whose work is interwoven with the daily life of us all. The remoter departments are likely to find their ends met chiefly by the skilled use of press and broadcasting facilities. But if the work of the latter class is to be understood by the people, and made effective among them, they must be equipped to use, besides editorial and advertising columns and the wireless, the poster and exhibition and film.[13]

The Post Office consistently spent more on publicity, advertising, and public relations than any other government body during the 1930s. Perhaps the London Passenger Transport Board was the only comparable entity in Britain at the time. The Post Office also spent a much higher proportion of its publicity budget on film than the Empire Marketing Board had done. In 1937 alone, for example, the Post Office spent a total of £85,000 on publicity. Of this £19,600 went to pay for the activities of the film unit. This was in contrast to the expenditure on publicity of £32,225 by the War Office, £15,900 by the Foreign Office, and £6,250 by the Ministry of Labour during the same period.[14] The Post Office had begun expanding its publicity in 1929, when it had started receiving a great deal of bad press about its activities and had become anxious to improve its image. It was not concerned with expanding sales – rarely a concern for a state monopoly, but rather with informing the public of what services were available, and to improve its public image generally. It became interested in using films in 1931 when the Telephone Publicity Advisory Committee arranged for the EMB Film Unit to produce a series of films publicizing the new automatic telephone system.[15]

The early cooperation between the EMB Film Unit and the Post Office resulted in the production of *Telephone Workers* (1932) and *The Coming of the Dial* (1932). Both were simple films intended to illustrate to the public how the new telephone exchange system worked. The Post Office had been very pleased with the films and agreed to commission the film unit on a regular basis. The Post Office agreed in March 1933 to set aside £3,200 for film publicity during the next six months. This was precisely the amount Grierson had predicted was required if the film unit was not to be affected by the economy cuts inflicted upon the Board's publicity activities.[16] This convenient arrangement had been made by Sir William Crawford, who was anxious to salvage as much of the publicity machinery as possible.

The Post Office also provided the film unit with much-needed sound equipment and acquired a British Visatone system for £1,050.[17] This was not a very sophisticated system and compared poorly to the sound facilities of the commercial studios and in any event, the unit could not afford the royalties on any of the three major sound systems; but even so, it was a great opportunity for the unit to experiment with sound and also to make films that, unlike its earlier efforts, would not be silent films facing a "fading market."[18] Henceforth, Grierson and his followers would devote a great deal of attention to sound, in both their films and in their writings.

In these early days, the Post Office was extremely generous to the film unit. It was also interested in the conduct of modern public relations, and the Post Office's monopoly on many types of mass communication in Great Britain made it an especially appropriate new home for the country's first official public relations department. It was widely anticipated that the Post Office would inherit the publicity apparatus built up at the Empire Marketing Board. However, even within the Post Office there were objections to taking over the film unit in its existing form. These came primarily from the Accountant General's Department, which believed that the Post Office was the wrong home for a unit that was taking on work for many other departments and semipublic bodies. Simon at the Post Office anticipated the difficulties the Post Office would face over possession of a film unit that was not solely employed on work for itself, maintaining that "if all the work is to continue I doubt if the Post Office is the proper department for it. It is not normal Post Office work and it involves services for so many different departments that an agency department like the Stationery Office would seem to be more suitable."[19] And the Treasury was similarly cautious:

The proposal that the film unit on transfer to the Post Office should continue to do non-Post Office work on an agency basis might well be objectionable if the amount of work was out of proportion to the amount of work done for the Post Office.[20]

The Treasury gave the necessary authority for the transfer of the unit to the Post Office for a trial period of six months, despite its reservations. Tallents managed to secure an agreement that gave the unit a great deal of autonomy:

The unit should be at liberty to continue its practice under the Empire Marketing Board of undertaking on repayment such marginal work for other government departments or public bodies as could appropriately be handled within the limits of its necessary overheads.[21]

The trade's response was immediate. The film unit's possession of sound recording equipment enabled it to make films that might fare well in regular commercial distribution. Documentary films would be competitive in a way they had not been before. Furthermore, the unit seemed on the point of evolving into an official film unit, carrying out work for both government departments and semipublic bodies. Neville Kearney complained that the refurbished film unit "cannot fail to compete unfairly with existing studios established and maintained as ordinary commercial ventures."[22] The subsequent development of the documentary film in Britain was very much shaped by the hostility generated in the transfer of the unit to the Post Office.

The film unit operated initially in exactly the same manner, and with exactly the same organizational structure, it had at the Empire Marketing Board. Grierson and the office manager, Stanley Fletcher, were the only members of the unit to join the Post Office's official payroll. The rest were technically employed by New Era Films, the company with which the unit had dealt at the EMB. This arrangement was no more than a convenient fiction. The company undertook to provide "operational services" for the unit. These amounted to the company arranging the accounts of the unit, carrying most of its members on its payroll, and obtaining theatrical distribution for its films.[23] Grierson frequently found this cumbersome arrangement convenient. He often used it to confuse his civil service masters and his enemies in the film trade. For example, when questioned by the Select Committee on Estimates, which scrutinized the activities of the film unit in 1934, Tallents and Grierson could claim that the arrangement with New Era amounted to the Post Office actually employing a commercial contractor. They were therefore able to suggest that the film trade's criticisms about public expenditure entering into competition with private enterprise were not justified.[24] Neither the trade nor the Treasury were convinced by this argument. Neville Kearney for one did not believe that this arrangement constituted putting work out to commercial tender. Meanwhile, F. P. Robinson at the Treasury had uncovered the truth about New Era, which no longer operated as a commercial enterprise, and he noted that "New Era did practically no work other than that for the Post Office."[25] Meanwhile, Grierson continued to use the contract with New Era to widen the scope of activity of the unit. His followers were able to continue working for other bodies on projects completely outside the brief of the Post Office in a manner that would have been impossible if they had been directly employed civil servants.

The activities of the Post Office Film Unit came to the attention of the Select Committee on Estimates as its probationary period of six months drew to a close, and Tallents had to justify the work of the film unit. His comments are interesting because they reveal some of the philosophical differences between a member of the new school of official public relations and those who still drew upon old-fashioned commercial advertising as the model for official publicity. Tallents believed that it was the task of the film unit to inform and educate the public about the services provided by the Post Office. It was to "bring alive" the Post Office just as it had attempted to bring alive the Empire at the Empire Marketing Board. This public relations function extended to include the staff of the Post Office itself, predating many of the current concerns and techniques of corporate communications. The idea was that morale would benefit if each worker knew how his job related to his colleagues. This was important for one of the country's largest employers. Tallents noted that the unit would "develop among the Post Office staff a better understanding of the department's scattered activities, and to encourage them to feel that their work is worthily represented to the public."[26] Elsewhere, Tallents elaborated upon the need he thought motion pictures would fulfill. Tallents was writing specifically about Post Office workers, but he thought his comments had wider application when he noted:

Lack of knowledge made the daily work of thousands of men and women, large bodies of them working remote from contact with the public, less interesting to them than it really was. They suffered from the lack in the public mind of an understanding of what they were doing; and they felt keenly the critical attitude of the public towards Post Office servants.[27]

It has been suggested by more than one person that the Select Committee that discussed the question of the GPO Film Unit was prejudiced against the documentary movement even before it began its deliberations.[28] In fact, the Select Committee was drawn precisely toward those aspects of the unit's activities that a worried Post Office accountant had suggested would attract critical attention. The Committee questioned the extremely vague terms of reference that Tallents gave it. It also found it hard to justify the Post Office engaging in the "semicommercial" activity of making films for other bodies on a fee-paid basis. On the other hand, it found much to commend in the idea of using films, as they put it, "to explain to the public what their work really was." It was here, for example, that the idea of a centralized official film service was first raised: "It would seem desirable that work should be centralized and not carried on in isolated units in different government departments."[29]

The Select Committee was very dissatisfied with the arrangements that had been made at the Post Office, believing it was the wrong home for a unit carrying out a service function for a number of other government departments. There was also a lot of sympathy for the trade view that

the action of His Majesty's Government in setting up a production and distribution unit under the control of a government department and serviced by public servants is scarcely consonant with the expressed intention of affording all possible assistance for the development of the growing British film industry.[30]

It was felt that the film unit should be run in accordance with civil service practice, not in such an arbitrary fashion. In other words, "the precise objective of departmental publicity for which Parliament is asked to vote money should be clearly stated and strictly maintained."[31] There was, however, an appreciation of the school of public relations with which the film unit was associated. One member of the Committee, the educationalist, Sir Kenneth Lindsay, was compelled to remark:

Departments today have got so complicated and so important, from the point of view of the consumer, who is the citizen . . . that they do need some explanation; and that the film, being one of the most easy methods, a new method of publicity, is perhaps the method par excellence of explaining to the citizens today what is happening.[32]

The Select Committee never contemplated complete abolition of the film unit. It recognized that films were a potentially important tool for departmental public relations and believed there would be a dramatic expansion in their use. So it wanted merely to formulate the rules that would govern film production, but it did impose limitations upon the Post Office's film activities. It mandated that the unit abandon producing films for other departments and outside bodies without prior authority from the Treasury. The unit was to limit itself solely to work for the Post Office, as soon as productions in hand, such as Basil Wright's film for the Ceylon Tea Propaganda Board, were completed. The Committee also believed that the film library should be handed over to a more appropriate recipient and demanded that the Post Office should operate it only until a more suitable home was found.

During the autumn of 1934 the Post Office was obliged to enter into negotiations with the Treasury to bring the running of the film unit and library into line with the recommendations of the Select Committee on Estimates. Tallents and Grierson were determined to minimize the effects of the Select Committee's recommendations and Treasury scrutiny upon the film unit. Unfortunately, the tactics they adopted did much to harm relations with the Treasury, with whom their stock soon fell quite low, which in the long run had very adverse effects upon the subsequent development of the official use of films.

The Treasury was anxious to extract from the Post Office a precise statement of the terms of reference for future film activities. Most important from the Treasury point of view was the concession it believed it had obtained from the Post Office: "It was agreed quite definitely that, at any rate for some time, the Post Office Film Unit must not do work for other government departments or outside bodies."[33] The Post Office also gave precise meaning to the type of films the unit would make. It would be restricted to producing straightforward advertising films and public relations films that were intended "to make known to the public the services, working methods and difficulties of the Post Office, with a view to enlisting the public in relation to Post Office work."[34] Actually this was still a very broad frame of reference. The Treasury also required that the film unit and library be reorganized. It was particularly eager to alter the questionable arrangement between the Post Office and the commercial contractor, which had attracted so much criticism from the film trade and the Select Committee. It conceded that the Post Office should exercise direct artistic control over the production of the films.[35] It was unaware that Grierson would interpret this understanding in very wide terms. The Treasury did not intend this to mean that the Post Office could retain a permanent staff of filmmakers on its payroll. Provisos were made that directors would be "working on a strictly temporary basis" and that their numbers would be "kept as small as possible." The Treasury did not want to be responsible for the demise of the film library because it would then be "attacked from two angles; by the educationalists and by those ministers and officials, e.g. the Board of Agriculture, who may desire a government propaganda library."[36]

The problem the Treasury faced was that there were no other agencies it thought capable of taking over the Post Office's film production and distribution. Treasury officials were unimpressed with the official Government Cinematograph Adviser as a possible alternative. In the evidence given to the Select Committee, his department had been depicted as chaotic and ill-run.[37] The Adviser and the Stationery Office were ruled out as candidates for taking over the agency functions of film production and display for government departments. As Robinson commented:

I think that it is clearly right for the Treasury to do all that is possible to prevent the setting up, under the aegis of the Stationery Office, of a central film bureau for the free issue of government films. This, however, is an important issue of policy on which I do not feel able to make a final decision.[38]

The fledgling British Film Institute did not impress the Treasury either. Robinson noted, after a very unsatisfactory meeting with R. S. Lambert, one of Institute's governors that "the Film Institute had not thought out very carefully or in any detail what they would do if they were to have the Empire Marketing Board films."[39] In the absence of a more appropriate home, the film library was allowed to stay for the time being at the Post

Office. The Post Office agreed to limit the library "to such films as can be said to have a bearing, even though indirect, on Post Office matters. The rest they will be prepared to hand over to whomsoever the government may direct."[40] The Treasury mistakenly believed that an understanding had been reached that was acceptable to itself and to the Post Office, although Tallents and Grierson were far from happy with the new restrictions. They were anxious that the work of the film unit and the library not be curtailed. They employed two sets of tactics to circumvent the recommendations of the Select Committee and the terms of the agreement with the Treasury. At times, the terms of agreement were interpreted in a manner unforseen by the Treasury, so that the letter, if not the spirit, of the agreement was fulfilled. Alternatively, there were occasions when Tallents and Grierson chose simply to ignore it.

The paradigm of the tactic of stretching the terms of the agreement between Treasury and Post Office was Grierson's "reorganization" of the film unit in the winter of 1934. This was intended to bring it into line with the Treasury recommendations regarding direct employment of creative staff. In November 1934, a Post Office Film Unit Committee was established to effect these changes. Grierson, who was directly responsible only to Tallents and therefore represented the film unit at this Committee, drew up his own plans for the reconstitution of the unit. His plan in no way called for a reduction in the size and scope of the unit. The staff were quite simply redivided between the payrolls of the commercial contractor and the Post Office. Grierson took this opportunity to place three film directors and a production manager on the books of the Post Office. An additional thirty people, including a producer and four more directors, were placed on the books of the commercial contractor.[41] The Treasury was soon startled to discover that the Post Office contended that in employing a total of thirty-seven people for its film activities it was obeying the Treasury demand that the number of people employed on films should be kept to a minimum.

The Treasury was very disconcerted by this supposed reorganization of the unit. As Robinson commented to Tallents:

I am rather disturbed at the proposal to pay direct from the Post Office Vote Messrs. Wright, Elton, and Legg, whilst you propose to employ through the contractor Cavalcanti, Spice and two or three others. What is the difference between the two groups and how does the employment of certain of them through the contractor square with the undertaking given to the Estimates Committee that the Post Office would itself assume responsibility for the creative side, obtaining from the trade on competitive terms operations services?[42]

Grierson's reorganization in no way brought about a reduction in the size of the film unit. The unit in many respects actually benefited from the new arrangements. Until the redivision of the staff between the books of the contractor and the Post Office, Grierson himself was the only person directly employed by the Post Office in a creative capacity. For the first time, film directors were now placed on the Post Office payroll. The reorganization also gave the unit some semblance of administrative respectability, something it had hitherto been denied. The Treasury was completely taken by surprise:

If the idea is that Wright, Elton and Legg are regarded as more permanent than the others, I can only say that I had understood that the intention was that none of your directors would be regarded as permanent or semi-permanent employees, they were to be taken on an ad hoc basis for particular films. We had not contemplated in fact that the contractor would be asked to employ any directorial staff or any other named persons but that he would merely undertake to perform specific services.[43]

Grierson's recommendations were accepted unchallenged by the Post Office Film Unit Committee, which felt it had fulfilled its obligations to the Select Committee and the Treasury. Grierson and Tallents had succeeded in maintaining the unit, but they had also made enemies at the Treasury.

At other times, Grierson and Tallents also simply chose to ignore the Treasury restrictions. A Treasury minute had stipulated:

The Post Office will not take a share in the production of films for outside semipublic bodies, and it will not undertake work for other government departments except with the specific authority of the Treasury. The Stationery Office will remain the department responsible for advising other departments in regard to the production of films.[44]

Within weeks after this minute was written, the Treasury learned that Grierson had provided the Ministry of Labour with one of his "young men."[45] Grierson had been acting as film adviser to the Ministry of Labour for some time, and at his suggestion, Arthur Elton had produced a scenario for a film for the Ministry. He hoped to make the film as a private individual but with access to the GPO Film Unit's equipment. The Treasury was not to be taken in by this casuistry. It believed this amounted to the Post Office unit making a film for another government department without the necessary Treasury authority. Overriding the Treasury complaints, Tallents blandly replied:

While recognising the force of the objections which you feel to any immediate undertaking of this kind, we do not think that our unit need necessarily be debarred, even at this stage, from helping another department . . . Our feeling is that in the long run it would be advantageous for us to undertake an occasional film for another department.[46]

Grierson and Tallents succeeded in turning the relatively benign Treasury attitude toward the documentary movement into downright hostility.

The Treasury had never been opposed to transferring the unit to the Post Office. Its only qualms had been about the semicommercial nature of the unit's activities. It had been easy to overlook these because the amounts of money involved were so small.[47] During 1934 and 1935, however, there was a growing suspicion within the Treasury that the Select Committee had not heard a full statement of the facts about the film unit and library. This feeling was reinforced by the action of Tallents and Grierson in refusing to obey the Treasury restrictions. From the Board of Trade it was learned that the unit's distribution of films in both the theatrical and nontheatrical markets was by no means as impressive as the Select Committee had been led to believe. In particular, the Treasury discovered that despite the claims made about the high quality of the unit's films, the Post Office found it extremely difficult to get theatrical distribution for its films. The Post Office's only successes in this field had come about through the good graces of the Board of Trade, which had given the commercial exhibitors some incentive to take up the films by registering them as "quota" films. The Treasury found that

normally educational and scientific films did not reckon for quota purposes but the Board of Trade had recently "stretched a point" and registered as British "shorts" three Post Office films . . . the only way in which the Post Office films are likely to be accepted in the theatres was if they were registered as British "shorts" for quota purposes.[48]

By this point, Tallents and Grierson were very suspect in the eyes of the Treasury. When the Ministry of Labour informed the Treasury of the part Grierson was playing in their negotiations for a publicity film to be made by Gaumont–British Instructional, they received the skeptical reply: "I should not set much store by the opinion of Grierson on a financial matter. He is a Tallents baby, and suspect accordingly in that field."[49]

By the mid-1930s, many government departments, including the Treasury itself, acknowledged the persuasive power of film and the duty of government departments to inform the public about their activities. At the same time, the most prominent advocates of the use of film in this manner had managed to cast strong doubts about their trustworthiness. Robinson stated the dilemma this situation posed in a memorandum entitled "Government Propaganda Films."[50] His report came in response to a suggestion from the Ministry of Labour that Arthur Elton should be appointed as its film officer on an established basis. He acknowledged that the British documentary film "amounted to a new school of cinematograph production." He was dubious about the work of the documentary movement and commented: "It is not clear how far the claims made on behalf of this new school are really justified." He was well aware of the part that self-advertisement had in establishing the reputation of the documentary movement. He therefore commented that, in judging its films, "press criticism which is favourable cannot be regarded as a wholly reliable guide." He had chosen to examine the movement's work himself and now concluded that he was "inclined to be skeptical on the question whether the work of the Post Office Film Unit is of so high a merit as is claimed."

The Treasury view was not shared by those in charge of the public relations departments of several government departments, and semipublic bodies. Within these agencies, there was great interest in both the public relations of the Post Office and the work of its film unit in particular. Hugh Quigley, head of public relations at the Central Electricity Board, was just one of many who thought the survival of the Post Office Film Unit vital. Quigley's opinion was respected. His board was then in the middle of a huge public relations campaign intended to transform British householders into a nation of electricity users. He thought it "a most valuable organisation for bringing the work of the great public boards before our educational institutions. There is no alternative to it."[51] Facing this widespread support for the film unit and its films, the Treasury seriously wondered if it had "so special a merit as to justify the Government utilising it wherever possible for the production of government cinematograph films." There were strong objections to allowing the film unit to become an official film service, as Robinson noted at some length:

From the practical point of view the Post Office unit has given an incredible amount of trouble. A policy based on the assumption that a particular individual or group of individuals are alone capable of producing a good film necessarily implies either that the Government shall itself undertake the whole process of making a film or that it shall enter into a contract with a commercial firm to carry out work under the direction of a government servant . . .If we could abandon the theory that Mr. Grierson and his school are alone capable of making satisfactory propaganda films the problem would become much simpler. A recognised film company would be engaged to make a film for a particular purpose and to undertake that, if it were so employed, it would secure adequate exhibition . . . If, as may well be the case, there are other schools of equal though somewhat different merit, is it desirable for the Government so to speak, to "hitch its wagon to a single star".[52]

The difficulty of obtaining adequate theatrical distribution for government films was a strong argument in favor of a system of commercial tender. Tallents and Grierson were in implicit agreement with this point. Grierson had noted that considerations of distribution should predicate film production in his very first memorandum for the Empire Marketing Board.[53] Meanwhile Tallents himself had only recently noted:

Arrangements for distribution are quite as important as arrangements for production, and should be envisaged from the start. There are very many films of the type which government departments are most likely to need, now stored in vaults without hope of effective distribution and large amounts of money have been wasted in production of this kind.[54]

Tallents had concluded that it would be possible for departments to obtain adequate distribution of their films without resort to commercial contractors. The Treasury was less sanguine and believed that it was extremely unlikely that films made for government departments would receive distribution on their own merits. It was thought that exhibitors would consider such films as "advertising films" for which they would demand a fee:

A figure of £2,000 has been mentioned in this connection . . . Before, therefore, a government department spends anything of the order of £1,000 for the manufacture of a ten minute film, it is essential that it should be sure of a circulation adequate to the cost.[55]

The Treasury did not consider that the Post Office's nontheatrical distribution system, still composed predominantly of schoolchildren, as a comparable venue for government films to the mass audiences of the commercial cinema.

Grierson found other ways to prevent the Treasury restrictions from checking the unit's expansion. The most important device continued to be the division of staff between the official and the commercial contractor's payroll. He was able to maintain that those staff members on the nonofficial books were at liberty to make films for other departments and semipublic bodies. In addition, members of the unit were officially allowed to complete films that were in hand before the agreement with the Treasury was made. Basil Wright's *Song of Ceylon* was one such project. Another was the film Grierson and Stuart Legg made for the British Broadcasting Corporation, *BBC: Voice of Britain*. Grierson hurried through negotiations concerning this film during June 1934 in order to get it started before the findings of the Select Committee rendered it outside his jurisdiction.[56]

Grierson and Tallents were always careful to emphasize that none of his unit's staff, including those working directly for the Post Office, were to be treated as established civil servants. They were therefore able to claim that even Arthur Elton's film for the Ministry of Labour, *Workers and Jobs* (1935), was not in defiance of the agreement with the Treasury. Grierson had been careful to guard himself when he listed Elton, along with Wright and Legg, as the unit's directly employed creative staff:

The directing staff on the Post Office list I should like regarded from the point of view of posts rather than personnel, as it may be in the best interests of the unit to vary the senior directors from time to time. The names indicated refer to the first holders of the posts.[57]

The Treasury did not appreciate the subtle distinctions Grierson made between the activities of the unit and those of its individual members. It

Figure 10. *BBC: The Voice of Britain* (Stuart Legg, 1934): Legg's attempt at a more popular treatment of actuality.

would not allow Elton to work for the Ministry of Labour in a private capacity while using the Post Office facilities since, as one official noted, "it was in fact, if not in form, having the film made by the Post Office Film Unit, a course which we had promised the Select Committee we would not adopt."[58] After they learned of the veto, Grierson and Tallents worked over Christmas 1934 to produce an alternative scheme. The Treasury subsequently discovered that the Ministry of Labour was to have the proposed film made by London Film Productions, who were to use Elton's scenario and to employ him as director for the film, which put the matter outside its jurisdiction.[59]

An important development during this period was the expansion of Grierson's influence into the private sector. Many public relations men, several of them previously associated with the Empire Marketing Board and subsequently the Publicity Committee that Tallents established at the Post Office, were very interested in the use of film. They often found that the commercial film trade was unable to produce films of the type they required. Jack Beddington, Director of Publicity and Advertising at Shell-Mex and British Petroleum, and later head of the Ministry of Infor-

Figure 11. *Workers and Jobs* (Arthur Elton, 1935): the efficient civil service finding work for Britain's unemployed.

mation's Films Division, noted that on several occasions when he had commissioned films for his company, these had proven

extraordinarily unsatisfactory both as to quality and cost . . . several of the biggest advertisers in the country have shared this experience, and are in consequence setting up units of their own almost exactly on a line with the Post Office Unit.

Beddington contrasted this experience with the consistently high quality of the films made at the Post Office Film Unit:

I think I can say, without fear of contradiction, that all those closely acquainted with the film business, both technically and commercially, are convinced of the superiority of Post Office films to all others in their own field, and I feel that this is very well borne out by the obvious jealousy of the trade for these films.[60]

This widespread support for the documentary movement within industry later proved crucial for the development of the independent documentary film. Beddington's own company was one of several concerns that sponsored documentary films on a large scale.

The GPO Film Unit also maintained connections with the private film-making sector. At the Empire Marketing Board Grierson had found some recruits within the commercial film industry. He had also inaugurated the policy of farming out staff members to the industry at times when the unit was not working to capacity. This had been an important way to provide experience for his followers, especially in the all-important use of sound recording. It had also been a means of adding to the unit's diminutive budget. The most important recruit from the commercial industry was the Brazilian filmmaker, Alberto Cavalcanti. Cavalcanti's presence at the film unit was to have a crucial effect upon the quality and type of films made at the unit. The most important instance of hiring out members of staff was the loan of Harry Watt to Robert Flaherty, who was then making *Man of Aran* (1934). Watt's interpretations of Flaherty's methods and style were to have a profound effect upon the late films made at the Post Office and at the Crown Film Unit.

The vastly different assessment of GPO films by the film trade and the documentary movement's supporters is largely explained by the fact that the film unit made several types of film. Often, they and their opponents were talking about different sets of films. Production at the Post Office fell essentially into three categories. Most of the unit's output consisted of simple and often blandly titled silent instructional films such as the *The New Operator, The Coming of the Dial,* and *How to Tie a Parcel.* In addition, each year, the unit lavished a large part of its budget on just two or three larger-scale productions. And finally, the unit constantly spent small amounts of money, but a considerable amount of its time, upon various "experimental" projects such as Len Lye's *A Colour Box* (1936).

Many of the documentarists' first efforts were simple instructional films. Stuart Legg's *Cable Ship* (1933) was the exemplar of films of this type. These films were invariably shot as silent films and on location. Both of these circumstances were partially determined by the tiny budget allocated to each film. These films used "real" people and natural locales to illustrate particular processes, events, or places. A great deal of emphasis was given to the voice-over narration that accompanied these films, if they were not actually released as silent films. The style adopted in these films descended directly from that evolved at the Empire Marketing Board. Their pedagogical values came from this earlier body of work too. Their intention was "to bring the workingman to the screen," and to reveal the drama of everyday existence. This, the documentarists believed, would awaken audiences to the superiority of the real over the make-believe of the fiction film. J. B. Priestley, who had recently completed a print documentary of his own, *English Journey,* found this argument fallacious:

They seem to imagine that in these elaborately designed moving pictures based on real life they have come nearer the truth than people working in any other medium, such as the printed word or the stage. But nearly all documentary films seem to me a very romantic heightening of ordinary life comparable not to the work of a realistic novelist or dramatist, but to the picturesque and highly coloured fictions of the romancer ... the film cannot help dropping out the dull passages, beautifying and heightening the rest, and then giving the whole thing a sort of glitter and excitement. What the documentary film producer is really saying is not, as he pretends, "I'll show you the truth about our ordinary life as nobody else has shown it," but something quite different, namely, "Oh, you think the steel industry or life in a fishing village dull, do you, well now you'll see!" And so you do: you see something exciting and romantic. But go and enter the steel industry, live yourself in a fishing village, and your final and exactly truthful impression would bear no resemblance to the film. In short, their very medium compels these young men to be romantic in practice, no matter how realistic they may be in theory.[61]

These instructional films took as their models Grierson's *Drifters* and his collaborative effort with Flaherty, *Industrial Britain,* although they rarely achieved the intimacy with their subject of these earlier films. There was always a gap between the filmmaker and the ordinary people he or she wanted to portray. This was partially a reflection of inexperience, but it was also indicative of the documentarists' class status. Their class backgrounds made it very difficult for them to relate to the real world of the ordinary working people they were so intent on "dramatizing." This lack of understanding becomes apparent in Thomas Baird's account of the reception of one of the unit's films:

I can remember one day when we showed a film called *Banking for Millions* to the workers of the Post Office Savings Bank. We gathered together some of those who work in the Savings Bank Headquarters in South Kensington to see what was, in many respects, a rather pedestrian film. It was a straightforward account of just what happens on the seven floors of the huge building. It was an account of office management in perhaps the most rationalised office in Great Britain. The actors were the 3,000 operators who handle postal orders, keep books and count counterfoils. The film described the technicalities of a score of miraculous machines which overprint, sort and count forms and orders. There was enough manipulation and machinery to make the best of us reel. But a few hundred eighteen-year-old girls cheered it all. Not for its technical dissertation, nor because it would help them to be more deft in their handling of their myriad postal orders, it was for another reason. For the first time many of them saw just what happened to the stacks of postal orders once they put them right way up. In truth, many of them saw for the first time just what their own job was. They had known it only as manipulation and sometimes rather dull routine. In the film they saw that it had something to do with the real world. In the film they saw this for the first time and they cheered. They were cheering themselves.[62]

Baird was guilty of precisely the sort of misjudgment Priestley had described. He believed this film had shown the drama that existed in monotonous and dull work. He thought that this revelation to the film's viewers and social actors had a spiritually uplifting effect. He did not appreciate that for the ordinary layperson the mere presence of one's own image on the screen was a cause for excitement, and was almost certainly the real reason for the cheering he noted.

Documentary filmmakers served their apprenticeship with these simple instructional films. It was a means of training them without putting a large amount of money at risk. Philosophically, this also encouraged the young filmmakers to think in essentially didactic terms. It permanently affected the manner in which they approached their material. It was a contributory factor in developing the elements of condescension and patronization that were often present in the Griersonian films. Another, and very practical effect of this type of filmmaking was that it made possible for the documentary movement to inflate the number of films it claimed to be producing. In 1939, for example, Grierson's group said they had made some 300 films during the previous decade.[63] A very high proportion of this total comprised the simple and cheap instructional films made by the Post Office.

Each year the GPO Film Unit made a small number of "prestige" films. This was deliberate policy, and it is largely for this group of films that the documentary movement is remembered. Budget, treatment, and usually length immediately distinguished these films from the simple instructional films. In the first two years of the GPO Film Unit, all the prestige films were made for other agencies. All three of the senior directors listed for the GPO Film Unit Committee had worked on films for outside interests. Basil Wright made *Song of Ceylon.* Stuart Legg made the film for the British Broadcasting Corporation. And Arthur Elton had produced *Workers and Jobs* for the Ministry of Labour. In subsequent years, however, the major films made by the film unit were intended directly for the Post Office. Even the prestige films had budgets that, by the standards of the feature film industry, were very small indeed. In 1935, for example, Tallents noted that the total annual budget for the film unit was less than £13,000. As he pointed out, this was less than the average cost of any one of the 189 British " 'long' films registered for quota purposes in 1933."[64] The largest amount the GPO Film Unit ever had to spend on a film was the £7,500 it received from the British Broadcasting Corporation for *BBC: The Voice of Britain.* Most of these films were made for much less. *Night Mail,* most famous of all British documentary films, was made for £2,000.[65] J. B. Priestley commented on the vast amounts of money then being poured into the reviving commercial film industry. He contrasted this with the documentary movement's penny-pinching parsimony:

Figure 12. *Night Mail* (Harry Watt and Basil Wright, 1936): "bringing alive" the jobs of the workers on the postal express.

Enormous sums of money were being handed over by the City, by those legendary "hard-headed" gentlemen who control our finance, to all manner of fantastic Central European characters, who had read with profit Hans Christian Andersen's story of the Emperor's new clothes . . . The City had about as much to show in the end as drunken sailors after a spree. And not a penny of this money lent to the earnest and enthusiastic young men who were making our documentary films.[66]

The consistently poor production values that the unit's small budget generally entailed contributed to the failure of the documentary film in commercial release. For example, when the unit acquired a sound system, this had to be the cheapest system available. As Harry Watt later noted, this resulted in Post Office films invariably having sound tracks of unacceptably poor quality.

Impoverished production values were not the only problem the documentary movement faced when trying for a regular commercial release. Their films suffered from the widespread prejudice among exhibitors and audiences against British film in general. The preference of the British exhibitors and their patrons for American fiction motion pictures over all other types of film was an obstacle to the documentary movement, which shall be examined elsewhere in more detail. Throughout this period American films dominated British screens, and the two Cinematograph Films Acts had comparatively little impact upon this situation. In 1936, for example, the Board of Trade noted for the Moyne Committee that 212 British long films had been registered for quota, compared with 506 similar foreign films.[67] This calculation made no allowance for the high proportion of the number of films in the British total that were quota quickies. British cinema audiences consistently showed a preference for American fiction films. As the trade press commented at the end of the decade:

The cheery musical, the farce, and so on – there can be no argument: they and the straight melodrama are the backbone of our kinemas, and it is no use pretending that patrons care from which side of the Atlantic they come.[68]

Song of Ceylon, BBC: The Voice of Britain, and *Night Mail,* the three major films made in the Post Office Film Unit's first five years all had very different approaches to their treatment of actuality. They shared a commitment to actuality for their material and a refusal to be limited to commercial methods and forms. As Grierson commented:

Whatever the difference of their developing styles – symphonic in Ruttmann, Ivens, Wright and Rotha, analytic in Elton and Legg and dialectical as yet in none of them – they have one achievement in common. They have taken the discursive cinema of the newsreels, the scenics and the "interests," and have given it shape; and they have done it with material which the commercial cinema had avoided.[69]

The price to pay for using material that commercial motion pictures avoided was that the cinema chose to avoid the documentary film as well. The GPO Film Unit only achieved major commercial distribution for its films when it adopted the style of the commercial cinema. *North Sea* (Watt, 1938), for example, was the biggest commercial success for the Post Office. It accomplished this by abandoning montage and the "creative" use of sound for scripted dialogue and the elaborate reconstruction of events in studio sets, all of which were hallmarks of commercial production. The narrative style of the feature film was adopted primarily after Grierson had left the unit. Until his departure, production was characterized by a deliberate rejection of studio artifice. This was partly the result of necessity but also sprang from Grierson's philosophical conviction of the superiority of "the real." Cinema audiences familiar with the polish of films made in Hollywood were accustomed to this type of film. The material the documentarists used and the manner in which they composed their films all combined to render their work inaccessible to the cinema audiences of the day. They were gradually coming to realize that their films would receive a good reception at film society shows and in the "art" cinemas, but that they would be ignored by mainstream commercial audiences. Associated Realist Film Producers admitted as much when they commented that Wright's *Song of Ceylon,* with its creative use of sound and its rich visual imagery, was of "great but specialised appeal."[70]

Grierson and his followers were aware of the difficulties even their major productions faced in commercial release. One attempt to accommodate audience tastes was made in the self-conscious adoption of a "popular" style for the unit's biggest production, *BBC: The Voice of Britain.* It was not a success, and Graham Greene was just one of many critics to pan the film, which was universally ignored by the trade. The experiment was not repeated.[71]

During this period, Harry Watt pioneered the story–documentary form. His first film in this genre was *The Saving of Bill Blewitt* (1936), which, significantly, relied heavily upon Watt's learning from two directors with previous commercial experience, Flaherty and Cavalcanti. *Bill Blewitt* was a simple film made for nontheatrical displays, to be shown primarily in schools, by the National Savings Movement and the Post Office Savings Bank. It showed how self-reliance and wise investment in the Post Office Savings Bank brought prosperity for an impoverished fisherman.[72] This was the inauspicious beginning of a type of production that was to win for the Post Office the popular following that eluded its other films in these first years.

Each year the Post Office released a small group of films for commercial exhibition. Initially New Era performed this task for the unit, but starting in 1934, Associated Talking Pictures took over commercial distribution. The original intention was to release films in groups of six, the usual manner in which short films were distributed. In fact, 1934 was the only year in which the unit managed to assemble six films in the *Weather Forecast* group. This group consisted of *Weather Forecast, Granton Trawler, Cable Ship, 6.30 Collection, Spring on the Farm,* and *Windmill in Barbados.* This was followed the next year by the *Post Haste* group, consisting of *Post Haste, Coal Face, Fishing Banks of Skye, Pett and Pott,* and *BBC: Droitwich.* In 1936, the only Post Office film released commercially was *Night Mail.*[73] The major productions for outside bodies were given separate release. This was an unimpressive performance, especially in view of the fact that all of these were short films. There is a dearth of information about the numbers of people seeing these films. This lack of knowledge is, in fact, indicative of the circumstances that led to the failure of the documentary in the cinema. So little is known about the distribution of short films in the 1930s largely because of their relative unimportance to commercial renters and exhibitors. Short films were always regarded as mere "fill ups," which the exhibitor expected to receive for nothing or for only a small charge. Short films became even less important as the decade progressed with the development of the double feature. This was a problem faced by all makers of short films. These filmmakers also found that the Cinematograph Films Act actually worked against their productions since it had been framed around the interests of producers of studio feature films. The Treasury was prompt to notice the implications of the major circuits' adoption of the double feature from 1935 onward. As Treasury official Percy Robinson noted:

It is unfortunate that just when the public is beginning to take an interest in documentary films the G.B. [Gaumont-British] crowd should be framing a policy which will tend to the exclusion of documentary shorts from theatrical programmes.[74]

Initially Tallents believed that the double-feature program would be a short-lived marketing device. He thought it was intended "to carry off the many feeble features which they have been producing, on the backs of the more popular feature films."[75] This is precisely how the double-feature system worked, but he did not think that it posed a threat to the commercial short film. Sadly, he was wrong. The Board of Trade revealed that in 1935, 1,600 of the 5,000 cinemas submitting quota returns reported that they no longer included short films in their programs.[76] The commercial position of short films deteriorated as the decade progressed. By 1939, less than one third of Britain's cinemas still showed single features. In that year, it was estimated that only 2.25 percent of the screen time of cinemas showing double features was taken up by short films.[77] The Board of Trade was quite certain about the cause of the decline of the short film. This was the result of "the increasing number of theatres which are now showing two long films, a newsreel and sometimes a Mickey Mouse."[78] The makers of short films who worked on a commercial basis also blamed the double feature for the decline in the demand for their output. H. Bruce Woolfe, for example, cited the example of New Zealand, the only part of the Empire that he knew had not introduced the practice of the double bill. There, the demand for short films continued unabated.[79]

The documentary movement was not driven by the same profit motive but nevertheless was still affected by the fact that the shrinking market for short films was perennially dominated by American producers. Their films were given away or were rented for very nominal charges, and they largely controlled the short film market. In 1929, for example, 150 British short films were registered for quota purposes, compared to 663 foreign short films. The relative position of the British short film industry declined dramatically. In 1936, only 85 British short films were registered, compared with 578 foreign short films.[80] The position of those firms making shorts on a commercial basis became very dire indeed. In contrast, sponsored documentary film production by the end of the decade was virtually the only area of short film production not in financial difficulties. Nevertheless, it too, found it difficult to compete for screen time with American short films to which cinema audiences had become accustomed.

Documentary filmmakers and commercial filmmakers alike complained bitterly about the disadvantages they suffered under the terms of the 1927 Cinematograph Films Act. When the system of quotas was introduced, no separate provision was made for short films. In addition, several categories of films were specifically excluded from the provisions of the Act. These included films of news and current events, natural scenery, advertisements and educational, industrial, and scientific films.[81] The intention in making these exceptions was to prevent filmmakers from taking advantage of the terms of the Act by producing quick and cheap films for which they could claim quota status. One practical effect was to exclude virtually all types of documentary films from quota protection. Renters and exhibitors were not inclined to take films that could not be counted as part of their quota of British films. It was only possible for the Post Office to get commercial distribution for the *Weather Forecast* group when the Board of Trade was kind enough to make an exception and grant this series quota status.

The documentary group was at the forefront of a lobby that demanded special provision for short films when the Moyne Committee met to discuss the legislation that would come into effect when the Cinematograph Films Act expired in 1938. The Post Office, the documentarists' central organizing body, Associated Realist Film Producers, and several commercial filmmakers all requested that a separate quota be established for short films, including documentary films, in any new legislation. Associated Realist Film Producers noted how their members' films could only obtain quota status if they could be shown to have "special exhibition value." The Board of Trade had defined this as meaning "box office value."[82] Proving special exhibition value entailed enlisting the support of the film trade to arrange a special press show. The trade demonstrated its lack of interest by rarely cooperating in arranging trade shows. As a result, as Associated Realist Film Producers noted, "evidence of 'special exhibition value' has sometimes to be obtained by the unorthodox method of soliciting advance testimonials from newspaper critics."[83]

The documentary movement believed that the films made at the Post Office and elsewhere should be given special quota status. This would be an incentive for their adoption by commercial renters and exhibitors. The Moyne Committee was extremely impressed with the case made by the documentarists and with the capacity of documentary films for effecting national publicity. On its recommendations, separate quotas for short films were introduced in the 1938 Cinematograph Films Act. Until the new Act took effect, however, the Post Office and other documentary filmmakers labored under the penalties of being excluded from the provisions of the 1927 Cinematograph Films Act.

Renters and exhibitors were, on the whole, conservative businesspeople and preferred to give their patrons the type of films to which they were used. This feeling was by no means universal, however, and one writer in the trade press was prompted to comment about documentary films:

I do not see why they should not be included in the kinema programme, for the public, though shy of the word "education" likes them more than the average showman believes.[84]

A strong motive for not including documentary films in their programs was that exhibitors associated such films with the Film Society and the nontheatrical distribution circuits. They regarded both these as direct competitors with their own interests. Periodically during the 1920s and 1930s, commercial exhibitors took groups showing free films to the courts, arguing on the grounds of public safety and unfair competition that these screenings ought to be suppressed. Grierson was often at pains to point out that nontheatrical screenings were not a threat to commercial exhibitors:

Education does not necessarily compete with entertainment. The educational audience may not be different in personnel from the entertainment audience. But it is different in mood. When the educational picture achieves entertainment value the theatres have been only too ready to take the film over from the nontheatrical field. The theatres, in other words, have the choice of profiting from any films which compete in entertainment value.[85]

The Cinematograph Exhibitors Association remained suspicious of anything associated with the "free show menace," as they characterized nontheatrical distribution. So, tainted by its association with nontheatrical distribution, the documentary movement actually weakened the appeal of its films to commercial exhibitors and audiences.

Nevertheless, one of the major achievements of the Post Office was developing an elaborate system of nontheatrical distribution. It built upon the Empire Film Library inherited from the Empire Marketing Board. One of the conditions of the agreement with the Treasury had been that the Post Office should dissociate itself from all those films that had no bearing on its own work.[86] The same sleight of hand that brought about the reorganization of the film unit was employed in the reorganization of the library. Grierson argued before the Treasury that the survival of the library was vital for allowing the Post Office to display its own films in conjunction with films of other types. He argued that this would create the "relief and contrast" necessary for "effective propaganda display."[87]

The film library was split into two parts, comprising of the Post Office Communications Film Library and the Empire Film Library. Both were housed in the Imperial Institute and administered by the same staff.[88] The following agreement governed this arrangement:

The Imperial Institute will undertake the day to day operation of the Post Office Communications Library as well as the Empire Film Library, but the Post Office will be responsible for determining the general policy to be followed in the administration of the Communications Library.[89]

The new Empire Film Library was officially opened as part of the Silver Jubilee celebrations in July 1935.

The library administered from the Imperial Institute operated a system of free film loans. In 1932, before the reorganization, the Institute lent out 5,575 films.[90] In 1936, the two libraries together lent out 23,500 films reaching an estimated annual audience of five million people. Films from the two libraries were generally sent out in conjunction with each other, with Post Office films accounting for about one-third of all loans, and the majority of films lent out were used in displays to schoolchildren. An early estimate of audience composition is indicative of later trends. In August 1934, it was estimated that 54 percent of all loans went to elementary and high schools, 13 percent went to juvenile organizations, and only 33 percent went to adult organizations.[91] The figures become even less impressive when it is appreciated that a display of these films would consist of perhaps three or four films in a program, which reduces considerably the number of aggregate screenings. The 1936 total of 23,500 films loaned implies a total of between 6,000 and 8,000 programs of films. Readjustment of audience figures must be made to take this factor into account. The numbers of adults viewing Post Office nontheatrical displays must have been but a fraction of the total audience of four million a year that Grierson claimed in 1935.[92]

Another means of distribution of films was a small fleet of mobile cinema units operated by the Post Office. These carried projection equipment that could be set up in any convenient auditorium. By the mid-1930s, this road-show method of distribution had been in use in Britain for over a decade. Grierson had been, as he often was, grudgingly impressed with the propaganda methods of the Conservative party. In this particular instance, he was aware of the manner in which the national government had made extensive use of road shows in the 1935 General Election campaign. An article in World Film News commented that two fleets of mobile cinema units operated by the government had succeeded in reaching 1,555,000 people.[93] The Post Office's own operation was on a much smaller scale. In 1936, the Post Office had four cinema vans that were reaching audiences composed of 500,000 schoolchildren.[94] The goal was to provide film displays for schools that had no film facilities or that only possessed silent film projectors. Extra evening performances for adult audiences reached 25,000 adults in the same period. The Post Office also regularly held film displays at public exhibition halls. The Treasury investigated displays of this type and concluded they were both ineffective and expensive. Percy Robinson, for example, reported discovering a near-empty auditorium playing Post Office films: "On the day on which I went to Manchester there was in the hall on the two occasions when I passed through it a mere handful of spectators."[95]

By 1938, the Post Office was claiming that 3,500,000 people saw its films each year.[96] In actual fact, the number of adults attending nontheatrical displays must have been far less than this. The documentary film had not become the great instrument for adult education that Grierson had anticipated. Grierson instead chose to write about the great progress of nontheatrical distribution, which he claimed would eventually outstrip the commercial cinema:

There is no stopping the growth of the non-theatrical (educational–propaganda) field. It meets a growing demand in the country for more knowledge of industrial and civic affairs. There is growing finance for production and distribution among those organizations whose interests are served by such education.[97]

Undoubtedly, nontheatrical film distribution did grow a great deal during the 1930s. It by no means justified the claims made by the documentary movement. Those claims were part of the elaborate policy of self-advertisement that the fledgling group of filmmakers needed. They hide the diminutive size of this type of distribution prior to World War II.

Subterfuge and self-advertisement did much to help the filmmakers of the documentary movement to escape the limitations imposed by their Treasury masters and by a series of Select Committees. Such restrictions had a very adverse effect upon the scope of work at the Post Office, and this, combined with the desire to spread the gospel of the documentary film elsewhere, led to a gradual filtering of talent out of the Post Office. Arthur Elton left to make films for the Ministry of Labour and then, in what became perhaps the most important transition toward commercial rather than official sponsorship, created the Shell Film Unit. Edgar Anstey left too, first to work for Shell, and then to run the American *March of Time* series British film unit. Stuart Legg went to the Strand Film Company, and Basil Wright left to set up the Realist Film Unit. Both were independent production companies geared to commercial sponsors. Finally, Grierson himself left the unit in June 1937. He resigned primarily to create Film Centre, an organization intended to take over the functions of Associated Realist Film Producers of bringing sponsors and filmmakers together.

In hindsight, this withdrawal from the Post Office seems almost systematic. In 1935, Tallents left the Post Office to take an appointment as public relations controller at the BBC. It became increasingly difficult to evade the Treasury without his assistance. Tallents continued to take an interest in the documentary movement, but he was no longer in a position to offer it his protection. His successor as Post Office public relations officer was Ernest Tristram Crutchley, a regular civil servant who like Tallents had a distinguished career in colonial and Dominion affairs. Like many of his peers, Crutchley was enthusiastic about the use of film publicity, but unlike Tallents, he was not easily swayed by Grierson. He preferred the advice of the professional commercial publicist, Highet, to the inspirational ideas offered by Grierson. Crutchley was not prepared to indulge in the tactics Grierson and Tallents had perpetrated. Grierson therefore faced the prospect of declining personal influence at the Post Office and working under a superior who would obey his civil service masters at the Treasury.

Grierson searched for an alternative home for the documentary movement. The prospects for expanding into other government departments were poor. Several departments had expressed an interest in establishing their own film sections, such as the Ministry of Labour. But the Post Office's work on behalf of other ministries had caused such a controversy that it was extremely unlikely that the Treasury would sanction the creation of film departments controlled by the documentary group within any of these ministries. At precisely the same time that the prospects for official sponsorship looked so bleak, there was a growing interest in documentary films within the public relations departments of a number of industrial concerns and semipublic bodies. The creation of Film Centre was intended to give Grierson control over the production of films of this type.

In the mid-1930s, the documentary group did not help its case by being increasingly irreverent toward government departments that it believed to be squandering the opportunity to use documentary films as a means of public information. They lost allies by making comments such as:

We are disappointed that the Ministry of Health leaves it to the Gas, Light and Coke Company and Cadbury's Chocolate to finance the health and housing propaganda we expect from it.[98]

Such comments were both tactless and inaccurate. In only the previous issue of *World Film News,* for example, an admiring writer had referred to Pathé's film, *The Great Crusade,* which dealt with the national slum clearance campaign, and which had been made in conjunction with the Ministry of Health.[99] A number of government ministries without a budget for expenditure on films frequently cooperated with commercial concerns that chose to make films on subjects of national importance. There were commercial companies that specialized in this type of production. National Progress Films, for example, made films in conjunction with both the Ministry of Transport and the Ministry of Health.[100] These films were financed by major industrial and commercial concerns, such as Pearl Assurance. These companies generally considered this to be prestigious advertising since they became associated with both the government and with a socially progressive stance. Government departments benefited by being able to participate in film production, without having to contribute toward its cost. Films of this type also secured considerable distribution in the cinemas, this too being arranged by the film company rather than the department concerned. Grierson's objections to such films were that they compromised national publicity by their involvement with advertisement for particular private enterprise concerns. This was, nevertheless, an important means by which departments were able to engage in film production without spending official funds.

Within the Post Office itself, the attitude toward Grierson and his group of filmmakers was increasingly ambivalent. There is no question that Grierson's superiors enjoyed the prestige their film unit had acquired. Crutchley himself thought Grierson "a fine artist and a film producer of eminence."[101] Elsewhere he stated, "I would underline . . . the testimony given to the superiority of the G.P.O. Film Unit in the realm of the documentary film. I am convinced of this superiority."[102] On the other hand, when Grierson announced his intention of resigning, the Post Office looked forward to the drastic changes in the policy and organization of the unit that it would be able to make. The Post Office was the leading exponent of the use of modern public relations by official bodies. Film was an important public relations tool that had been largely developed by the documentary movement. When the opportunity came to place film policy under the direct control of the civil service, it was eagerly grasped by the Post Office. In the final analysis, the Post Office preferred to control its own publicity rather than delegating it to a group of filmmakers with definite ideas of their own concerning the use of film publicity.

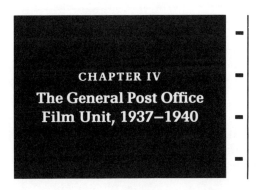

CHAPTER IV

The General Post Office Film Unit, 1937–1940

We were convinced that, unless our films, with their message of the dignity of the ordinary man, could compete with commercial film on its own ground, that is, in the cinemas where people paid to see and enjoy them, we would have failed. This meant, of course, that our films must be entertainment.[1]

The Government cannot afford to ignore the efficiency of cinematograph films as a medium for the dissemination of news and explanation, especially in times of emergency.[2]

Grierson's resignation provided the opportunity for a complete reappraisal of the GPO Film Unit. In the six months prior to Grierson's resignation, the Stewart Committee, an internal committee of inquiry, discussed the changes that might be made when he left. Its most urgent concern was to establish "proper administrative control" over the unit to replace the complete autonomy it had under Grierson. It also intended to revise the unit's structure since it was considered that "the organization of the unit is, judged by civil service standards, somewhat loose, perhaps necessarily so."[3]

As Post Office film officer, Grierson had been directly responsible only to the public relations officer. This arrangement had permitted him to have a great deal of independence in both the day-to-day running of the unit and also in determining overall film policy for the Post Office. The Stewart Committee began by recommending Grierson's post be abolished altogether. It suggested instead that a regular civil servant be made responsible for the unit.[4] So in August 1937, A. G. Highet was promoted to the post of Controller of Publicity with executive control over the film unit. As the committee noted in its report:

Highet, who has been appointed to the new post of Controller of Publicity will be responsible for the executive side of publicity activities: advertising, exhibitions, posters, ceremonies, the design of leaflets and booklets, etc., and in addition, the

79

general control of the film unit . . . The technical administration of the unit will be in the hands of Mr. J. B. Holmes who has been appointed to the new post of Production Supervisor.[5]

The appointment of J. B. Holmes was also indicative of a change of heart at the Post Office. Holmes's background was in instructional and educational films, but he had begun his career with Bruce Woolfe and commercial filmmaking, not the Griersonian school. His appointment in preference to one of Grierson's men completed the split with the first generation of the documentary movement.

Alberto Cavalcanti and Harry Watt both stayed with the Post Office Film Unit. They had never been part of Grierson's inner circle. They, along with the changes in the bureaucratic control of the film unit, were to bring about a fundamental change in its approach to filmmaking. Holmes's appointment proved to be little short of a disaster. Highet soon discovered that Holmes was a competent filmmaker but relatively ineffectual as head of the film unit.[6] Cavalcanti was soon appointed senior producer in his place, and Holmes joined Watt as senior director.[7] This triumvirate controlled production at the film unit until it was taken over by the Ministry of Information at the beginning of the war. Under their guidance, there was a complete break with the rest of the documentary movement. There are also indications of hostility between the Cavalcanti and Grierson camps dating from this time.

The other major change based on recommendations of the Stewart Committee was the separation of film production and film distribution. Beginning in August 1937, film display and distribution were no longer the film unit's concern, and they were placed under Highet's direct control. This division of responsibility was symptomatic of the way in which the Post Office viewed film publicity and the operations of its film unit after Grierson's departure. The film unit was regarded simply as the most efficient way of making films for Post Office publicity. It was not considered as the group of information experts, those "men of spirit and imagination" Grierson had envisaged. Crutchley and Highet believed that films should have the same public relations function that Tallents had proposed. Crutchley was given the opportunity to state his views when yet another Select Committee on Estimates in 1938 investigated the publicity expenditure of the Post Office and several other bodies, including the War Office and the National Fitness Council. He stated:

The objective of our film unit is to be educative and communicative, not to sell things exactly. It is designed in fact, to satisfy the very large public curiosity about public services, and how the Post Office machine works.[8]

This is exactly what Tallents had been talking about when he stated that the purpose of the film unit was to "bring alive" the Post Office to the general public.

Figure 13. *We Live in Two Worlds* (Alberto Cavalcanti, 1937): J. B. Priestley.

Crutchley found the new arrangements for the film unit worked well. As he reported to the Director General of the Post Office:

Mr. Highet has been highly successful in establishing his influence and control in circumstances which the previous history of the unit rendered extremely delicate . . . As a result we have more systematic working to more definite programmes and the introduction of valuable constructive criticism of films during their making. This year's films are in general opinion well up to the high technical standards set by Mr. Grierson, and I am satisfied that the morale and enthusiasm of the workers in the unit remains high.[9]

Grierson had never had the time for long-term planning of GPO films, and there had never been an attempt to produce coordinated series. Instead, individual films tended to be commissioned depending on immediate needs. After Grierson's resignation, the GPO Film Unit had a more programmatic approach to production. For example, in 1937 and 1938, the unit made a series of films dealing with the subject of international communications. The best known of these were the film made with J. B. Priestley's cooperation, *We Live in Two Worlds* (1937), and *Line to the Tschierva Hut* (1937). The series was an unusual example of international cooperation in documentary filmmaking made in conjunction with the Swiss Telephone Company, Pro-Telephon Zurich.

During the same period, the unit also made a series of films, all with Scottish themes, for the forthcoming Empire Exhibition to be held in Glasgow in autumn 1938. These included the major film *North Sea* (1938), as well as *Mony a Pickle* (1938) and *The Tocher* (1938), especially made with Scottish audiences in mind. Similarly, the unit also made a series of films dealing with the British workman in the workplace and in his leisure time, including the now famous *Spare Time* (1939), *Men in Danger* (1939), and *British Made* (1939), which were intended for display in the official British Pavilion at the 1939 New York World's Fair.

The revamped film unit was not fully occupied with these films. Crutchley told the Select Committee that he thought the unit would be able to undertake work for other government departments.[10] He also thought that it would be advantageous for the increasing number of government departments making use of film publicity to have a central government filmmaking organization. Crutchley feared incurring the wrath of the Treasury and the film trade, and therefore he did not suggest that the GPO Film Unit become this central filmmaking organization as both Tallents and Grierson had wanted. As Crutchley stated later: "I personally felt that as things stood, we should, if we expanded ourselves very much, run considerable risk of trouble from the film trade."[11] Several other departments, nevertheless, argued for the expansion of the film unit in order to fulfill their requirements for films.

Within the Foreign Office and the Joint Film Committee of the British Council and the Travel Association, it was widely felt that the GPO Post Office Film Unit was the only trustworthy part of the documentary film movement. It was also thought that it was the only group capable of making the type of films they wished, meaning by this presumably that the directors and producers there were more likely to do as they were instructed than at some of the new commercial production houses. For example, the unit was the only part of the documentary movement asked by the Joint Film Committee to make films especially for the New York World's Fair. Highet inherited Grierson's place on the Joint Film Committee and was able to liaise between it and the film unit. The GPO Film Unit had a special ally at the Joint Committee and also in the News Department of the Foreign Office in Rowland Kenney. Kenney had been interested in film propaganda, which dated back to the time when he and Grierson had sat together on an Inter-Departmental Committee on Trade Propaganda and Advertisement Film Sub-Committee in 1930. Kenney was also the special film representative on the Vansittart Committee. He suggested to the Joint Film Committee "that the GPO Film Unit should be expanded to deal with the propaganda concerning government departments in this country which it is desirable to send abroad."[12] Unfortunately, Kenney's suggestion was ignored while the Vansittart Committee considered the creation of a National Films Council, whose primary responsibility would be film propaganda overseas. Nothing came of this proposal prior to the war, but the ensuing discussion effectively stifled more practical suggestions such as the expansion of the GPO Film Unit.

Several other government departments looked to the Post Office to provide a lead in home publicity, an area where it was now regarded as something of an official authority. As the Select Committee on Estimates put it in its report:

It is a well know public fact that the publicity work of the Post Office has a considerable influence upon the public mind in relation to public affairs.[13]

The Post Office was approached by departments wanting films made by the unit or seeking its advice when they were commissioning productions by other film units. For example, in 1939, the film unit produced two films for the Ministry of Health, *Health for the Nation* and *Men in Danger.* This department was one of several to favor expanding the unit to meet its needs.

Finally, the planners of the Ministry of Information anticipated that the GPO Film Unit would become the official film production unit in the event of war. They too, wanted to expand the facilities available at the Post Office. The GPO Film Unit was thought to be fundamentally different from the independent documentary filmmaking units because it alone was wholly within official control. As G. E. G. Forbes, Highet's assistant, explained:

Ability in the production of documentary films is not in itself adequate equipment for the effective presentation of news and explanation as regards the work of a government department. The scale and complexity of such work makes it difficult for persons of artistic temperament to grasp its essentials so clearly as to be able to present them intelligibly to the public; and the difficulty cannot be overcome otherwise than by constant experience in this field combined with direct and intimate association with the daily workings of the government machine. The special position of the film unit has enabled it largely to overcome this difficulty . . . In time of emergency it is desirable for the Government to have at its instant disposal a film-producing organisation of a kind to which the departments generally, and especially those concerned with defense, can surely grant access to secret information and secret localities; and this condition cannot be fulfilled otherwise than by the continuous maintenance of a film-producing organisation directly staffed and controlled by the Government.[14]

It was therefore agreed that, on the outbreak of war, the Post Office Film Unit would at once come directly under the control of the Ministry of Information.[15]

Widespread official support for the GPO Film Unit had some very concrete effects. First, the Treasury was prepared to countenance filmmaking for other departments. This was a complete volte-face from its policy toward the unit under Grierson. Second, the facilities of the unit were greatly extended. Early in 1939, for example, the Treasury provided funds for a new sound system. The new RCA Photophone system cost ten times as much as the unit's first sound system.[16] It gave the unit facilities comparable to those of the best commercial film producers. This was all evidently in preparation for the anticipated expansion of the unit's work in wartime.

Whitehall tended to treat the GPO Film Unit very differently from the rest of the documentary movement. This was symptomatic of the growing gulf between it, under Highet, Cavalcanti, and Watt, and the rest of the documentary movement led by Grierson and Paul Rotha. Beginning in 1937 those documentarists who had chosen to remain outside the Post Office were mostly concerned with the production of films for industry and some semipublic bodies. There was a considerable amount of animosity between Grierson's group and several government departments, particularly the Foreign Office and the Joint Film Committee. On two occasions this hostility came out into the open. In 1938 the Joint Film Committee decided to withhold a grant of £750 it had offered toward the costs of production of the films made for the Films of Scotland Committee.[17] This series of films was the first coordinated production program undertaken by Film Centre. This petty decision was viewed by the documentary movement as an attempt to sabotage the growth of the independent documentary film. The Joint Film Committee's explanation was that it thought the films "unsuited for inclusion in a general list of British pictures to be supplied to H. M. Missions abroad for display to foreign audiences."[18] In other words, the images of industrial Britain that populated the films produced to project Scotland overseas did not sit well with a group that had a much more pastoral notion of Britain. The second occasion for hostility was the prolonged and very public dispute over which films were to be included in the official exhibit at the New York World's Fair. Grierson's actions in both these affairs made him persona non grata with both the Post Office and the Foreign Office.

The GPO Film Unit's good official standing combined with the fundamental changes in the type of films it made that took place after Grierson's departure were responsible for considerable hostility that emerged between itself and the independent documentary units. There was also a personal element involved. The staff of the Post Office Film Unit had security of employment. The employees of the two major independent documentary units, Strand and Realist, worked from job to job. They were never sure from where their next contract would be coming. As Bruce Woolfe later commented, beginning in 1938, the prospects for most branches of industry grew grim as war seemed imminent, and one result was a slackening in the demand for sponsored short films. Potential

Figure 14. *The Saving of Bill Blewitt* (Harry Watt, 1936): the Post Office Savings Bank transforming Bill Blewitt into a small businessman.

sponsors had other things on their minds besides documentary films. As Bruce Woolfe put it: "By the Autumn of 1939, short film production was almost at a standstill and the industry faced as bleak an outlook as at any time in its chequered history."[19]

The differences between the two wings of the documentary movement were clearest in the films the GPO Film Unit produced during this later period. These diverged markedly from both the unit's own earlier productions and the films made by the rest of the documentary movement. Cavalcanti led the GPO Film Unit away from theoretical discussions about public education and "art" toward films that relied heavily upon the narrative techniques of the commercial film industry. In essence, this was exactly the type of influence Grierson had tried to exclude from the documentary film. The story-documentary made its first appearance while Grierson was still at the Post Office. Harry Watt produced this type of film with *The Saving of Bill Blewitt* (1936). The film employed many of the methods of the commercial fiction film. It had scripted dialogue, some studio sets, and, most significant, it was built around a wholly fictional story. However, it also was made largely on location and employed nonprofessional actors, who were real people acting out events that might very possibly happen to them during the course of their day-to-day lives. In some respects this anticipated the production techniques and the aesthetic of Italian neorealism. *Bill Blewitt* and many of the other films made by the Post Office exhibited the traits that Raymond Williams has defined as the essential elements of all types of realism: a contemporary setting, social inclusiveness, and narratives rooted in secular as opposed to mystical or spiritual explanation.[20] *Bill Blewitt* certainly had all these qualities, although its solution to the problems of the worker turned small businessman – the Post Office Savings Bank – was perhaps a less radical solution than most realists would expect. The fact that the film lacked the production values and sophistication in technique of a commercial fiction film made this no less of a break from the earlier documentary film tradition. *Bill Blewitt* was a rejection of the earlier Griersonian tradition of didacticism in favor of a much more humanistic approach that was less intimidating to film subject and audiences alike.

Watt's promotion to the position of senior director at the unit allowed him to develop the story-documentary on a much grander scale. Watt perfected the story-documentary in *North Sea*, a film he made specifically for presentation at the Empire Exhibition in Glasgow. The film had its basis in true events. Watt wrote the script for this film after reading a series of reports about storm warnings and distress calls from ships that occurred each winter.[21] He "dramatized" these events by making them specific and told the story of one ship caught in the middle of such a storm. Most of the film was shot on location, but as in the making of *Night Mail*, Watt also made use of elaborate studio reconstructions. As in *Bill Blewitt*, all the actors were real people, not professional actors. The most important aspect of the film was the series of performances that Watt was able to extract from his "actors."

North Sea was the most widely distributed of all the films made by the GPO Film Unit. It was eagerly taken up by the commercial distributors and was widely distributed overseas too. Forbes noted the film was "strikingly successful," and commented:

North Sea . . . has earned over £4,000 in rentals (a sum believed to exceed the earnings of any other non-theatrical film) and has been generally acclaimed by the Press as setting a new standard in this field, despite the fact that its release coincided with the release in this country of the far more costly film *The River*, produced under the auspices of the American Government and heralded with a remarkable amount of publicity.[22]

Receipts from overseas distribution of the film, combined with those from distribution in England, must have covered the film's production

Figure 15. *North Sea* (Harry Watt, 1938): GPO films made increasing use of studio sets.

cost of £6,000. The Post Office was gratified by the amount of publicity this film had been able to attract for so little cost:

A total of 1126 column-inches in the British press were devoted to reviews of *North Sea* as the most successful documentary film produced to date. This amount of space would cost more to buy than the film cost to make.[23]

On the whole, Grierson's intimates were not initially very enthusiastic about *North Sea*. They found it too tainted by Robert Flaherty's romanticism. It was also perhaps too close to the tastes and style of commercial cinema, and too successful in theatrical release too. The film's style was very different from the journalistic approach that was increasingly common among the rest of the documentary movement.

Aesthetically speaking, the Griersonian school had always emphasized editing of both sound and image as the most important aspect of "interpreting" reality. They attempted to give form and meaning to actuality footage by the manner in which they chose to cut the material. In the early days of the movement, Russian montage theory and practice were clearly the biggest single influence on their work. The debt of *Drifters* and many of the films that followed it to *Battleship Potemkin* was constantly acknowledged in the early films and writings of Grierson's inner circle. Later there were some important stylistic changes, and their films relied much more heavily upon the quick, illustrative cutting of the *March of Time* style of photojournalism. These later films became a mixture of staged reenactment and voice-over narration or direct address that served to explain the images the viewer saw.

The story-documentary, in contrast to this other tradition, relied primarily upon conventional feature film continuity editing. In this type of film, the burden of the film was carried within the narrative and the performances of the actors. Watt had learned how to treat people in films from his apprenticeship under Robert Flaherty. Watt believed real people, or "social actors," were capable of far better, or "more real," performances than professional actors were able to turn in.[24] Their "performances" – such a term is itself problematic in this context – were quite different from those of the professional film actor. Their very awkwardness in front of the camera was perhaps their greatest asset. It was proof of their bona fides as real people. Watt's actors performed upon studio sets, mouthing dialogue that had been written for them in reconstructions of events in which they had not taken part. Nevertheless, their very manner left no doubt that they were real people and not professional actors.

Watt's intimate portrayal of a group of workingmen in *North Sea* contrasted greatly with the portrayal of the workingman in earlier Griersonian documentaries, which deliberately refused to have rapport with their subject. Their workingman was a heroic figure, best thought of in the abstract. The worker was to be deified, as he was in the Russian films. Edgar Anstey for example, made a very revealing statement – only partially ironic – about his belief that "the workingman can only be a heroic figure. If he's not heroic, he can't be a workingman, almost."[25]

Many of Grierson's acolytes found it impossible to become genuinely close to their material, even when they actually entered the houses of the people they were attempting to depict. The paradigm of this was the series of interviews with slum dwellers in 1935's *Housing Problems*. Such films alienated both their subjects and popular audiences. Watt, with his easy familiarity with his actors and his sensitivity to audience tastes, suffered neither of these drawbacks.

Cavalcanti and Humphrey Jennings, who made his first major film for the unit during this period, were concerned with different types of film. Cavalcanti continued to develop the expository film. As a documentary filmmaker, perhaps his own finest achievement in this area was the film on international communications, *We Live in Two Worlds*. As an executive producer he was responsible for the series of films on the nation's health, John Monck's *Health for the Nation* and Pat Jackson's *Men in*

Figure 16. Humphrey Jennings filming *Spare Time* (1939).

Danger (both 1939). Perhaps the most important development in this type of film was the high degree of technical competence these films achieved. This was a reflection of both experience and the large budgets these films had in comparison to the earlier projects. The most exciting of this series of films was Humphrey Jennings's first major film, *Spare Time.*

Spare Time was made especially for display in the British Pavilion at the 1939 New York World's Fair. It was an early example of Jennings's aural and visual poetry on film. It indicated the direction that Jennings's use of visual and aural metaphor followed during the war. The film was heavily influenced by Jennings's connections with Mass Observation, which like the British documentary movement, was in many respects an attempt at an ethnography of the British working class. *The Times*, for example, thought the film was "an example of cinematic Mass Observation." Grierson's wing of the documentary movement disliked the manner in which Jennings refused to romanticize ordinary people. They mistook his approach for condescension, particularly in sequences such as the famous Kazoo Band march, of which *The Times* commented, "nothing could be queerer or of greater anthropological interest."[26] Perhaps Jennings's biggest fault, in the eyes of Grierson and his followers, was that he took little part in the proselytizing and theoretical discussions that were so much a part of the movement. He was also very much an individual creative artist, which also conflicted with the documentarists' essentially collaborative approach to their craft.

One reason for the stylistic differences between the films made at the Post Office and by the rest of the documentary movement was the GPO Film Unit's official standing. Production at the film unit became much more closely related to official demands and the civil service point of view than elsewhere. Members of staff were no longer able to make major films that reflected their interests rather than official needs. In contrast, under Grierson, for example, the unit had made *Coalface,* a film that had absolutely nothing to do with the Post Office. The film, which was finished when trade opposition to the Post Office was at its height, was finally released as a pseudonymous "Empo" production. Rogue films of this type ceased after Grierson's resignation. As a rule, later productions were much more closely related to official publicity policy and any major film required the prior approval of Highet, the civil service master of the unit, before production commenced. In addition, the Treasury exercised control over film production for outside bodies to seek Treasury approval before the unit began work on their behalf.[27]

The treatment of material and structure of films made by the GPO Film Unit also reflect the fact that they were made by a directly controlled official film unit. The treatments adopted in most of these films detailed a very specific view of Britain and British society. In Grierson's time, the unit produced films that showed the British public as hardworking, patriotic, and in need of guidance from a competent governing élite. The paradigm of films of this type was, ironically, *Workers and Jobs,* the film Grierson had wished the unit to produce but that the Treasury had insisted should be undertaken as an independent production. In that film, Elton showed the neat and orderly manner in which the unemployed deported themselves at the Labour Exchange. Authority was personified in the humane and competent civil servant in charge of the Exchange. Not surprisingly in a film made for the Ministry of Labour perhaps, the biggest problem facing workers seemed to be arranging for employers and employees to come together, not massive structural unemployment. Other films, not made by the Post Office, often featured senior politicians as the voice of authority. For example, Walter Elliot M.P. appeared in *Enough to Eat,* a film about malnutrition in Britain. The image of competent, concerned, and responsible authority was an important feature of the Griersonian documentary. In many respects this was a visualization of Grierson's notion of "stewardship," the manner in which governing élites had to exercise responsibly the power they had been given, and to show that they were responsible.

Significantly, members of the senior civil service were not featured in a

Figure 17. *Health for the Nation* (John Monck, 1939): the Ministry of Health providing "good housing, water supply, sanitation, and drainage and all the health services."

GPO film until after Grierson's resignation. Soon after the assumption of control over the unit by a civil servant, however, Harry Watt began a film dealing with the Accountant General's Department of the Post Office. In a very lighthearted but clear elucidation, Watt showed the manner in which this department exercised extensive control over the country's finances. *Big Money* was liked by the audiences and by the civil service, who thought it presented an admirable picture of themselves. As Hugh Croom-Johnson noted, after seeing the film at the premiere of the Post Office's major film, *North Sea,* it was "much the best film of the evening, giving an admirable impression of the civil service generally."[28] A series of less frivolous films treated the civil service in a similarly favorable way. *Health for the Nation,* for example, showed the measures being taken by the Ministry of Health to "provide good housing, water supply, sanitation and drainage and all the health services."[29] The film was sponsored by the Ministry; so obviously, as Paul Rotha noted in condemning the film:

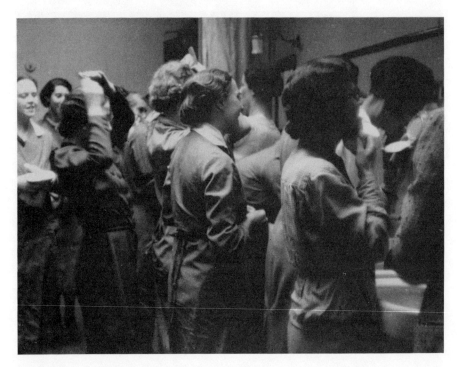

Figure 18. *Health for the Nation.*

It left one with the impression that there was nothing the Ministry wouldn't do to improve the lot of the working man. It did not suggest that better working conditions come about in spite of the Ministry and not because of it.[30]

There are also elements of an "official" style in the later films of the GPO Film Unit, which are not found in the films made by the rest of the documentary movement. The approach of many of their films raised questions and suggested contradictions by the juxtaposition of image with image and image with sound. The GPO Film Unit's approach to film structure on the other hand often implied consensus. The story form and the use of continuity editing suggested solutions rather than raising questions and positing contradictions. The way in which these films were constructed discouraged the film viewer from interrogating the material. The Post Office saw the story-documentary as the ideal vehicle for official propaganda. Crutchley, who was one of the planners of film publicity for the Ministry of Information believed that the story form would be a vital means of undertaking official propaganda during the war.[31] This proved to be the case, and the story-documentary became a staple form of production at the Crown Film Unit, the Post Office Film Unit's wartime descendant.

Many factors were responsible for a growing schism between the GPO Film Unit and the rest of the documentary movement. The unit enjoyed official favor largely denied to the independent documentary units. Some of its films received acclaim in the commercial cinema, which perennially eluded the films made by Grierson's followers. The unit had facilities and constant financial support for which the independent units could only wish. Perhaps the greatest cause of contention, however, was that Grierson did not exercise much influence over the unit. Ironically, the best equipped and funded production unit, which he himself had founded, was no longer under his control. It undermined his vision of the documentary group as a movement, as a group of people all working together for the same objectives. It also benefited from the kudos and international reputation that he had helped build.

Grierson felt that he and the GPO Film Unit were no longer working toward the same ends. It was increasingly concerned with straightforward departmental propaganda, which he himself had never advocated. The GPO unit had also successfully adapted itself to the commercial cinema. It was widely felt that both these changes were a move away from the informational and enlightening ends of the orginal movement. Cavalcanti was generally blamed for these changes. Rotha commented in retrospect about the later films made at the Post Office:

Photographically, they were of a high standard. They were muddled, however, from any social point of view. No film told its story clearly. They each started with some universal conception and then led nowhere. It was due, perhaps, to Cavalcanti's insistence on good technique at all costs . . . It showed where the pursuit of technique for its own sake can lead if a social conscience is absent.[32]

The GPO Film Unit's films certainly did have a point of view. They were wedded much more closely to official publicity ends than they had ever been in Grierson's time. Many of them had an element of humanity that films made by the independent documentary units rarely achieved. Others, like Humphrey Jennings's *Spare Time,* managed to get too close to their subject for the documentarists' idealized vision of ordinary people.

By 1939, John Grierson and Paul Rotha, often divided on so many other issues, were united in their belief that the GPO Film Unit was the tool of its official masters. They believed it had surrendered the independence that Grierson had jealously guarded. The unit was no longer part of the small group of autonomous information experts, using art to interpret the world to the public. It was seen as a straightforward producer of official film propaganda. This became plain in the events of that year at the New York World's Fair. The GPO Film Unit's recent work was displayed in the

British Pavilion there. This included the series of films that had been made especially for exhibition. The rest of the documentarists' films were shown at a separate display at the fair, much to the embarrassment of the officials in charge of the British Pavilion. This was indicative of the differences that existed between the documentarists and the Foreign Office, and British officialdom generally. It also led the planners of the Ministry of Information to envisage the GPO Film Unit as the nucleus for official filmmaking in wartime and the exclusion of Grierson and his followers from their plans.

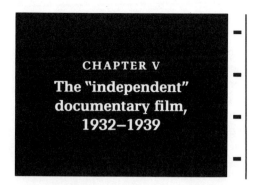

Even films which are primarily produced in the interests of large capitalists can be effectively used to bring this new world of our citizenship into the imagination without inevitably alienating the support of those who finance them.[1]

Let cinema attempt film interpretations of modern problems and events, of things as they really are today, and by so doing perform a definite function. Let cinema recognize the existence of real men and women, real things and real issues, and by so doing offer to State, Industry, Commerce, to public and private organisations of all kinds, a method of communication and propaganda to project not just personal opinions but arguments for a world of common interests.[2]

The castor oil without the accompanying chocolate cream, which is the dose the documentarians try to administer precludes their enjoying any wide distribution over the vast cinema exhibiting network.[3]

Cadbury's, very interested in the sale of chocolate creams, was careful to steer clear of the castor oil that Dallas Bower associated with the documentary movement. Commercial and industrial concerns, such as Cadbury's Chocolate, Austin Motors, and the London, Midland and Scottish Railway Company invested very substantial sums in the production of publicity and advertising films in the 1920s and 1930s. As Sidney Box noted in 1937: "Several industrial concerns in Great Britain are allocating more than £10,000 a year to propaganda by film."[4] These companies were a source of finance that the documentary group was never able to tap. They remained solely interested in conventional advertising and "industrial" films.

Films made for these major commercial concerns were shown either as paid advertisements in the commercial cinema or on a nontheatrical basis, using roadshop displays. By the mid-1930s, advertising films were included on a regular basis in the programs of most British cinemas as they have continued to be until the present day. They reached virtually all of the cinemagoing public. Nontheatrical audiences for these films were much smaller and cost far more for the advertiser. In 1934, for example, Cadbury Brothers estimated that their annual nontheatrical audience totaled only some 350,000. Each member of this audience cost the company between seven and ten pence per head.[5]

In the 1930s, production and distribution of films of this type grew rapidly. Several concerns, such as the London, Midland and Scottish Railway Company, actually had their own in-house production units. There were also many small film production companies such as Publicity Films, Revelation Films, Steuart Films, and others that specialized in making this kind of film for clients. The Grierson group was not involved in opening up this field. This seems surprising because industrial sponsorship was the logical alternative to official support. Grierson himself, of course, had pointed this out in his early reports for the Empire Marketing Board and for the Film Sub-Committee on Trade Propaganda and Advertisement.

In 1927, in his second report for the Empire Marketing Board, Grierson had expounded at length on the potential importance of "commercial, industrial and educational films" for reviving both the British film industry and British trade in general. He maintained that the film trade generally handled such films very poorly. He believed there was "clearly a case for the organisation of supplementary production units and supplementary exhibition arrangements."[6] In these early years, Grierson had expected a great deal of development in the nonofficially sponsored documentary film. However, industry and commerce rarely provided the wherewithal for the production of documentary films during the 1930s. Only one company, Shell Oil, set up a documentary film unit of its own. In addition, a small number of publicly owned or public utility concerns regularly sponsored programs of documentary films. The most prominent sponsors of this type were Imperial Airways and the gas industry. The Strand Film Company made a number of films each year for Imperial Airways, having first been involved in the coproduction of Paul Rotha's *Contact*. The gas industry was remarkable for the number of films dealing with contemporary social issues in a fairly direct way, which it commissioned with the Strand Film Company and the Realist Film Unit. In addition, there were also some companies, such as the Orient Shipping Line and the Southern Railway Company, that provided sporadic and occasional sponsorship. Most of the expenditure on film publicity by purely private enterprise concerns went into straightforward advertising films, which aimed to entertain and to sell the product to the cinema audience without education or uplift. They were well aware of the dictum, "It is no use blinking the fact that a cinema audience planks down its money at the box office to be entertained . . . there may be a little pill, but there must be a lot of jam."[7]

Semipublic bodies were much more likely to sponsor documentary films. Typically, these were agencies that were instruments of government policy, but lay outside the bureaucracy of the traditional civil service. The most prominent sponsors of this type included the National Council for Social Service and the Land Settlement Association. Both were ostensibly autonomous organizations, which in fact were closely tied to government policy, especially in connection with the designated Special Areas and unemployment. The National Council was intended to encourage the spirit of volunteerism – the unemployed would help each other until work returned, while the Land Settlement Association's goal was to resettle unemployed workers on rural smallholdings. These organizations developed an outlook on publicity and public relations quite similar to that of the public service and publicly owned industries. The "independent" documentary movement grew on the coattails of this new school of public relations. This school grew within concerns that were not motivated by the traditional incentives of private enterprise and agencies that operated on the periphery of conventional public policy.

This approach to public relations was imported largely from the United States. It developed there in response to the demands of government during wartime and the desire on the part of oligopoly concerns like Standard Oil to improve their public standing. Theorists like Lippmann, and practitioners like George Creel, Edward L. Bernays, and "Ivy" Lee noted that the interests of government departments and big corporations were often best served by public education about their activities. Bernays explained the rise of the public relations expert in this way:

The new profession of public relations counsel has grown up because of the increasing complexity of modern life and the consequent necessity of making the actions of one part of the public understandable to other sectors of the public.

Bernays commented elsewhere on why public education was such an efficient means of winning approbation:

If the public is better informed about the processes of its own life, it will be so much the more receptive to reasonable appeals to its own interests. No matter how sophisticated, how cynical the public may become about publicity methods, it must respond to the basic appeals.[8]

The development of public relations in Britain during the 1930s was often linked to specific individuals who had been associated in some capacity with the Empire Marketing Board. Public relations men who had worked with Sir Stephen Tallents at the Board were subsequently imbued with the idea that information and education were the key to public relations and that the documentary film was a vital part of this. Major government departments were slower to develop public relations machinery than they had been in the United States. The departments where public relations developed in Britain, the Post Office and the Empire Marketing Board, were engaged in commercial activities to an extent that was unusual for a government agency. As Sir Stephen Tallents commented:

> The Post Office of today is a combination between a great business corporation and a government department. As such its publicity – to use, in default of a better title, a word which nobody likes and which is at some points inadequate to our subject – must be organized to combine, with such modification as its special position demands, the well tried methods of commercial advertising and the almost wholly unpractised methods of government publicity.[9]

The growing range of agencies that had the attributes of both government and commerce, like the Post Office and the public utilities, provided the documentary movement with a wide variety of potential sponsors.

Grierson's inspiration for the development of the independent documentary film, as with so many things, came from the United States. Grierson had been particularly impressed there by two things. He noted the extent to which American trade and industry benefited from the incidental publicity for their products in American feature films. He suggested that "the strength of American film publicity has lain in the fact that American products have been part and parcel of the atmosphere and setting and have been made desirable by the star or story associations of the picture."[10] He also noted the very great number of films that were made in the United States each year with industrial sponsorship. He cited Will Hays, the Republican head of the U.S. Motion Picture Producers and Distributors Association, who in 1930 claimed that 100 million feet of industrial films were being shot in the United States each year.[11] Grierson believed that the sponsored film could be much more artistically creative than the commercial feature film. *Nanook of the North,* for example, had shown how this could be the case. As Grierson noted, *Nanook* was "financed by Revillon Frères and was in the first place an advertisement for furs." There was little to compare with *Nanook* in Great Britain. Grierson was completely unimpressed with the industrial film in Britain. He characterized the efforts of the firms who sponsored films about their activities as "a complete failure." He noted films were generally made " 'in the air,' without any regard to special audience requirements. A vague decision that 'a film of the plant would somehow or other be useful' means almost invariably a bad film."[12] Paul Rotha noted that the continual carelessness of producers of industrial films had created a tradition of slipshod work. These people made films "on the disgraceful basis of so much per foot, cut to measure without skill or thought."[13]

Grierson suggested remedies for this "senile" school of filmmaking, as he termed it. He proposed that films should be made that dramatized industries as a whole, not the sectional interests of particular companies, just as his own *Drifters* had done. Furthermore, Grierson noted elsewhere, he envisaged industrial films as creative and potentially inspirational pieces of filmmaking. He also wanted the exclusion of any elements of the fiction film world from industrial films. Grierson exhorted industrial film-makers to base their films on the real world, not on escapism:

Look into your subject matter. If you have brains enough and imagination enough, you are bound to find something interesting at the heart of it. Why apologize for your subject with an extraneous leg-show when you may find in the subject itself a theme more lastingly impressive.[14]

Generally, though, few commercial concerns were interested in paying for films that dramatized their industry but that gave their own business no more attention than they gave to their rivals. A small clique of men, bound by professional, personal, and family ties provided the initial wherewithal for film production outside official auspices. Paul Rotha gave credit to a small group of public relations men with a social con-science, particularly Jack Beddington, of Shell-Mex and British Petro-leum, Frank Pick at the London Passenger Transport Board, Snowden Gamble of Imperial Airways, H. E. Medlicott at Anglo-Iranian Oil, Alexan-der Wolcough of the Asiatic Petroleum Company, Thomas Tallents of the Orient Shipping Line, and A. P. Ryan and S. C. Leslie at the gas industry for their patronage of British filmmaking.[15] All were involved in some aspect of corporate development of the Empire or in consumer-orientated commercial enterprises.

The documentary movement frequently characterized these individu-als as farsighted businessmen who were prepared to put the interests of the community as a whole before those of their own sectional interests. Their willingness to sponsor documentary films was evidence of their commitment to public education. Some critics were very cynical about this. As Arthur Calder-Marshall commented:

When a film is financed by interests other than those of the entertainment indus-try, the financiers are out to get results, either in sales or states of mind . . . Mr. Grierson may like to talk about social education, surpliced in self-importance and social benignity. Other people may like hearing him. But even if it sounds like a sermon, a sales talk is still a sales talk.[16]

Commercial concerns were rarely prepared to pay for films – or for any other type of public relations exercise, for that matter – if they were to get no return of any kind on their investment. Self-interest always played a

Figure 19. *Housing Problems* (Arthur Elton and Edgar Anstey, 1935): working-class men and women given the opportunity to speak for themselves to city planners and government.

part in sponsorship. The gas industry was often cited as the paradigm of a selfless sponsor of films dealing with narrowly defined social issues. These films were in fact closely tied to elaborate and long-term public relations policy. Beginning in 1935, each year the Gas, Light and Coke Company, the major supplier of gas in Greater London, and the British Commercial Gas Association sponsored the production of a group of films. Each year, there would be one or more films dealing with important social issues, such as housing, education, malnutrition, and pollution. The best known of these films include *Housing Problems* (1935), *The Nutrition Film: Enough to Eat* (1936), *Kensal House* (1936), *The Smoke Menace* (1937), and *Children at School* (1937). These films comprised a large part of the body of work upon which the reputation of the documentary movement was built. Grierson's followers frequently praised the gas industry for fulfilling its obligations as a large corporation and for providing the funds for films that should rightly have been made by government departments. A. P. Ryan, who became publicity manager at the Gas, Light

Figure 20. *Housing Problems.*

and Coke Company after resigning as press officer at the Empire Marketing Board, was credited with having "associated gas and public service
for the first time in film."[17] Ryan was responsible for arranging sponsorship for *Housing Problems,* the first of the gas industry's films to deal
with a pressing national crisis.

   S. C. Leslie succeeded A. P. Ryan in 1936, and under his control the
image of the gas industry promoted in the films it sponsored was that of a
socially conscious organization with interests transcending crass commercial profit. The gas industry's films attracted a substantial part of the
annual nontheatrical audience of ten million that Grierson claimed in the
later 1930s.[18] They also provided a large part of the work undertaken each
year by the independent documentary units.

   Film sponsorship was part of an extensive and carefully orchestrated
campaign to improve the public standing of the gas industry, particularly
among local government officials. Sir David Milne-Watson, Governor of
the Gas, Light and Coke Company, hired A. P. Ryan to create a publicity
department for his company in 1931. This new department was part of a
wider effort to "modernize" the image of the gas industry, which in compar-

Figure 21. *Housing Problems.*

ison to the electricity industry was increasingly characterized as old-fashioned and antiquated. The gas industry felt compelled to do this because for the first time it faced competition from the electricity industry for control over the supply of power for cooking and heating. The gas industry found that some municipalities, especially those with their own electricity undertakings, were increasingly prejudiced against the use of gas, especially by council tenants. At that time, the gas industry found town councils were building new housing estates that were completely dependent upon electricity, with no provision for the supply of gas. Some local authorities had even taken the step of filling in the gas pipes on existing council property with cement.[19] The gas industry had to act to make gas more popular among both consumers and the town planners, who in the final analysis decided which form of power consumers should receive.

The publicity department of the Gas, Light and Coke Company found that it had to improve its own image as well as advertising its services and the new, modern-looking appliances it was making available. For the general public, the publicity department poured out imaginative and interesting materials along the lines pioneered by the Empire Marketing Board and Shell Oil. The creation of an easily identified symbol, the

Figure 22. *Enough to Eat* (Edgar Anstey, 1936): nutrition – a natural subject for films sponsored by the gas industry.

animation character, Mr. Therm, was an important part of this popular campaign. Mr. Therm appeared constantly in the gas industry's film and press publicity in the 1930s.[20] As had been the case at the Empire Marketing Board, documentary films were a relatively small part of this large-scale publicity campaign. They succeeded, however, in attracting a large amount of publicity in the press. The primary intention behind the films was to associate the gas industry with social progressivism in the eyes of the planners responsible for slum clearance and new housing estates. In this way, gas was portrayed as an integral part of housing units in the new housing estate shown in *Housing Problems* and was part of the campaign for cleaner air in *The Smoke Menace.*

The gas industry films received some theatrical distribution, but generally they were shown on a nontheatrical basis. In 1938, for example, Sir David Milne-Watson estimated that the gas industry's films had been seen by one million people that year through various forms of nontheatrical distribution. He suggested that his company's sponsorship of films had not been "dictated by directly commercial motives." He believed that the films were intended to establish

Figure 23. *The Smoke Menace* (John Taylor, 1937): pollution – another natural subject for gas-industry-sponsored films.

relations of improved understanding and increased confidence between our industry and its public, and not least in the minds of those more highly critical and influential sections which are particularly difficult to reach through traditional channels of persuasion.[21]

When the ultimate intention of the gas industry's film sponsorship was to improve its image, and thereby maintain and hopefully, increase, sales of gas, it is difficult to accept Milne-Watson's claim that no directly commercial motives were involved. As Arthur Calder-Marshall commented: "The Gas, Light and Coke Company is ... finding in the performance of a socially useful task a first-class advertisement."[22]

British film exhibitors had no doubts about the films made by the gas industry, regarding them as straightforward advertising films that would only be shown on payment of a fee to the exhibitor. Furthermore, the films made by the documentary group were only a small part of an extensive film publicity campaign intended to cover the whole gamut of audiences. The campaign spanned from cookery films starring Mr. Therm for display in commercial cinemas and nontheatrical venues such as Women's Institute meetings to social documentaries aimed at more serious audiences in special screenings arranged for local city councils, adult educa-

Figure 24. *Children at School* (Basil Wright, 1937): the gas industry finding in "the performance of a socially useful task a first-class advertisement."

Figure 25. *Children at School.*

tion classes, the film societies, and so on. This diversified public relations effort deliberately targeted different types of audiences.

Public utilities such as the gas industry were obvious candidates to be approached as alternatives to sponsorship by government departments. Public utilities could make only limited use of conventional advertising. They had to persuade whole bodies of people not simply individuals, about the merits of their product. For example, the gas industry achieved nothing if it persuaded a householder to change to gas, if the local council was not prepared to supply it. The image of the industry as a whole had to be improved and passed on to decisionmakers as well as the general public. Public relations men like S. C. Leslie were convinced that sponsorship of occasional essays in photojournalism gave returns in the form of improved public standing for his company. This opinion was shared by a writer in *Kine Weekly*, who believed that the gas industry's documentary films were an "advertising medium" whose "exploitation in town halls and other civic temples should prove of inestimable value to the public and their sponsors alike."[23] In Hugh Quigley, the electricity industry had a public relations expert who was equally conscious of the value of documentary films for refurbishing the corporate image. He believed that the documentary group alone had the capacity to produce films of this type. He had found the "capacity of the film producing industry to do industrial films . . . very limited indeed."[24] It was the gas industry, which found itself burdened with an old-fashioned image, and therefore, it, rather than the electricity industry, was most willing to provide backing for the documentary group.

The other important commercial sponsor for documentary films was Imperial Airways. In many respects this airline, and a series of publicity campaigns that showed the manner in which it was using air routes to bring together distant parts of the Empire, was the direct descendent of the Empire Marketing Board. It, too, needed to "bring alive" the different outposts of the Empire. It regularly sponsored productions by the Strand Film Company, which included *Heart of an Empire* (1936), *The Future Is in the Air* (1937), *Air Outpost* (1937), *Watch and Ward in the Air* (1937), *Wings over Empire* (1939), and *African Skyways* (1939). Imperial Airways, like the gas industry, was not governed by the traditional motives of private enterprise. Air travel was a new commodity, and like the Post Office in its marketing of the telephone, the aviation industry literally had to create a market where none had existed. Air travel could not be advertised as competing with rival forms of transport. Sponsorship of documentary films was intended to create an image for air passenger transport, and did this by linking the industry to business and colonial development. Films made for Imperial Airways were invariably concerned directly with the company's own activities, unlike those sponsored by the gas industry. In this respect, they recalled the earlier tradition of the industrial film. The Imperial Airways films were important, however, because they provided a regular income for the two independent documentary units, the Strand Film Company and the Realist Film Unit.

The Shell organization was the only major industrial sponsor of documentary films that was neither a public utility nor publicly owned. Shell-Mex and British Petroleum, on the advice of Jack Beddington, sponsored occasional productions, the most notable of these being Paul Rotha's debut film, *Contact,* which was made in conjunction with Imperial Airways. After this, Grierson was asked to produce a report on the use of film publicity for the Shell group. As a result of this report, in 1934, the Asiatic Petroleum Company set up a film unit, under the control of Alexander Wolcough and headed at first by Edgar Anstey and Arthur Elton. This was the beginning of Elton's involvement with the Shell Film Unit, which spanned the next thirty years. During the 1930s, the Shell Film Unit became a steady producer of high-quality documentary films, often with a science and technology emphasis.[25]

Shell's interest in films derived from Jack Beddington, who, as assistant general manager and director of publicity for Shell-Mex and British Petroleum, was responsible for his company's consistently high publicity standards. Beddington, like so many of the public relations men with whom the documentary movement collaborated, was associated with Sir Stephen Tallents, and both served as members of the Post Office Publicity Committee. Beddington, like Frank Pick, believed that the big corporations had a social obligation to support artistic endeavor. He believed the Shell Company ought to be a patron of the arts, although as Sir Kenneth Clark once commented, the art resulting from this policy was very rarely outstanding.[26] For Beddington, as for Tallents, the artist had an important social role to play as the purveyor of knowledge to the general public. He agreed with John Stuart Mill's dictum that, "It is the artist alone in whose hands truth becomes impressive and a living principle of action."[27]

The development of the independent documentary movement was facilitated by the growing number of semiofficial and noncommercial enterprises interested in film publicity in the 1930s. There was a proliferation of organizations that, although very definitely tools of the government, were created and operated outside the traditional civil service hierarchy: the British Council, established to improve British cultural relations overseas; the National Fitness Council, created to develop health education in Britain; the National Savings Movement, intended to encourage small savers to invest in the government; and the Scottish Development Council, all worked in this way. In his excellent book on the British Council, for example, Philip Taylor has written a closely argued work on the creation of the modern apparatus for national publicity overseas in the 1930s.[28] The development of modern public relations and publicity within these other quasi-governmental bodies, working on public opinion within Great Britain, is a subject that awaits a full study.

All of these organizations spent substantial amounts of money on film publicity. Some agencies, such as the British Council, were primarily engaged in the distribution of existing films. For others, such as the Scottish Development Council, which set up a special Films of Scotland Committee, production of films was an important part of their work.[29] All these bodies believed that film was a particularly effective form of publicity. The National Fitness Council, for example, was set up at a time when the government was concerned about the shortage of healthy army recruits, and its goal was to educate Britain's general public in health and nutrition. It was so convinced of the value of films that by 1939 it was devoting one-third of its total annual publicity budget of £31,000 to the production and distribution of films.[30]

It was obvious to all concerned with the documentary movement that a film unit or group of film units, working on a proper commercial basis and not attached to a government department, had to be established to cater for production for outside sponsors. Production for outside sponsors by the Post Office Film Unit could only be sporadic. It could never escape from the charge of unfair competition leveled at it by the film trade. It was crucial for the subsequent development of the independent documentary movement that Paul Rotha, not Grierson, lead the way in erecting independent production on a regular basis to meet these needs.

Paul Rotha was never one of Grierson's "young men." He worked with Grierson only briefly at the Empire Marketing Board and was never on the payroll at the GPO Film Unit. Rotha was the only member of the documentary movement to build a reputation for himself independently of Grierson's patronage. Prior to meeting Grierson, Rotha had already established himself as a major British film writer and theorist with *The Film Till Now*, first published in 1930. This was one of the very first attempts to produce a systematic and global history of the motion picture, and its publication actually predates Terry Ramsaye's better known *One Million and One Nights*. He went on to write *Documentary Film*, the first basic text on documentary theory and history in 1935. This has gone through revision in subsequent editions and remains one of the standard books on the politics and aesthetics of documentary filmmaking. Rotha emerged as an important filmmaker in his own right. Proper assessment of Rotha's contribution to the development of the documentary film in Britain has constantly been hindered by the tendency of authors to overemphasize the role of Grierson and his inner circle over that of Rotha. It is only comparatively recently that there have been attempts at reappraisal that have placed Rotha firmly back in the center of the documentary movement.[31] Even these efforts have failed perhaps to give sufficient credit to Rotha for the development of the independent documentary film. The independent units developed interests and an approach to their material quite different from those predominating in that part of the documentary movement that remained under direct official control.

Rotha entered industrial film production immediately after a brief tenure with the Empire Marketing Board Film Unit. He was first employed upon the Imperial Airways–Shell coproduction, *Contact*. Jack Beddington arranged for British Instructional Films, the commercial company with most experience with films of this type, to be the production company working with Rotha on the film. This was the beginning of a long and very unhappy working relationship between the left-wing Rotha and the conservative H. Bruce Woolfe at British Instructional Films, and its later incarnation, Gaumont–British Instructional. Beddington once noted to Kingsley Wood that he subsequently regretted having "forced" Rotha on to Bruce Woolfe.[32] The conservative production company and Rotha, the difficult and socialist artist, did not get on together at all.

Rotha worked with Bruce Woolfe for two years. During this time, he gradually developed an ability to bring contemporary social issues into industrial films made for commercial sponsors. *Shipyard* (1934) and *The Face of Britain* (1935) were ostensibly straightforward films for industrial sponsors. *Shipyard,* made for Vickers Armstrong and the Orient Line, was a close study of the effects of building a ship within a closed shipbuilding community. Shipbuilding was one of the most depressed industries in Britain in the 1930s, and Rotha's film went directly to the heart of the prospect of unemployment that faced the community once the ship had been completed. *The Face of Britain* dealt with the hopes for a cleaner countryside with the increasing use of electricity by industry. Rotha, inspired by Priestley's recently published *English Journey,*[33] felt obligated to also deal with the subject of mass unemployment in both of these films. The desire to deal with such pressing social issues, and the deteriorating relationship between himself and Bruce Woolfe chronicled in Rotha's autobiographical *Documentary Diary,* made Rotha anxious to set himself up as an independent producer and director.[34]

Rotha wanted to dissociate himself from any of the big commercial producers, and his employer, Gaumont–British Instructional, was an offshoot of Britain's biggest production combine. At the same time, however, Rotha still believed that the proper place for the documentary film was in regular theatrical release.[35] He did not acknowledge the difficulties in distribution a small independent production company faced if it was not tied to one of the big production or distribution companies. In any event, in 1935, when Donald Taylor offered Rotha the position of director of production at the Strand Film Company, Rotha gladly accepted.

The Strand Film Company, like the earlier concern, New Era Films, was a commercial company that was at first owned by a major film producer and distributor before being appropriated by the documentary movement. Both were transformed from failing producers of feature films into full-time production companies making documentary films. For the Strand Film Company, this proved to be quite a profitable venture. Rotha claimed that the company soon began to flounder after he ceased to be associated with it in 1937. In fact, the evidence suggests that the company was consistently a financial success. In 1938, for example, the company had so much work on hand that it was compelled to move into bigger and better facilities at Merton Park.[36] In addition, its zoological film series were a huge commercial success, so much so, that a separate company, Strand Zoological Film Productions, was set up to produce the series.

When Rotha was appointed director of production at Strand, he brought with him as assets the series of contacts with sponsors that he had made while at Gaumont–British Instructional. These contacts included Imperial Airways and the National Book Council. They provided the reconstituted company with its first work. Rotha's other main contribution was the style as a documentary filmmaker that he had evolved while working at Gaumont–British. This was quite different from that that had emerged at the GPO Film Unit. Rotha's connections were important because they enabled the new company to commence production assured of regular sponsorship. Rotha's possession of a personal style of filmmaking, which had developed outside the Grierson coterie, was even more important. For two years, Rotha was in charge of a documentary unit that, although closely related to Grierson and the documentary movement, developed its own interests and style of filmmaking.

In February 1937, the Strand Film Company was joined by another documentary film unit when Basil Wright established the Realist Film Unit. Grierson, who was scheduled to leave the Post Office in June of that year, was clearly behind this move to enter the field of the independent documentary film. In fact, Realist soon began to usurp Strand's position as the center of independent documentary production, and this was made possible by the confluence of two other factors. Perhaps most important was the temporary removal of Paul Rotha from the scene. He had been invited to give a lecture tour of the United States and was out of Britain during the latter half of 1937 and the first half of 1938.[37] His position at Strand was taken over by Stuart Legg, who was very much a Grierson man. It appears that Legg was prepared to acquiesce in the expansion of the competing production company directly controlled by Grierson at the expense of his own unit. In addition, Donald Taylor was increasingly interested in making films for commercial exhibition. Under Taylor and Legg, the Strand Film Company made more travelogues and zoological films and fewer of the socially conscious films like the ones produced by Rotha. The other factor behind the relative decline of Strand was the creation of Film Centre. Grierson's "film consultancy" quickly and quietly took over from Associated Realist Film Producers the function of mediating between sponsors and filmmakers. Rotha was the secretary of that body and his absence must have greatly facilitated the takeover by Film Centre. Film Centre soon proved itself very biased toward Realist in its allocation of contracts. For example, Realist took over the production of films for the gas industry. Grierson's advice must clearly have been important in deciding how such favors were awarded. The Strand Film Company and the Realist Film Unit were the basis for what is characterized here as the independent documentary movement. Film Centre also played an important part in the development of this movement. It became the agency that allocated contracts among the different production companies.

Publicity was also important. The members of the documentary group continued to state their case and to make themselves known through articles in the lay press and in a variety of trade journals and literary periodicals. Basil Wright, for example, became film critic for *The Spectator* in 1938. Grierson and Rotha both regularly contributed to *The Times* and the other quality newspapers. The publicity effort came into its own, however, with the creation in April 1936, of *World Film News.* This was a small but influential journal, which at its height had a circulation of perhaps 4,000. *World Film News* in a sense reflected some of the major contradictions within the Griersonian philosophy. In its early issues, its banner headlines and broad political cartoons made it look very much like a mass-market tabloid newspaper – and yet this was not the constituency of this magazine at all. This was very much an indication of the way in which Grierson's essential élitism was grafted on to a belief about how the mass media could be used. The magazine's early readership was built upon the circulation of the recently defunct Edinburgh-based art magazine *Cinema Quarterly,* but unlike its predecessor, was published from London, the center of film sponsorship. It was vital to the documentary movement because it had to have access to the pages of a quality film journal, and *Sight and Sound* had become increasingly reluctant to deal with the documentarists, particularly after the fracas between the Post Office and the Film Institute in 1934. *World Film News* became a podium for the documentary movement and a showcase for their films. It was a useful meeting place for filmmakers and film sponsors and a good way of keeping them informed of each other's activities.

An important consequence of the creation of *World Film News,* over which Grierson exercised absolute editorial control, and Film Centre, where he was equally prominent, was to take over the initiative in leading the independent documentary movement from Rotha and Associated Realist Film Producers. Rotha had established Associated Realist Film Producers in December 1935. To be fair, in later years, Rotha admitted that the inspiration for the idea of a cooperative body for documentary filmmakers came initially from Grierson himself. As early as March 1934, Grierson had begun to think that such an organization would be useful.[38] Rotha, who represented Associated Realist Film Producers before the Moyne Committee, explained to the Committee what the functions of this body were:

Associated Realist Film Producers is an independent, authoritative body acting as a consultant film organisation to government departments and other official bodies, to the various public services, university and education authorities, industrial and commercial organisations, and others anxious to make their activities known to a wide public. Associated Realist Film Producers is not itself a commercial production or distribution company but co-operates with existing film companies in the production and distribution of films. The Association co-ordinates and develops the field of documentary cinema by grouping together producers and directors who have established themselves among the leading makers of documentary films.[39]

The association had some real substance. In addition to carrying out the tasks of coordination of production and liaison between producers and filmmakers, it also represented the documentary movement at the national level. Rotha was, for example, the most eloquent witness on behalf of the documentary movement to appear before the Moyne Committee. This influence was short-lived, however, and its most important functions were soon taken over by Grierson's Film Centre.

Film Centre was ambitious. Its first major project was very close to Grierson's heart. Within weeks of its creation, Film Centre announced plans for a whole series of films that were to be the basis for a comprehensive screen image of Scotland, to be made for the Films of Scotland Committee. Grierson was a key figure in the creation of the Films of Scotland Committee as well as Film Centre, which was given the task of allocating the production of the Films of Scotland series.

The film output of these two independent units deserves a degree of critical attention that it has not so far received. The tendency in critical writing has been to concentrate on a very small number of films made by the two units, particularly Strand's *Today We Live.* Close scrutiny of just these films has been made at the expense of analysis of the complete body of work of the two units. This is unfortunate because during the five years between the creation of the Strand Film Company and the outbreak of World War II, there was a significant growth in the technical sophistication and range of documentary film production, for which the two independent units were largely responsible. During this time, each unit developed its own individual approach, and it is possible to discern a distinctive unit style and structure, which were also quite different from that which prevailed at the GPO Film Unit in the later 1930s. The independent units were also – sponsors willing – able to venture into areas of concern denied to the GPO Film Unit. During the later part of the decade, most of the impetus of the documentary movement came from the independent units.

At the Strand Film Company, Rotha developed a polemical style that he used in a number of socially conscious films. This style was later taken up and elaborated upon by the Realist Film Unit. Most considerations of the work of the Strand Film Company have perhaps failed to appreciate that most of its films were of a straightforward and commercial nature. For example, Rotha's own *Contact* was the only film made for Imperial Airways that diverged markedly from the traditional type of travelogue and industrial film. All the other films made by Strand for Imperial Airways were very much part of this earlier tradition. Only a handful of Strand's annual output consisted of films of a socially aware nature, yet generally these have received emphasis in surveys of the British documentary movement.

The films on social issues do merit much of the attention they have received. Films such as *On the Way to Work* (1936), made for the Ministry of Labour, *Here Is the Land* (1937), made for the Land Settlement Association, and *Today We Live,* made for the National Council for Social Service, were all important for the manner in which they were able to bring issues such as unemployment to the cinema screen, albeit in a limited and compromised way. Such films, sponsored by government and quasi-official bodies, always tended to concentrate on alleviating the symptoms of an ailing economy rather than demanding fundamental structural changes. This reluctance to contradict the philosophies and interests of their sponsors led Arthur Calder-Marshall to characterize British documentaries as "grimly obsequious, like boys toadying to masters or clerks smarming to the boss."[40] The documentary movement's response to such accusations was, and still is, that it was better to make compromised films rather than not to make films at all.[41] However, there was perhaps greater ideological consensus between the documentarists and their civil service and corporate masters than such claims imply.

Paul Rotha was responsible for a series of innovations at Strand. He was also the producer of the few films dealing with social issues that were made there. Furthermore, Rotha, like Grierson, had an unusually extensive degree of control over films being directed by others under his supervision. Both felt that a film producer had an important creative function and was entitled to a great deal of authority over the director, although it is perfectly true that the distinction between these roles was by no means as hard and fast in documentary filmmaking as in feature film production. In this, as in so many things, Grierson was as pedantic as ever:

Only one thing gives the producer importance: the fact that he makes directors and, through directors, makes art. It is the only thing worth an artist's making: money not excepted. Directors can be no larger than the producer allows them to be, and their films no bigger (except by noble accident) than his own imagination permits.[42]

Grierson and his followers had a very malleable notion of film credits. Many of their films were genuinely collaborative pieces, and so film credits assigning responsibility for specific accomplishments did not mean very much. Credits were used to promote the group as a whole rather than individual reputations. Collaboration was often not acknowledged in these films. Paul Rotha particularly had an active influence upon many films attributed to others, for example, Stanley Hawes's *Here is the Land*, yet this often went unacknowledged.

Rotha brought to his work a style in which photojournalism in the manner of *The March of Time* and reconstructions of actual or fictitious events were neatly blended together. Some issues of *The March of Time* series dealt with the impact of the industrial depression in Britain, not only immediate issues such as unemployment and malnutrition but also longer-term problems relating to issues such as national health standards and housing. This type of treatment had much in common with Rotha's style. The films used voice-of-god narration to accompany film images, tempered with a sensitive use of ordinary men and women functioning as social actors.

In *Shipyard* and *The Face of Britain*, Rotha developed this type of structure further by opening each film with a historical prologue. These prologues were usually elaborate pieces of photomontage that attempted to put the issue under discussion in its historical context and were a device later employed in many of the films made at Strand. In both *Today We Live* and *Here Is the Land*, an explanation of how the present state of economic and political affairs had evolved preceded a description of what was being done to alleviate the effects of the industrial depression. This description often took the form of using real people as social actors in scripted reconstructions. This blend of photomontage as "history" and reconstructions as "present reality" was a new approach to "the creative interpretation of reality" as Rotha termed it.[43] This attempt to blend the voice-over style of *The March of Time* with narrative elements of the fiction film was well suited both to the Strand Film Company and its sponsors.

The documentary movement felt compelled to explain the historical background of the situations it was describing in some form or other, and historical exposition became an increasingly important element in its films. By the time John Taylor made *The Smoke Menace* (1937), this form of exposition was fully developed. The Realist Film Unit also began to seek other ways of incorporating historical exposition into its films. Here, there was a growing penchant for the use of reconstructions of historic events. For example, *Advance Democracy* (1938) included reconstructions of important events in the history of the labour movement. There were also extensive historical reconstructions in *New Worlds for Old* (1938) and *The Londoners* (1938). Reenactments of this type were sometimes interwoven with the earlier approach, so that several types of exposition were included within the same film. A recurrent theme in these expositions was that central government and corporate Britain had between them begun to resolve the problems of industrial recession and its consequences, particularly as they related to public health.

The overall structure of films made by the independent units was often very eclectic because of the manner in which diverse narrative and expositional elements were blended together. There was a gradual movement away from the impressionistic form Rotha had developed in early films like *Contact* and *Shipyard*.[44] Few of these later films had the lyricism of Basil Wright's *Song of Ceylon* either. This was a deliberate abandonment of poetic forms in favor of a much starker approach thought more appropriate to socially purposive films. Filmmakers wanted an approach that would be appealing to popular audiences, so they chose to borrow from the techniques of the feature film, rather than the earlier didactic model appropriated from the Soviet Union. They were also anxious to provide an adequate explanation of the subjects they were treating, and therefore tried these different ways of providing a historical context. Editing was very important in the earlier films made by the independent units. It was important, for example, in the impressionistic prologues in *Here Is the Land* and *Today We Live*. Editing strategies became less important in the later films, which derived their impact from characterization, scripted dialogue, and the voice-over narration. In these later films also, images were not required to speak for themselves when story, character, and narrator could provide most of the verbal cues.

The content of the films made by the independent documentary units ranged over a much wider field of topics than those made by the official GPO Film Unit. Nevertheless the filmmakers were rarely able to step completely outside the limits their sponsor imposed upon their work. Occasionally films were made that called for radical political change, such as Realist's film for the Co-operative Movement, *Advance Democracy*. Generally, however, films made at the independent units implicitly or explicitly supported the status quo. They highlighted only those things that were being done to improve and alleviate. This situation was perhaps inevitable given the ultimate reliance upon big private enterprise and government-funded bodies for financial support and the documentarists' own impossible stance as the unaligned presenters of the facts.

Certain themes recur within the body of films made by the independent units, the most prevalent being that benevolent corporations and government put the public's well-being before their own interests. Improvements in the way people were housed, fed, educated and clothed,

Figure 26. *Today We Live* (Ruby Grierson and Ralph Bond, 1937): the voice of the National Council for Social Service on the radio.

and the social services offered to them if they were misfortunate enough to become unemployed, was constantly stressed. This benevolence was given substance in the form of another favorite element in these films, the presence of the "expert." The figure of the expert, the scientist or the knowledgeable government official, recurs constantly in these films. This notion of the important social role of the expert was close to the heart of the documentarists' own theories.

The documentarists perceived themselves as the communications experts, demanded by Sir Stephen Tallents, who would interpret the modern world to its citizens. In films made on an independent basis, the figure of the expert, the man in authority, was defined and nuanced in a variety of ways. In *Workers and Jobs,* for example, Arthur Elton personified the competence of the Ministry of Labour in the figure of the benign and efficient civil service clerk, who had all the latest communications technology at his disposal, and who was tied into a network of employment exchanges that spanned the country. In this way, documentary films attempted to give bureaucracy a face. This image of the expert was enlarged in later films. In *Today We Live,* for example, the expert comes to pervade the lives of the unemployed coalminers in a Welsh village and the villagers in the Cotswolds. The men from the National Council for Social Service enter the homes and meetings of these people, prompting and giving shape to their ideas and intentions. They state the case for the National Council and suggest what people can do to fall in line with its plans. It is in fact a voice on the radio – literally the voice of god – that suggests to the characters in the film that they become interested in the National Council. In many of these films, the radio and the telephone are shown as the great panacea, whether it is finding work for the unemployed, helping a group build a village hall, or rescuing the crew of a shipwrecked trawler.

The representation of the working class in these films was as systematic and coherent as the portrayal of the official bureaucratic expert. In those films associated with Paul Rotha, there was a real effort to escape from the cold and distancing manner in which ordinary people were presented in earlier documentary films, such as *Aero-Engine* and *Industrial Britain*. These earlier films had been almost clinical in their detached studies of the industrial workforce; they represented workers only as manual labor and gave no thought of people's lives outside the workplace. When documentary crews made a rare excursion into working class homes, as in *Housing Problems*, they tended to retain their detachment and alienating approach. In contrast, two Strand films, *Here is the Land* and *Today We Live*, attempted a much more sympathetic portrayal of working class family life, and were not films that could be accused of "slumming." Rotha had developed a familiarity with ordinary working class men and women that reached its maturity in the films he made for the Ministry of Information during the war. In essence, Rotha presented the worker as completely blameless for his own unemployment. Workers were shown as anxious to take advantage of the services of government bodies and organizations such as the Land Settlement Association. As in the Post Office films, it was an essential part of these films that all roles should be played by real people, not professional actors.

By the late 1930s, the independent documentary movement had created adequate apparatus for making films and for publishing its work. So much so that sponsored film production was virtually the only section of the film industry to be unaffected by the financial collapse of the film industry during 1937–8.[45] The fundamental shortcomings of the independent documentary movement lay not in production but in arranging the commercial distribution and exhibition of its films. The failure of documentary film in regular commercial release, except for occasional films such as *Night Mail* and *North Sea*, was related to the circumstances of commercial display in the 1930s. It was also an indication of the gulf between the ambitions of the documentary movement and the desires and tastes of the audiences attending the commercial cinema.

Dallas Bower once commented: "You rarely see a genuine documentary film in a popular cinema-hall. The miner does not want to see his own backyard and precious few viscountesses are interested in or care two hoots in hell about slum clearance."[46] All the evidence supports Bower's statement. Each year a tiny number of documentary films made by the independent units were registered with the Board of Trade for regular commercial exhibition.[47] Grierson and Rotha were both anxious to reach the audiences in the commercial cinemas. This was where the biggest audience resided, even though from the very beginning Grierson was aware that the documentary movement would also have to exploit nontheatrical distribution. Rotha, much more of a populist than Grierson, was particularly enthusiastic about getting films into the cinemas. As he reported to the Moyne Committee, "the documentary film certainly at the present and for several years to come relied primarily upon public theatre distribution."[48]

Three major obstacles faced the development of the independent documentary film in the commercial cinema. In the first place, the legislation governing film exhibition in the 1930s adversely affected the distribution and exhibition of documentary films during this time. So, too, did the nature of the film distribution and exhibition industry in Britain. The evidence is overwhelming that exhibitors and distributors had little time – or space in their film programs – for the documentary film. A third factor, perhaps both the most important and yet the most difficult to substantiate, was the nature and extent of the demand for documentary films among cinema audiences in the 1930s.

The 1927 Cinematograph Films Act was framed before the emergence of the documentary film. It was unintentionally prejudiced against the genre by its exclusion of most types of actuality film from its provisions. In addition, the Act had not established separate quotas for long and short films. Cinema exhibitors and renters wishing to fulfill their quota obligations could show an increased proportion of British long films rather than a combination of long and short films. The Act nevertheless had compelled exhibitors and renters to handle an increasing proportion of British films. This led to the rise of the notorious quota quickie, the cheaply made and technically British film, often only seen by the cinema cleaners.[49] Having fulfilled his quota obligations in this manner, the exhibitor could then get down to the real business of showing American feature films. There was no interest in documentary films because they could not be counted against American films for quota purposes. The producers of short films and documentarists joined together to demand a separate quota for short films, for which documentaries would be eligible. This demand was made before the Moyne Committee, which met during 1936 to discuss changes in legislation pending the expiration of the 1927 Act.

Rotha and other representatives of the documentary movement complained to the Moyne Committee about the unfair manner in which the existing Act was interpreted by the big commercial concerns. They noted how several series of – in their eyes – trivial short films made by the major commercial studios, such as *Musical Gems of Scotland,* had been given full quota status, when this had been refused to such worthwhile documentary films as *Beside the Seaside* and *The Key to Scotland.*[50] Rotha went on to note that the only way in which quota status could be obtained for documentary films was to prove that they had "special exhibition value." The onus was upon the filmmaker to prove that his film had this value. For the documentary filmmaker, this was often difficult to prove because it entailed arranging a special trade show for renters and exhibitors. The film trade were rarely interested in attending these shows. As Rotha noted, the usual manner in which documentary films were released and publicized, through the film societies and the critics in the quality press, had prejudiced the trade against participating in the procedures necessary to have a film deemed as having special exhibition value.

The documentarists had an unusual ally in their campaign for a separate quota for short films, the Film Producers Group of the Federation of British Industries. This alliance was unlikely because of the earlier conflict over unfair competition between the documentary movement and the commercial trade. The Film Producers Group argued:

There has always been an annual deficit of short British films available to meet short quota requirements. The production of short British films, other than purely entertainment films, but containing an important entertainment element, is being widely developed in this country, and it is thought desirable from many points of view that the production of good films of this type should be encouraged.[51]

The Film Producers Group was joined by the Association of Cinematograph Technicians in arguing that the short film industry was also important as a training ground for technicians who subsequently entered the feature film industry.[52] Because of this concerted demand from this diverse group of lobbies, separate quota provisions for short films were embodied in the Cinematograph Films Act (1938). However, the onset of World War II drastically altered the nature of film distribution and exhibition in Britain, and this makes it very difficult to surmise what the effects of these new provisions might have been. Presumably they would have gone some way to making documentary and other types of short film more attractive to commercial exhibitors and renters.

The documentarists' campaign to change film legislation was faced with massive indifference from the distribution and exhibition sides of the film industry. The whole subject of documentary films was of so little importance to the Cinematograph Exhibitors Association (CEA) that they were not even mentioned in its memorandum for the Moyne Committee.[53] Theo Fligelstone, President of the CEA claimed in his evidence before the Moyne Committee that exhibitors and renters simply reflected the tastes of their clientele when they refused to book documentary films. As he put it: "No documentary film . . . has ever set the Thames on fire." He reported, for example, that the Empire Marketing Board films he had handled had done very poorly. He believed that if there were high-quality short films made in Britain, then renters and exhibitors would take them. Fligelstone was convinced that such films would have to be of an entertainment character because, as he put it, "the public will not be educated."[54] The documentary movement was never able to overcome this prejudice against their films. Fligelstone was typical of the men who controlled commercial film exhibition in Britain in the 1930s and 1940s. They all believed that their audiences came to be entertained, not educated and that uplift and escapism were rarely compatible. Exhibitors took great pride in their ability to read their audiences. On the rare occasions when documentary films received an airing in the commercial cinema, it seems that their view was vindicated.

Evidence of audience tastes before World War II, especially in relation to documentary films, is very difficult to obtain. Progressive showmen such as Sidney Bernstein, head of the Granada theatre circuit did periodically send out questionnaires to their audiences. Such attempts to gauge audience tastes were, however, sporadic and selective, and at best were very broad market research tests. There was no concerted attempt to ascertain audience tastes comparable to Simon Rowson's statistical analysis of the composition of cinema audiences. Grierson himself suggested that market research aimed at exploring audience tastes would be amply rewarded. He asked:

Production methods, films forms, dramatic appeal are discussed and rediscussed by the men who make films. There are professional critics. There is a progressive body of criticism. Laws are formulated – and believed – which govern manufacture. Why not a similar analysis of the public's reactions to films?[55]

Naturally enough, the documentarists argued that the evidence supported their claim that there was a demand among cinema audiences that was being frustrated by the exhibitors and distributors. Renters argued that there was no such demand. They believed that audiences were content with the double features and comedy shorts served to them by the regular commercial exhibitor.

Paul Rotha told the Moyne Committee about the Newcastle audiences who wrote to their local film critic, complaining that he had failed to alert them to *Shipyard,* which played briefly and without publicity in a local cinema. He blamed this on the exhibitor who had failed to publicize the film. Rotha claimed this was but one of many instances when audience demand was frustrated by the policies of exhibitors and renters.[56] Bruce Woolfe also reported that cinema audiences he had questioned had expressed a desire to have short actuality films included in their evening's entertainment, if these films had some entertainment element.[57] The documentarists did have a small number of popular successes to support their case. They pointed to the successful bookings of *North Sea* and *Night Mail*. Significantly, however, the two independent units never made films that had the widespread popular appeal of these two films.

Audience tastes were very strongly influenced by the organization of renting, booking, and programming films in the 1930s. Exhibition and distribution were increasingly under the control of a small number of circuits. By 1936, for example, over half of the first-run cinemas were controlled by just nine large theater circuits, which between them owned 652 cinemas, including most of the larger metropolitan first-run houses.[58] There was a growing tendency for these to show only double-feature programs, which left no room for the display of short films. Many distributors of short films, such as Zenifilms, which handled many films for the documentary group, went out of business. Their demise was blamed upon the rise of the double feature.[59] Producers with short film interests believed there was opposition within cinema audiences to the new type of program. Bruce Woolfe, for example, believed

the double feature was unpopular and that people would rather see shorts in the commercial cinema . . . everywhere we go we make enquiries and we find . . . that in ninety-five per cent of the enquiries that we direct that the people prefer to see short films. They do not want to see the sort of stuff that they say is a poor imitation of the first film that they saw, they do not want to sit through an hour of this horrible stuff in order to get through to the first feature.[60]

The exhibition side of the industry did not agree. As the editor of *Kine Weekly* noted, film exhibitors would sometimes take short films if they had entertainment value, although they complained: "What we protest against is the strenuous advocacy of them as the means of spreading culture and uplift."[61]

By the late 1930s the documentary film movement claimed an annual nontheatrical audience of ten million people for its films. There was a tendency to give increasing emphasis to this type of distribution, in view of the persistent failure of the documentary film in the commercial cinema. Thomas Baird and Grierson both argued that nontheatrical distribution, although it dealt with far smaller audiences than commercial distribution, was potentially much more important. This was because the films for this type of distribution could be purely informative, which was impossible for films in regular commercial release. Grierson had spelt out this possibility a decade previously when he wrote:

The drift in the industry towards mass appeal and nothing but mass appeal shuts out the possibility of any but the most highly popularized informative films, and is likely to deny any considerable outlet to films which are on the face of them instructive or propagandist.[62]

The documentarists constantly asserted that their nontheatrical audiences had a disproportionate amount of social and political influence. Their goal was to reach the policymakers and leaders of public opinion, and those who set the agenda for public debate. It is true that some of the films that were shown nontheatrically were able to generate an enormous amount of attention in the press, as *Enough to Eat* did.[63] Yet the same contradiction was apparent in *World Film News* of using an essentially mass medium to narrowcast information to very specific audiences. Furthermore, attention from the critics rarely translated into increased attendances at nontheatrical showings of documentary films.

By the late 1930s, then, there were two independent documentary units, in addition to the official unit maintained by the Post Office, with a tradition of making films for large-scale sponsors. The movement had also erected a small but growing means of distributing films on a nontheatrical basis. This tradition of production and the system of nontheatrical distribution were both resources that were heavily drawn upon during the war. That was the long-term impact of independent documentary production. The immediate effect of independent documentary activity was much slighter. Documentary films remained films made by élites for élites. Furthermore, these were Britain's cultural and literary élites, rather than those exercising a great deal of political influence. This tended to keep the impact of these films, in political terms, fairly small. Within conventional political circles the documentary movement remained suspect. Grierson, who was never fully trusted when he was working for a government department, was trusted even less when he was not. He constantly provoked those in positions of authority. The documentary movement barely had time to recover from one crisis brought on by Grierson's lack of discretion before it was faced with another. For example, the controversy over the Films of Scotland had barely died down when Grierson's demands for explicit film propaganda for the United States on the eve of World War II succeeded in creating a great deal more ill-will. In many ways, Grierson was the documentary movement's greatest liability as well as its greatest asset.

In addition to the problems created by clashes of personality, the independent documentary film was also hindered by the inconsistencies that inevitably followed from trying to make films reflecting the standpoint of an unbiased observer, when these were funded by private enterprise or semigovernmental bodies. Grierson and his colleagues became masters at persuading organizations to pay for films that were only peripherally related to their work. Even so, the values of those bodies pervaded the films made by the documentary group. There was no escape from the fact that, "He who pays the piper calls the tune."

CHAPTER VI

The British documentary film, trade propaganda, and national projection, 1926–1939

The relationship of film values to trade returns is possibly better understood in the States than it is here . . . the British film business has not yet taken itself seriously enough as a national asset nor looked enough to its national duty.[1]

We knew all too keenly that the sending out free of hundreds of wall-maps of the British Isles dotted with symbolic thatched cottages would hardly evoke a constructive response among Americans towards the British people. The whole of British information sent abroad by the Foreign Office or the British Council was mid-Victorian amateurism and positively dangerous to the Britain of the 1930s.[2]

John Grierson was always concerned with overseas as well as domestic projection of national life. His enthusiasm for reaching the general public in other countries, particularly the United States, came to be shared by others within the documentary movement, especially Paul Rotha. The image of national life that the documentary movement wished to export changed during the course of the late 1920s and 1930s, as did its motives for national publicity. Grierson's first connection with Britain's official publicists was actually his first position in any official capacity. He was commissioned to write a series of reports for the Empire Marketing Board on the use of films as national publicity, particularly in the United States and Russia. Grierson's last exchange with British officials, prior to accepting the job of Film Commissioner for Canada, consisted of a plan he tried to press on the Ministry of Information and the Foreign Office for the creation of an extensive nontheatrical distribution scheme for documentary films in the United States. This was to be administered by himself and other senior documentarists. These two exchanges set the time frame for a discussion of the involvement of the documentary movement in national and Empire publicity during the 1920s and 1930s.

Grierson's early contribution was welcomed by the bodies and government departments concerned with the very narrow issue of improving British trade. This subject consumed the time of several Imperial Conferences in 1926, 1930, and again in 1932.[3] His later plans, however, were rejected by those organizing Britain's prewar and early wartime information services at the Ministry of Information, the Foreign Office, and the British Council. Grierson's opinion was respected when his advice coincided with the aims and interests of those eager to develop British and Empire trade. It was repudiated when it conflicted with official plans for national projection. In addition, the manner in which the documentary movement chose to state its case in the late 1930s had eroded most of its standing with those arranging national publicity in the uneasy months prior to the outbreak of the war.

The documentary movement obtained its early support and financial backing from the campaign to improve Empire trade. The film activities of the Empire Marketing Board were one of the offspring of this interest in Empire trade. During this period, Grierson had the benevolent support of several senior officials belonging to those departments most immediately concerned with British and Empire trade, in particular, in addition to Sir Stephen Tallents, E. L. Mercier at the Department of Overseas Trade. Both men were subsequently involved in the development of British film publicity overseas. Tallents had myriad personal connections with Grierson, in addition to his direct involvement with the film activities of the Post Office, the Imperial Relations Trust, and the postwar British Council Film Advisory Committee. Mercier was behind the Department of Overseas Trade's constant interest in film publicity, particularly the overseas distribution of industrial and documentary films. He participated in successive inquiries into the subject in 1928, in 1930, and again in 1937. Mercier maintained this connection with film publicity and was appointed deputy director of the Films Division of the Ministry of Information in 1940.

Mercier and the Department of Overseas Trade were interested in films and the views of the documentary movement only insofar as these might improve Britain's international trade position. Tallents, in contrast, had an elaborate philosophy about the intentions and priorities of national projection and film publicity. He believed that there was an urgent need for the British people to illustrate and promote their national image overseas, and specifically to show the role of old-fashioned patriotism and institutions like the Empire in the modern world. As he wrote in his influential pamphlet on this subject:

In the case of good international understanding, within the Empire and without it; for the sake of our export trade; in the interest of our old tourist trade; above all, perhaps, in this discharge of our great responsibilities to the other countries of the Commonwealth of British peoples, we must master the art of national projection and must set ourselves to throw a fitting presentation of England upon the world's screens.[4]

Tallent's constant use of cinematic metaphors like "projection" was an indication perhaps of just how important he and others thought films could be as overseas publicity. By 1939, by the stance they had come to adopt, by their unfortunate tendency to generate adverse publicity for the government departments with which they were at odds, and by their association with Tallents, who was himself persona non grata with British publicity planners after the collapse of British publicity machinery during the Munich crisis, the documentary movement had estranged virtually all official supporters. However, this had not always been the case, and a decade earlier Grierson had been able to tap a pervasive interest in film publicity.

In the mid-1920s, it was estimated that only 5 percent of the films shown on the cinema screens of the Empire were of British origin.[5] A number of pressure groups such as the British Empire League, the League of Empire, and the Navy League all lobbied for some form of protection for the British film industry. They advocated a protective quota system along the lines of the German *kontingent* plan, which limited the quantity of American imports into the country. In an address before the Empire Film Institute, Sir James Parr explained why these august bodies were so anxious. The position he developed was quite close to that argued by John Grierson at just about the same time. Parr argued:

It is horrible to think that the British Empire is receiving its education from a place called Hollywood. The Dominions would rather have a picture with a wholesome, honest British background, something that gives British sentiment, something that is honest to our traditions, than the abortions which we get from Hollywood . . . the American film is everywhere, and is the best advertisement of American trade and commerce. Trade follows the film, not the flag.[6]

The agreement between the documentary movement and the various patriotic and trade lobbies was reinforced by the generally pitiful state of the British feature film production during this period. There were several reasons why the trade lobbies doubted the ability of the British film industry to act as the agent of British trade publicity overseas. First, the industry was so enfeebled by American domination that it was difficult to conceive of it competing with U.S. producers, except in the very long run. For example, in 1925, the film industry was at such a low ebb that there was only one major studio production, George Pearson's *Satan's Sister*, then being made in the whole of the British Empire. When that film went on location to Jamaica, no major feature film was being made in a studio anywhere in the British Empire.[7] The feature film industry was also tainted by its intimate association with American film interests, especially in the renting sector. In the late 1920s, for example, just three American companies controlled over one-third of all films being rented in Great Britain.[8] This rendered the power of calls to patriotism dubious to say the least.

Many politicians and public servants regarded the British feature film industry as a willing accomplice to the American takeover of the Empire's cinema screens, and this view prevailed throughout the interwar years. Sir Arnold Wilson, a Member of Parliament associated with both the film industry and national projection, and who served as a member of the Board of Trade Advisory Committee on Cinematograph Films, felt compelled to ask: "What proportion of producers and exhibitors care tuppence for the British Empire or anything to do with it?"[9] In contrast to feature films, documentaries, and to a lesser extent newsreels, were viewed as a national product. They did not suffer from association with American film interests in the way feature films did. It was natural that publicity planners soon looked to them, rather than the feature film, to carry the burden of overseas publicity.

Grierson's first contribution was unsurprisingly and perhaps opportunistically shaped by the nature of this debate. The emphasis in his early comments about national publicity was very much upon the benefits to trade and commerce that would accrue from a more extensive display of British films on international screens. As Grierson put it when paraphrasing Will Hays: "One foot of film equals one dollar of trade."[10] Grierson believed that the British feature film would never be able to compete on equal terms with the American feature film, especially in the vital area of incidental publicity. He noted:

In matters such as technical slickness, finished performance, modern atmosphere, and popular appeal, no other mass of film production begins to compare with the Hollywood product. These factors in combination give a "last word" air to the most humble and incidental prop . . . It would be useless to attempt to compete with American production in the matter of massed incidental publicity.[11]

There was an element of glamour in American films that the British film industry "tied to the provincial and meretricious dramatics of the modern London stage" could never hope to emulate. In a report for the Inter-Departmental Committee on Trade Propaganda and Advertisement in 1930, Grierson elaborated on how this incidental publicity worked in American feature films to promote specific American products and services in overseas markets:

It is for example, extremely doubtful if directors like Mr. Cecil B. DeMille are in receipt of retaining fees from the American Plumbers Association. It is much more likely that the excellence of the plumbing arrangements so often manifest in their films, is prompted by a desire to add showman's value to a flash of female

Figure 27. *Cargo from Jamaica* (Basil Wright, 1933): promoting Empire produce.

nudity. It is, so to speak, by hitching its wagon to the naked stars, that the fame of American plumbing has been spread all over the world.[12]

Grierson suggested as an answer to American domination of feature film production that British filmmakers should concentrate on the second feature and short film market. This was dominated by interest shorts, which usually comprised travelogues and other actuality-based films. Grierson thought that these short films could be dramatized in such a way so as to render even the most prosaic subject exciting. As he noted about Victor Turin's film on collectivization in Russia: "Turin demonstrated in the first reel of *Turk-Sib* you can create suspense and build up a huge mood of expectation even for something as ordinary as water."[13] He thought the quality of existing short films was almost universally poor, so that it would be possible for British producers to take over this portion of the market. He noted that films of this type were "generally so dull that the competition for really distinguished films of man and his work is almost nil."[14] Basil Wright's *Cargo from Jamaica* (1933), made toward the end of the Empire Marketing Board period, was the kind of alternative Grierson had in mind. Films like this were intended to sell the Empire and its products – in this case, bananas – in an interesting manner that captured the imagination of the viewer without the alienating banalities of a commerical travelogue.

Grierson's views were of great interest to the Department of Overseas Trade, which as early as 1928 had begun to study the subject and had commissioned a special report.[15] In 1930, Grierson wrote a report for the Department of Overseas Trade's Committee on Trade Advertisement and Propaganda, and as a consequence it established a special Film Sub-Committee of which he became a member. Here Grierson's views were formally introduced to the Department of Overseas Trade and the Foreign Office, which was represented by its News Department's Rowland Kenney. This Sub-Committee concluded that it would be desirable to create a central body to administer official overseas film publicity.[16] This foreshadowed Grierson's later demands for the creation of such an agency and the widespread demand for a National Films Council in the years immediately prior to the war. Strongly influenced by Grierson, this committee came to think of film publicity almost exclusively in terms of actuality film. Unfortunately, it did not itself evolve into the specialized film advisory body Grierson wished. The main committee came to the conclusion:

While we feel that it is of importance that this type of publicity should be developed, the subject is so complicated and in some respects so technical that at the present we do not feel competent to advise as to the steps to be taken.[17]

Nevertheless, the committee had achieved something. Grierson's ideas for the development of the short actuality film had been given wider currency. Henceforth, Grierson was sure of some support from the Department of Overseas Trade. This would prove extremely valuable after the abolition of the Empire Marketing Board.

The Department of Overseas Trade had an interest in documentary production throughout the 1930s. Its direct involvement amounted to membership of the Joint Film Committee alongside the British Council, the British Film Institute, the Travel and Industrial Development Association, and the Post Office. It also organized another inquiry into the distribution of films overseas during 1936–7. The Department of Overseas Trade was close to the stance of the documentary movement in many respects. Grierson, for example, advocated films in which whole industries, rather than individual companies, were publicized. The Department of Overseas Trade echoed this sentiment when it advocated films in which "specific advertising is subordinated to the general interest."[18]

The documentary movement derived real practical value from the Department of Overseas Trade's interest. For example, this led to the initial ascendency of documentary films in the plans of the Joint Film Committee. Toward the end of the decade, however, as the movement talked less about trade propaganda and more about "propaganda for democracy," there was a discernible withering away of its support within the Joint Committee. Another benefit was the way in which the Department of Overseas Trade acquiesced in the documentarists' appropriation of the Travel Association's film unit, and this had lasting significance. Grierson acted as the Travel and Industrial Development Association's film adviser until 1938, and his sister Marion ran its film unit until it was taken over by the British Council in 1939.

The Travel Association film unit was created in 1932, and from the beginning, always had a shadowy existence. Initially, it was attached to the Empire Marketing Board Film Unit, employing the same staffers and facilities. Subsequently, it went first to the GPO Film Unit and finally became part of the Strand Film Company. Through all these changes Marion Grierson was head of production. It was the only production unit working continuously through the 1930s exclusively concerned with films intended for overseas distribution. Like all attempts to develop official film production and distribution, the Travel Association suffered from an acute shortage of funds. Even the most ambitious of the unit's early efforts, such as the paired films *So This is London* and *So This is Lancashire,* showed all too clearly the signs of forced economies. One result of this parsimony was that a large number of the Travel Association films, such as *St. James Park* and *London on Parade,* had to be made as silent films. In fact, it was only when the unit was taken over by the British Council in October 1939 that is was able to embark upon more prestigious and expensive productions.[19] Taken out of the hands of the documentary movement, the unit began the production of a series of Technicolor films, intended for distribution in the United States on a theatrical basis.[20]

The documentary movement had appropriated the only official film organization solely interested in overseas publicity. Despite the somewhat meager achievements of the Travel Association, the documentarists were anxious to give it and its film unit full credit. As Arthur Elton noted in *World Film News:*

Now the Empire Marketing Board is dead, the Travel and Industrial Development Association is the only group not under obligation to specialised commercial or political interests in a position to make detached films reflecting the national life of the country.[21]

One consequence of the documentary group's interest in the Travel Association was that its film activities often got far more press attention than other bodies interested in the use of films overseas, including its senior partner, the British Council. The Secretary-General of the British Council reacted with much chagrin to the manner in which the Travel and Industrial Development Association was presented as "the only, or at any rate, the most important organisation for cultural propaganda in existence."[22]

The documentary movement's links with the Travel Association amounted to running the film unit and publicizing the work of the Association. The documentarists never took over the Association's distribution of films overseas, which in fact both they and the British Council found wanting. The British Council thought that the Association was not qualified to arrange the intricacies of overseas film distribution. As one British Council official asserted:

The Travel Association do not know much about foreign countries and are therefore not really qualified to select the most suitable films to be shown in each country. Anybody could have told them that as there are no railways in Albania it was hopeless to send that country *Night Mail,* and that a church film, *For All Eternity,* would probably cause offense in modern Germany.[23]

For its part, the documentary movement felt that the Travel Association did not give sufficient planning to its distribution, especially in the United States. Thomas Baird noted how, for example, in the United States, the Travel Association simply handed over control of its films to the American YMCA, who fitted them into displays as it wished.[24] Nevertheless, despite these criticisms of the Travel Association's distribution methods, this connection remained important for the documentary movement. It meant that, whatever else happened, the movement always had a place in at least one of the agencies responsible for British film publicity overseas.

The documentary movement's success in influencing the Travel Association contrasts strongly with the checkered history of its relationship with the British Council. In comparison to those agencies interested exclusively in the relatively concrete task of expanding British trade, the British Council had a high-minded, if somewhat nebulous notion, of the image of Britain that should be projected abroad.[25] It was an image that relied more on the superiority of Britain's high culture, rather than on any sustained cultivation of the forms of British popular culture overseas. The Council believed that this image should be geared to governing élites rather than the general public of the countries to which it reached out. However, this élitism did not preclude the British Council from taking an active interest in cinema, the mass medium par excellence. The British Council was heir to the widespread belief in official circles in the efficacy of film propaganda. And from its inception the British Council was interested in the use of films. As the chairman of the Council noted only months after its creation:

It occurs to me that the finest propaganda and the most widespread that we could possibly do is in the form of a film, which would picture the manifold activities of life in England today.[26]

The Council had no funds to produce films until it was given the task of providing films for the British Pavilion at the New York World's Fair in 1939. Until that time, its film activities were restricted to the selection of films made by other bodies and to arranging their overseas distribution. It also attempted to influence the filmmaking activities of other agencies such as the newsreel companies and the Post Office Film Unit.

The British Council primarily worked through the Joint Film Committee, where it was joined by a number of other interested bodies. This Committee first met in April 1936, and its chairman was Philip Guedalla, a prominent popular historian, who had had some experience with motion pictures serving on the Board of Trade Advisory Committee on Cinematograph Films. Guedalla's personal opinions, his open antagonism toward Grierson, and a tendency to make flippant comments about film publicity to the press gradually steered the Joint Committee toward a collision with the documentary movement. Other members of the Committee included Rowland Kenney, Oliver Bell, General Manager of the British Film Institute, L. A. de L. Meredith and A. F. Primrose of the Travel Association, E. L. Mercier of the Department of Overseas Trade, Lieutenant-Colonel Charles Bridge of the British Council, and John Grierson, in his dual capacity as Post Office Film Officer and Film Adviser to the Travel Association.[27] The most important change in the membership of the Committee occurred when M. Neville Kearney, a representative of the Film Producers Group of the Federation of British Industries and the British Newsreel Association, took over Grierson's membership of the Committee, during 1938.[28] The Committee's initial brief was to investigate all types of films, and it was specifically commissioned to "stimulate the distribution abroad of all types of British films: 'Documentary,' 'Entertainment' and 'Newsreel.' "[29] From the beginning, however, the Committee thought of national projection primarily in terms of documentary films. It was also concerned with newsreels to some extent, but not at all with feature films. The Committee limited its interests to different types of actuality film because it felt that the feature industry "neither needs or desires assistance from outside."[30] Since these statements coincided with the revival of the fortunes of the British feature film industry, there were perhaps grounds for its position.

During 1937 newsreels gradually assumed equal importance with documentary films in the Joint Committee's plans. This change in the Committee's priorities set the tone for a massive disagreement that subsequently ensued over two issues. In the first instance, a great deal of animosity was stirred up between the documentary group and the Joint Committee over the films made for the Films of Scotland Committee. That particular debate was less about who should actually pay for the films than about the nature of the screen image of Scotland. It merged with a second issue, which concerned the provision of films for the forthcoming New York World's Fair. The relationship between the documentary group and the Joint Committee was initially quite amicable. It ended with great differences of opinion over these two issues during 1938–9. These differences reflected not only the exclusion of the documentary group from the proceedings of the Joint Committee but also the ascendancy of different government departments, with different aims and interests from those that had created the Joint Committee.

There were always substantial differences of opinion between two camps at the Joint Committee. At first it was dominated by the trade lobby, which looked to film as a means of improving British trade and which supported the documentary movement. Later, this was superseded by the Foreign Office and the British Council, who were interested in using film to project a loftier image of Britain abroad. After the Joint Committee had been in operation for a year, Croom-Johnson, a British Council official, commented on the manner in which the trade view predominated over the cultural view. His criticisms are interesting for the way in which they illuminate the British Council's own policy concerning the use of film publicity. He voiced two main criticisms. In the first instance, he thought that the predominance of the Department of Overseas Trade at the Committee was reflected in the fact that it was "engineering minded." As he noted:

They like to see an impressive piece of machinery at the end of a film and did not seem to take much account of other forms of British culture.[31]

Croom-Johnson found the Committee's emphasis on trade propaganda unfortunate and also substantially at odds with the Council's own concerns. The Committee believed, he noted,

that the foreigner is only impressed with England as a manufacturing nation. I rather feel this is not the impression we want to create . . . while admittedly nobody will complain if British trade increases as a result of our activities, we must be careful that people do not look upon us as being (as Aagard once accused us of being), "just a smoke-screen for British trade penetration."

Croom-Johnson also felt that the Committee was "apt to underestimate the mentality of foreign film audiences," aiming at the level of, as Guedalla once put it, "a low-class Maltese tobacconist." This was anathema to the British Council, which was interested in persuasion of élites not the masses. As Croom-Johnson concluded on the subject of film publicity:

By "playing down" to film audiences we shall not gain the interest of the unintelligent (who don't matter to us anyway) and shall lose the sympathy of the intelligent Anglophile student and the moderately intelligent newspaper readers at whom we should presumably aim.[32]

In the late 1930s, the British Council view came to predominate at the Joint Committee, and there was little sympathy for the documentary school's point of view. The starkness, honesty, and preoccupation with industrial processes and the urban working class that were the hallmark of so many Griersonian films had no place in the British Council's rural and dignified conception of the image of Britain. This position was typified by a British Council representative's reaction to two of the outstanding documentary films of the later 1930s, *The Smoke Menace* (1937) and *Children at School* (1937). Both films were deemed "technically well made and full of interest," but were not thought suitable for national publicity overseas. The films were faulted for exactly those features that the documentary group utilized. They were thought to be "too impersonal and scientific, and there seemed to be too little local colour and movement." The films were considered "too objective and unbiased." *Children at School* was thought "too informative to hold the interest of any but a relatively instructed audience." *The Smoke Menace* "revealed too much that is unfortunate in our social system."[33]

By 1938 both the Joint Film Committee and the British Council expected the newsreels to carry the burden of British film publicity overseas. The Joint Committee advocated "the judicious exploitation of the newsreel, which is far more convincing than any fabricated propaganda product." During 1938, the Joint Film Committee negotiated with the newsreel companies to procure an increased proportion of British news items in newsreels overseas. It was believed

essential that news of this country should receive its proper share of attention in foreign film programmes and should not be edged off the screen by American items admitted for commercial reasons or subsidised items from other European states.[34]

Approaches were made to the newsreel companies in both London and Paris. Paris was especially important because it acted as the central exchange for news film between the different European countries.[35] The Committee came to an agreement with Gaumont–British News, to pay a subsidy to the company and to support the Newsreel Association's proposal to have the duties on newsreel film abolished. In return, Gaumont–British undertook to increase the number of British newsreel items distributed abroad. The British Council learned that the following agreement had been made with Gaumont–British News:

For a moderate subvention, British news items will be made available over a far larger area than hitherto, and in some cases special news items will be worked up into a more extended form; for example, the recent record-breaking flight of the R.A.F. could be worked up into a general essay on the achievements of British aviation, civil as well as military.[36]

The Joint Committee was so satisfied with the results of its negotiations with the newsreel companies, and so convinced of the efficacy of newsreels, that when it was given the responsibility of arranging films for the British Pavilion at the New York World's Fair, it announced it was doing so "mainly on a newsreel basis."[37] *British News,* which was made on a rotation basis by the five newsreel companies, especially for the Fair, was thought to be one of the major accomplishments of the British Pavilion.[38]

As soon as the Joint Committee had substantial funds for filmmaking, it turned away from the documentary group and toward the newsreels. This change in emphasis became clear in the actions of both the Joint Committee and the documentary group during the related issues of the films for the Films of Scotland Committee and the provision of films for the New York World's Fair. The public and private statements of the documentary group and the Joint Committee reveal the growing chasm between their thinking on national film publicity. These debates were highlighted by the events of Munich and the imminence of war.

In both these disputes, agreement was made all the more difficult by the conduct of both sides. The Joint Committee was disabled by a Department of Overseas Trade decision not to publicize arrangements for the Fair until only months before it was opened. Public attacks on the Committee were often made in ignorance of its plans. In addition, its chairman, Philip Guedalla, was often guilty of refusing to treat the subject with sufficient gravity. The documentary movement was equally culpable of irresponsible behavior, although this was a result of taking these matters very seriously indeed. Repeatedly, Grierson made rash and inadequately briefed statements to the press. The situation was exacerbated by his willingness to make personal attacks upon "the inelastic imaginations of some of those who guide our national needs of propaganda."[39] As a result of their behavior over these issues, Grierson and his followers acquired a reputation for capricious behavior that did a great deal of harm.

In late 1937, the Films of Scotland Committee was set up under the auspices of the Commissioner for the Special Areas and the Secretary of State for Scotland. Its commission was to produce a series of films for immediate display at the forthcoming Empire Exhibition, which was to be held at Glasgow in 1938. These films were also to be the permanent basis for a series that would project Scotland overseas, as a part of the film distribution plans of the British Council and the Travel Association. Grierson played a crucial role, by proselytizing in public and private influence, in the creation of the Committee. He had influence with Walter Elliot, who had been involved with documentary films since the days of the Empire Marketing Board and was now the Secretary of State for Scotland. He also had the support of Sir Horace Hamilton, the newly appointed Permanent Secretary at the Scottish Office.[40] Grierson ascribed the creation of the Committee not to his own work but to the activities of the press during the previous two years:

Both the Committee and the funds placed at its disposal were largely the result of newspaper initiative . . . we Scots wished to see the fair face of our country projected on the screens of the world and particularly so in the year of the Empire Exhibition.[41]

Grierson believed this was the first committee of any kind that wished to associate itself with films that would emphasize the modern and forward-looking aspects of a nation's screen image. He compared this attitude with that of previous film committees with which he had been associated. These were

generally composed of old-fashioned people. They either think the cinema a slight and rather vulgar business the common people go in for, and therefore to be treated with amused contempt, or they consider it an ignoble, but necessary means of addressing the multitude – to be treated seriously, but without respect.[42]

The British Council was quick to offer the relatively small sun of £750 toward the cost of the Committee's first series of films, on the understanding that these would be suitable for display as a part of its overseas film distribution system.[43] The Joint Film Committee was given the task of deciding whether or not the films would be suitable for distribution by the Council. Grierson and Film Centre, meanwhile, were given responsibility for producing the first series of films. From the beginning, Grierson assumed that this would comprise six or seven films, providing a comprehensive picture of Scotland's social and economic reconstruction, for use abroad as well as for display at the Glasgow Exhibition.[44]

The first series of films for the Films of Scotland Committee was according to Grierson's usual hyperbole, "the first planned production endeavour in the field of documentary film."[45] It was also the only occasion when complete responsibility for the national screen projection of an entire country was delegated to the documentary movement. As Grierson pointed out on more than one occasion, a disproportionate number of documentary films made in the 1930s had Scottish settings, including *Drifters, Night Mail,* and *North Sea.* This was the first time, however, that the documentary movement had responsibility for a series of films with the explicit intention of projecting that country as a whole. Grierson was very enthusiastic about the opportunity that this new venture represented:

There is nothing like the films for showing the life of the country, and here was the prospect of all sorts of people being interested in Scotland in 1938, and a chance to focus their interest in the life and achievements of our country.[46]

Seven films were eventually made for the Films of Scotland Committee, including Basil Wright's *The Face of Scotland,* Donald Alexander's *Wealth of a Nation,* Alexander Shaw's *The Children's Story,* and Mary Field's *They Made the Land.* There were also three instructional films: *Seafood, Sport in Scotland,* and *Scotland for Fitness.*

There is evidence that the films received a relatively poor response when they were shown in Glasgow. A. G. Highet, who was responsible for Post Office publicity at the Glasgow Exhibition, noted the public reaction to the Films of Scotland film display. He told the Joint Film Committee that newsreels actually had been much more popular than the documentary films:

The cinema had not been well attended when documentaries alone were being shown and the attendance had gone up when newsreels were included in the programme.[47]

The Joint Film Committee was even less enthusiastic about the films than the general public. After a screening, one British Council representative maintained they were

uninspired from the point of view of national publicity. For the most part they were too frank – not enough selection and (literary) composition. There was very little of the colourful or the modernistic, very little excitement, in short, no showmanship. In the average, they were rather dismal and grim . . . the films would have a very narrow range of interest, they might even be harmful if shown to any but enlightened and already sympathetic audiences.

These were exactly the same criticisms that had been raised by the Council against *The Smoke Menace* and *Children at School* earlier that year. On this occasion, however, it was thought that the actual subject matter as well as the treatment chosen by the filmmakers was the cause, and the British Council's reviewer concluded:

Perhaps many of the defects are inherent in the subject itself – Scotland is, after all, to a great extent rather austere, solid and small-scale. Its large-scale aspects such as its moors and shipbuilding industry were not treated at any length.[48]

The British Council decided that the films were not suitable for overseas distribution and that it was not consequently liable to pay the £750 it had originally offered toward the cost of the films.

The British Council's behavior over the Films of Scotland and its decision not to incorporate them into its overseas distribution scheme is symptomatic of the manner in which politicians and public servants tended to exclude the whole question of Scotland from their thinking in the 1930s – a subject that warrants a scholarly study in its own right but that is outside the present terms of discussion. For present purposes, the Council's actions, and the documentary movement's response to these actions, illuminate the diverging opinions of the two bodies. They also arranged the terms upon which the controversy over the films for the 1939 New York World's Fair was fought.

The documentarists believed, correctly, that the Joint Committee had rejected the Scottish films because they did not conform to the official stereotypical image of Scotland. As Rotha commented for the Joint Committee:

It would have been easy to have filmed the showpieces and the popular associations – the games at Braemar and the Monarch in his glen. A skirl of pipes and pattern of plaids would, after all, have been as handy a set of symbols as St. Pauls or the Eiffel Tower. But the people who planned these films and the creative technicians who made them knew that the art of national projection goes deeper than specific splendours.[49]

The documentarists assumed that since the Scottish films would not be a part of the British Council's overseas distribution plans, they were not to be included in the display at the British Pavilion at the World's Fair either, which was then going through the planning stages with the Joint Committee. This assumption was made without actual knowledge of what the Joint Committee's intentions were regarding the Pavilion cinema. After all, the decision not to pay anything toward the cost of the Films of Scotland was made only the day after the Joint Committee was formally asked by the Department of Overseas Trade to take on the problem of the New York World's Fair.[50] The decision about the Scottish films must have been reached with the Fair in mind. In fact, the Joint Committee qualified its rejection of the Scottish films. It agreed to consider the films for display to specialized audiences at both the Fair and in the displays arranged by British missions overseas.[51]

The British Council's decision on the Scottish films, and its inferred rejection of the films for the World's Fair, produced a great deal of angry comment from both the documentary movement and many of its influential supporters. Robert Hurd of the Saltire Society, for example, declared the Committee's decision "unfortunate and tactless, for the films are good and they project modern Scotland in a lively and convincing manner."[52] He thought the Fair would be a repetition of the Paris Exhibition, where Scotland had been "relegated to Section Z or placed in an equally inconspicuous position." Meanwhile, the producers and directors of the Films of Scotland series produced a memorandum for the Joint Committee in which they noted that while the Committee had not deigned to recommend the films for official circulation abroad, all seven of the films had since been taken for distribution by commercial renters in Britain.[53] Grierson was prompted to demand the abolition of this shortsighted Committee:

The situation must be altered by national protest, even if that bungling Committee of the South has to be scrapped for one less parochial . . . if we cannot have a reasonable Committee representative of the best interests of Scotland then it would be far better for Scotland to go ahead on its own in producing films for overseas distribution.[54]

In the face of a great deal of adverse publicity, and especially because the question of the Scottish films had become entangled with the issue of films for the World's Fair, the Council and the Joint Committee began to retreat. It was announced in January 1939 that three of the films, *The*

Face of Scotland, They Made the Land, and *The Children's Story,* had been accepted for display at the World's Fair.[55] There were also suggestions that a partial payment of £300 should be made toward the cost of the films. There was even a revision in the Council's attitude toward the films. It was now felt that "they are, in the main, neither bad, nor uninteresting; their main fault is a too rigid determination not to emphasise the picturesque character of Scotland."[56] But this contrition came too late. The Scottish films were now only part of the bigger battle being fought to decide what image of Britain would be exported in the films to be displayed at the World's Fair.

The timing of the 1939 New York World's Fair made it a significant focus for competing corporate and national displays. Within the Joint Committee and the British Council, opinion was divided over the subject of the provision of films for the World's Fair. Some considered it as the opportunity to demand funds to begin producing films, not merely distribute existing films. As Colonel Bridge from the British Council noted:

If we can put up a considered scheme for the production of a special film for New York which would of course be of value to the Joint Committee in other places, it would provide a good opportunity for seeing what the Treasury attitude is to this matter.[57]

Others, including the Joint Committee chairman, Philip Guedalla, refused to believe that the film display would be of any great significance:

A small theatre occupying only a part of the exhibition building of one country and situated in the ground of a World's Fair is unlikely, at best, to attract more than brief visits from a floating population.[58]

There were different expectations about the importance of the films to be displayed in New York, but there was basic agreement as to the type of film to be displayed there. The Joint Committee had no qualms in agreeing with the suggestions coming down from the New York World's Fair Advisory Committee to make "the percentage of films showing the pageantry of English life fairly high."[59] The Committee also agreed to have a "strong newsreel element" in its programs.[60] The Joint Committee arranged with the Newsreel Association for the five British newsreel companies to provide a collaborative newsreel, *British News,* assembled especially for the Fair. The intention was that if this proved a success, then, at the end of the Fair, the Committee would consider distributing the newsreel abroad. The Joint Film Committee also decided to commission the General Post Office Film Unit to make two films on the subject of the British people at work and play. The Post Office Film Unit made *Spare Time* and *British Made.* The arrangements for the Fair greatly increased the Joint Film Committee's budget: £10,000 was allocated for films for the Fair, £3,900 of this was to go to the newsreel companies for the production of *British News.*[61] None of these arrangements were made public, however, because of the wish of the Department of Overseas Trade that there should be no publicity until immediately before the Fair.

In the absence of any real information about the Committee's plans for the Fair, the documentary movement began to argue that nothing at all was being done. Donald Taylor, for example, called for "an authoritative inspiration and a planned production" of films for the Fair.[62] Meanwhile, Paul Rotha, who had only recently returned from his extended lecture tour of the United States argued:

It would be a national disgrace if this opportunity should be wasted as a result of there being no considered policy and lack of co-ordination.[63]

Grierson joined the debate with an article in *The Spectator.* He chastised the Joint Committee for not sufficiently appreciating the urgency of the present situation. It was of paramount importance, Grierson believed, that Britain should present itself as a "functioning democracy" at the forthcoming Fair. In view of the increasing likelihood of war with the totalitarian powers, it was essential that Britain align herself with the United States. This, he felt, necessitated demonstrating in the films for the Fair and elsewhere that Britain was moving toward a fairer and more egalitarian conception of how its society ought to be organized. As Grierson wrote: "I want a picture of Britain as a functioning democracy, for it is the only picture on earth I am interested in, and I begin to wonder if I may not have to press for it."[64]

Grierson elaborated upon the image of British democracy that he wished to purvey at the World's Fair elsewhere:

When Britain appears in its international role as a pillar of democracy, the picture they expect from here is a somewhat detailed picture of just those personal freedoms and social goods the pillar upholds . . . We have a great deal to tell about our contribution to constructive democracy for we have a fine record in matters of housing and health, education and the public welfare as any country. If we don't tell it, it is because we are, as a nation, still very diffident about appearing in our working clothes.[65]

He did not believe that the Joint Committee was going to provide the image of Britain, as he implied in his comment:

Our only concern is that the picture of Britain presented in New York shall be a picture of a living country and living people, and not simply a decorative picture of odds and ends of ceremonial.

He was also doubtful the newsreels, the Joint Committee's chosen vehicle, could provide the type of picture of Britain for which he called:

Appreciating the newsreel presentation of Britain during the past few weeks, and, in particular, their shallow picture of Britain's social and political disposition, one's doubts increase.[66]

Grierson's comments met with a warm reception in the national press. As the *Evening Standard* commented:

To suppose that Britain can be "put over" successfully in the United States by excerpts from newsreels which tend naturally to dwell on the topical "shows and circuses" of the day – Parliament's State opening, Ascot, the formal trappings of British pageantry – would be a profound mistake. It will not be made, we may be sure, by those responsible for the choice of totalitarian films, German or Russian.[67]

In a leading article, *The Times* came out in favor of using documentary films as a primary form of national projection at the Fair. It believed "there is good reason to give the film of fact a larger share of the programme than it enjoys in the ordinary public cinema in either country." This was because the documentary film was "the distinctively British contribution to the art of the moving pictures" and also because it was most suited for the immediate task of portraying national life.[68] *The Times* believed that something similar to the Scottish film series was needed for Britain at the Fair. As *The Times* had commented on another occasion:

It is the short film of the documentary kind, and not the popular feature film, that presents the most authentic picture of our national life.[69]

The British Council and the Joint Film Committee lost a great deal of face as a result of the documentary movement's campaign. The accusations of lack of planning and policy struck home. Many people listened to Grierson when he noted:

We have been shipshod in our film relations all over the world . . . There has been no first-rate planning anywhere – no first-rate minds who understand the field of international relations and the structure of the film industry, to strike out a policy – no machinery to mobilise the great goodwill of our industry in effecting that policy.[70]

The British Council's position was made much worse by – in the Council's own words – the "rather light-hearted" manner in which Guedalla handled the subject of films in a series of press interviews. For the *Daily Express,* he characterized the documentarists' campaign as "the beauties who don't want to be left out of the beauty-show." Asked for an indication of the general policy of the Joint Committee on the Fair, Guedalla commented:

Anything that is a pleasure to look at and advantageous to Britain will be shown – and that doesn't mean pictures of glue-factories by night, photographed wrong way up, with crude Russian music.[71]

Guedalla's comments evoked a pained response from the British Council, which conceded that he had created an "unfortunate impression." It was agreed, however, that public interest has been aroused and we should take immediate steps to satisfy it, particularly as our intentions have been grossly misrepresented.[72]

The British Council believed that the documentarists were behind the campaign of adverse publicity it had received. It noted that the campaign had "proceeded on a complete absence of information as to the Council's intentions." It was thought that the best way of gagging the documentarists would be to recruit them:

Although Messrs. Grierson and Rotha are believed to have acted foolishly in the matter, they are good producers, with excellent ideas, and it would be a pity to antagonise them for lack of careful handling. Cannot we enlist their help for the second special film to be made for the Fair.[73]

Within the senior ranks of the Council, there was also tacit support for the documentary movement. After Grierson's *Kine Weekly* article, in which he called for proper publicity planning, Lord Lloyd, the head of the British Council, himself wrote to Grierson, commenting that he agreed with "almost every word" of what he had written.[74]

Official respect for Grierson's ideas was not matched with an equal regard for his actions. In fact, Grierson's attacks, and especially a press conference he gave in Edinburgh in February 1939 alienated some of his long-standing supporters. Niven McNicoll, previously his staunch advocate at the Scottish Office, was compelled to comment after the Edinburgh press conference:

I shall be very sorry indeed if he has said anything to raise personal issues or otherwise to inflate controversy over these films. I dislike that method of "diplomacy."[75]

This attitude toward the documentary movement was exacerbated by the eventual outcome of the debate over films for the New York World's Fair.

The Joint Film Committee never wavered from its original intention to rely primarily upon newsreels as the main means of national projection. *British News* was regarded as one of the real successes of the British Pavilion. This was especially true after the Fair reopened in 1940, when the information carried in the newsreel was often more up to date in its reports on the changing situation in Europe than the indigenous American newsreels. As a Foreign Office official reported to Duff Cooper, the British Minister of Information, in the spring of 1940:

British News was one of the most successful, and, from the publicity point of view, most promising features of the New York World's Fair.[76]

In addition to the newsreel, the British Pavilion cinema showed many documentary films. Nearly all of these were films made by the GPO Film Unit, and not by the two major independent documentary units, including *Night Mail, Spare Time, Calender of the Year,* and *Workers and Jobs.*

Night Mail was actually the second most popular film at the Pavilion, after a special film about the Coronation.[77] As the Minister at the Department of Overseas Trade commented to Philip Guedalla:

It is a remarkable tribute to you and your committee that throughout the whole of the Exhibition there was hardly an empty seat in the film pavilion.[78]

The Joint Committee produced a display that was successful on their own terms. Spectacle and pageantry were the key element in their program of films. This corresponded with the tone of the British Pavilion as a whole. Pageantry was the hallmark of the entire Pavilion. Significantly, the highpoint of the Exhibition was the Royal visit, which was, as the Commissioner General wrote, "a splendid climax to the first six weeks of the Fair."[79]

The documentary group's response to its virtual exclusion from the official exhibit was to arrange a separate display for its films. Under the auspices of American Film Center, an organization funded by the Carnegie Foundation and with close connections with Film Centre in London, a competing display of British documentaries was arranged in the Little Theatre of the Science and Education Building at the Fair. This display was the outcome of visits by Grierson, Rotha, and Thomas Baird to the United States during the previous two years. Grierson had visited North America in connection with his work for the Imperial Relations Trust. Rotha and Baird had both received scholarships to undertake lecture tours and disseminate the idea of the documentary film. This history of cooperation between the documentary movement and various educational bodies in the United States, especially the Carnegie Foundation, culminated in the display of the documentarists' films at the Fair.

Richard Griffith, Rotha's American colleague, claimed that the documentarists' display was a great success. He termed it

the only local exhibit of films in operation throughout the Fair . . . to present a complete picture of the modern effort to reorganise society on a modern basis.

He compared this to the official film display at the British Pavilion, which he characterized as

a heterogeneous collection of travelogues and "interest" films, incompetent enough and dull enough to alienate the most passionately Anglophile group.[80]

He did not note that many films on display at the official exhibit had actually been made by members of the documentary group. To have done so would perhaps have spoiled the simple dichotomy he and the others made between their display of films illustrative of the scientific, social, and economic reconstruction of Britain and the pageantry and spectacle of the films at the official exhibit. There was a definite ideological division between the documentarists and the officials arranging the official image of Britain, but it was not as clear-cut as Griffith suggested. This ideological difference was compounded by the documentarists' decision to organize their display on a completely independent basis from the official display. This came at precisely that time when it was vital that national publicity should be presented in a united manner. By this action the documentarists effectively excluded themselves from the official plans for national publicity overseas being made immediately prior to the outbreak of war and during the early months of the war.

Plans for official film publicity overseas in wartime were notable for the manner in which they specifically disregarded the documentary movement, with the exception of the tame General Post Office Film Unit. One of the first consequences of these official plans was that the special relationship between the Travel Association and the documentary group was ended. All the Travel Association's film activities were taken over by the British Council in October 1939. A newly christened British Council Films Department was then placed under the control of M. Neville Kearney, who resigned from his position as secretary of both the Newsreel Association and the Film Producers Group of the Federation of British Industries to take up the appointment.[81] Kearney was a former Foreign Office man himself and just the kind of person the Foreign Office wanted to organize overseas film publicity. He had also been involved in several disputes with the documentary group and had done all he could to curtail their activities, such as leading the lobby that sought to contain the work of the GPO Film Unit during 1933–4. Kearney's presence at the British Council ended the possibility of the documentary movement being an influence there. He was also largely responsible for the constant disputes over films that arose between the British Council and the Ministry of Information during the war.

After the Films Division of the Ministry of Information had been in existence less than a year, Kearney believed that the "documentary boys" had taken over control there. As he wrote to a colleague at the Foreign Office:

One cannot avoid the suspicion that the ultimate object is eventually to centralize in the hands of one body – i.e. Film Centre "Documentary Boys" – the whole influence of films in the reordering of things social both during the war and when it comes to an end . . . the Films Division of the Ministry of Information itself is now largely composed of the same "Documentary Boys," their satellites being selected to produce or direct all Ministry films or despatched to one place or another as advisers.[82]

Kearney maintained this belief in a documentarists' conspiracy at the Ministry of Information throughout the war. In 1942 he commented:

The "Documentary Boys" are in clover. It is like putting mice in a cheese shop! Those inside and those outside the Ministry go into a huddle and think of every conceivable subject about which a film could be made – and then those inside proceed to get authority and dish out the films to those outside! It is a wonderful system.[83]

The documentary movement was equally scornful of the policy and procedures of the British Council and the Foreign Office during the war. In 1941, for example, their own periodical, *Documentary News Letter,* called for an end to the British Council Film Committee and Film Department. The Committee's work was chastised for being "tied to the ill-laundered apron strings of the Foreign Office" and symptomatic of "the spinelessness of British film propaganda." The Film Department represented "an attitude of mind which is entirely divorced from the urgencies of the moment." As for the Film Committee, this had

an old-fashioned and reactionary outlook which can certainly do this nation nothing but harm amongst free and progressive peoples all over the world.[84]

Because of this history of animosity, the documentary movement's wartime participation in national publicity overseas took place primarily through the Ministry of Information. Its actions before and during the war, compounded by the widespread belief that it had infiltrated the Films Division of the Ministry of Information, contributed greatly to the antagonism that developed between the British Council and the Ministry of Information.

Immediately prior to the war, Grierson was involved in another project concerning overseas publicity. Had he not been, he would most certainly have played a larger role in the dispute with the British Council, and the repercussions so much more serious. Beginning early in 1938, Grierson acted as Film Adviser to the Imperial Relations Trust. The Trust was set up in late 1937 as a result of an anonymous gift of £250,000. Lord Baldwin was the chairman of the Trust. Its stated purpose was to improve Empire relations and understanding. On the advice of Sir Stephen Tallents, Lord Baldwin set up a Film Committee, of which Lord Clarendon was the chairman and Tallents a prominent member. Grierson undertook a series of reports on the use of film in the Dominions and colonies on behalf of this Committee. The interest in Empire rather than national projection was, for both Grierson and Tallents, a return to earlier priorities. Grierson's investigations into film in the Dominions ultimately led to the creation of national film units in Australia and elsewhere. His report on the use of film by the Canadian government was the basis of the report he wrote for the Canadian government, which led to the National Film Act, the creation of the National Film Board, and his own eventual appointment as Canadian Film Commissioner.[85]

Grierson's travels in North America during this time reaffirmed his early belief that Britain's most pressing film publicity task was to reach filmgoers in the United States. Many of his contributions to the debate on the selection of films for the World's Fair were made while he was in North America. He believed this gave him a unique perspective and a special awareness of the type of film publicity that Britain had to produce:

Opinion is so fiercely democratic in both Canada and the United States these days and so fearful least Britain sidestep the democratic issue that our cultural relations with America in the year to come depend upon the skill with which we articulate our faith as a democratic society.[86]

In the year prior to the outbreak of war, the most urgent and compelling task for both Grierson and Paul Rotha was to establish closer film relations with the United States. The campaign for films for the World's Fair was just part of this wider concern.

Grierson's demand that Britain must export an image of herself as a "functioning democracy" followed closely the impact of the British documentary film upon filmmaking in the United States. A substantial although uncoordinated distribution of British documentary films had been set up in the United States, and there was a considerable demand for these films, especially from the "little theater" circuit. Early in 1938, Grierson began to demand that this distribution become planned and purposive and his protégé, Thomas Baird, was commissioned to produce several memoranda on this subject. Baird found a great deal wanting in the nontheatrical distribution of films, especially when it operated under official auspices. Since the British Council was debarred from working in the United States, this distribution amounted to that run by the Travel Association. The Travel Association, copying the practice of the Canadian Motion Picture Bureau, simply handed its films over to the American YMCA for inclusion in its programs as it saw fit. Baird considered this completely ineffectual from the viewpoint of national publicity. He believed films were being distributed

to no great advantage . . . they reach a reasonably wide but unselected audience. Their identity is lost and the British audience is reduced to a minimum.[87]

Because of these shortcomings, during August, September, and October 1939, the documentary movement pressed for the creation of a new system of official film distribution in the United States to be put under their own immediate control.

In September 1939, Grierson, who was in Hollywood, began to bombard the Ministry of Information and the British Ambassador in Washington with telegrams and memoranda. Grierson's isolation from the publicity planners was not merely geographical. He was so uninformed about the planning arrangements made for the Ministry of Information that his first two telegrams to the Ministry were addressed to Alexander Korda, whom he mistakenly believed had been appointed Director of the Films Division.[88] He cabled that the most important task for film publicity in the United States was to develop the "fast growing influential non-theatrical field" and to expand the distribution of documentary films there. He suggested appointing Basil Wright, Paul Rotha, and Thomas Baird to take charge of this scheme. The next day, Grierson cabled again to ask for "carte blanche" so that he could begin work in the United States.[89]

There was no room for Grierson in the plans of the Ministry of Information. He had blotted his copybook even further by sending these messages in open telegrams when talking about a subject as sensitive as British publicity in the United States. There was considerable alarm within the Ministry when it was learned that Grierson had not been satisfied with the official silence, which was his only reply from the Ministry, and had decided to approach directly Lord Lothian, the British Ambassador in Washington.

Grierson produced a memorandum for Lord Lothian on British information services in the United States. He reiterated that the key to influencing American opinion lay in the provision of open and honest information about events in Britain. He also thought that the "democratic gambit" ought to be played by Britain. He noted that Hollywood was "wide open to suggestions for democratic propaganda which can be fitted into the terms of ordinary entertainment."[90] He also argued that documentary films were potentially more important than feature films because they reached the "discussive levels of American opinion," which was the same argument he had used to legitimate nontheatrical distribution in Great Britain. He therefore again suggested that the scheme for the nontheatrical distribution of British documentary films in the United States be got under way, estimating that this would cost $50,000 initially. He again suggested that Wright, Rotha, and Baird be brought over to America to organize the scheme.

Sir Joseph Ball, former director of the Conservative party's Research Department and the first Director of the Films Division and his assistant G. E. G. Forbes, a colleague of Grierson's at the Post Office, were both "far from happy about Grierson's activities." Ball explained why this was so:

Even if we assess the documentary movement as highly as Grierson and his associates suggest in their communications to the press, the fact remains that an enormously larger public in all countries is reached by commercial films distributed through commercial channels, and it would be disastrous to lose the goodwill of the commercial people in the attempt, even in the successful attempt, to increase the output of the distribution of documentaries.[91]

Unfortunately for the Ministry, Lord Lothian chose to take an official interest in Grierson's plans. By mid-October 1939, these plans had been so modified that British documentary films were now to be distributed under the auspices of an organization known as International Film Center.

International Film Center was set up jointly by the American Committee on Intellectual Co-operation and American Film Center.[92] Grierson proposed that the British government should distribute films through International Film Center, which would also distribute films for other countries in the United States. The Ministry of Information and the British Council spent the next six months discussing the proposal. Both these bodies were interested in increasing British propaganda in the United States, but were cautious about becoming involved in anything like the Grierson scheme, which entailed quite overt publicity. They had other reasons for being lukewarm in their attitude toward this subject. In the first instance, they agreed with Ball that commercial distribution was the best means of reaching the American public. Second, it was widely felt that Grierson's plans contained a strong element of "jobs for the boys." Third, and most serious of these objections, neither the Council nor the Ministry wished to delegate responsibility for British film publicity in the United States to the documentary movement. As Joseph Ball commented:

The ... individuals nominated by Mr. Grierson for the proposed posts are all associated with him in the activities of his "Film Centre," a very small private company ... Such a group would not be considered by the other documentary organisations as representative of the movement in general as to justify a monopoly for its members of the influential and lucrative posts now in question; and even if their resentment could be ignored it is probable that the appointments would be severely criticised by numerous members of the House of Commons, who are known to distrust Mr Grierson and his associates.

Ball also concluded that the appointment of Grierson as the head of the National Film Board of Canada did not solve the problem posed by the documentary movement:

The Film Publicity Division learns with anxiety that he has been appointed Canadian Film Commissioner, and does not regard the fact that his advice can therefore now be obtained without special payment as any reason for relying on it.[93]

The Ministry of Information, the British Council, and the Foreign Office met twice during January 1940 under the chairmanship of Sir Stephen Gaselee, to discuss the issue of nontheatrical distribution of British films in the United States.[94] They were all concerned about International Film Center, which it was thought

would naturally become suspect of being a British Government propaganda instrument, even if the films chosen for circulation by it were not the ones the British Government would have chosen.[95]

Those bodies gathered together at the meetings in January 1940 were compelled to take International Film Center seriously, however, by the news that it would be arranging the displays of documentary films in the Science and Education Building at the reopened World's Fair in May 1940.

The Ministry of Information pushed for the appointment of an official to the British Library of Information in New York, who would work with, but not for, International Film Center. The Foreign Office also saw merit in these proposals:

If the British Section of the International Film Center can get into operation before the Fair opens, the control of the use of British films at the Fair would be much simplified. Lord Halifax is informed that the Committee appointed to select suitable documentary films for display in the British Pavilion Film Theatre at the New York World's Fair in 1939 suffered considerable embarrassment by reason of the fact that British films which it had rejected as being unsuitable for display to American audiences nevertheless secured a showing in the Science and Education Theatre through the activities of the commercial firms by whom the rejected films were owned.[96]

In fulfillment of these plans, in May 1940, Richard Ford, a Ministry of Information man, was appointed to the British Library of Information. His function was to work in conjunction with International Film Center in arranging the distribution of British films in the United States. The appointment of just one official was the sole outcome of the campaign the documentary movement had begun the previous September. The Ministry of Information and the Foreign Office had been compelled to make a decision, but this was not the one for which the documentarists had petitioned.

Meanwhile, in the employment of another country, Grierson was able to undertake many of the projects to which he had aspired in Britain. Canada was in many respects a combination of Scotland and the United States, and was much more receptive to his ideas than English civil servants and politicians could ever be. He had wanted to be placed in charge of national film publicity. He had always wanted to influence public opinion in the United States. He was always interested in developing the large-scale distribution of documentary films on a theatrical and nontheatrical basis. He was able to do all these things in his capacity as Canadian Film Commissioner, and ultimately during the war he acquired responsibility for managing information policy in Canada on a much wider scale than this. The National Film Board of Canada had particular success with its series, *World in Action.* This series was eventually seen in 7,500 American cinemas.[97] *World in Action* gave Grierson the success in the commerical cinema and in the United States that he had always wanted. Significantly, this success came when Grierson abandoned the aesthetic and style of the British documentary film school in favor of news reportage and the techniques of *The March of Time* and the newsreels. Grierson had to return to North America, where so many of his ideas and impulses had been shaped, before he was entrusted with the executive power he had craved during the fifteen years he had spent in Britain since his first visit to the United States.

In England the leaderless documentary movement found in the early months of the war that the planners would countenance the units making some films for overseas. They would not, however, allow the documentarists to take part in deciding overall strategy. At the first meeting of the Joint Committee after the declaration of war, for example, it was decided that the GPO Film Unit and the Strand and Realist units must be given work to keep them in operation. Strand and Realist were both asked to prepare treatments for films for overseas. Work was found for the documentary units because

the Ministry of Information was anxious that documentary film companies should, if possible, be kept going . . . it was important that small companies such as British Films, Realist Film Unit and the Strand Film Company, etc. should be given a chance to produce films . . . it was important to keep the small companies in being as the larger companies could look after themselves. [98]

The Joint Committee found no incongruity in placing another company, British Films Ltd., with its long-standing connections with the Conservative party, on the same footing as Strand and Realist. They were all considered, quite straightforwardly, as production companies that could produce films that would conform with the Committee's wishes on demand.

The documentary movement was never apt, however, to fall in so easily with the wishes of its paymasters. Furthermore, it would not remain silent about the direction that it felt should be taken by official publicity policy, and its headlong attack on the film activities of the British Council in 1941 was a prime example of this kind of behavior. The documentarists were not content to make films that expressed the viewpoints of others. M. Neville Kearney's suspicions about the "Documentary Boys," as he termed them, and their involvement with the Films Division of the Ministry of Information had some basis in fact. At the Ministry the documentary group attempted yet again to influence overseas publicity during the war.

We seem to have a boxed compass or a complete cycle – i.e. "Documentary Boys" controlling the issue at the Ministry of Information, with their prototypes ranging far and wide . . . it is ingenious, but it seems to me all wrong. It also appears a little sinister.[1]

At the outset of the war all concerned with the moulding of opinion expected that the film would play a part of ever increasing importance. That expectation has been realised.[2]

In 1939, the Vansittart Committee put forward a proposal to establish a National Films Council.[3] In the same year, the Treasury was approached by powerful film trade interests, including Sir Michael Bruce, public relations officer for the Odeon chain of cinemas, who asked for a "central government committee" to regulate the commercial production and distribution of government propaganda films.[4] In addition, the lengthy and well-publicized debate over the selection of films for the New York World's Fair had just been acrimoniously settled, with the documentarists' decision to compete with the official film display with a presentation of their own. During this widespread discussion about film publicity, the planners of the Ministry of Information considered arrangements for film publicity on two separate occasions. Each time, the planners gave special attention to the value of documentary films as a means of propaganda. Neither group of planners was, as Paul Rotha once claimed, "ignorant of the fact that there had been an efficient official machine for filmmaking in being without interruption since the EMB Film Unit in 1929."[5]

During the summer of 1938, the Home Publicity Planning Sub-Committee met to discuss domestic publicity machinery for the future Ministry of Information. The Sub-Committee's members included E. T. Crutchley, Stephen King-Hall, H. V. Rhodes, and Lady Williams.[6] They agreed that Crutchley's public relations department at the Post Office would provide the personnel and a model for a similar organization at the Ministry of

Information. As part of these plans, the Post Office's film production and distribution machinery were also to go to the new Ministry.[7] The GPO Film Unit, which they thought "has had some outstanding successes in the 'documentary' field," was to be the nucleus for an official film unit. As Crutchley explained:

Film production units organised to supply the theatrical market and concentrating much more on box-office appeal than the interpretation of the public consciousness will find it difficult at first to adapt themselves to new and constantly changing requirements and it will be a great advantage for the publicity division to have film production resources of its own.[8]

The Sub-Committee did not progress from discussion of film production arrangements to extensive thought about the nature of the films that would be required by the Ministry. The only concrete proposal for film production was that

a most useful immediate task for this organisation would be short educational films dealing with (a) gas masks and (b) trench digging.

The Sub-Committee made no other detailed suggestions for film production because it believed that radio would carry the burden of government publicity in wartime:

Because of its speed and universality and because people who will neither read printed matter nor hear speaking will listen to the wireless, broadcasting will prove to be the most important of all publicity media if it continues in wartime.[9]

Overseas and domestic film propaganda were discussed in much more detail by the International Propaganda and Broadcasting Enquiry. This second group of Ministry of Information planners met under the chairmanship of Ivison Macadam during the summer of 1939. Macadam noted that the British film industry had made it clear during the discussion of the proposed National Films Council that it wished to be active in the production and distribution of government propaganda films. He concluded that "mere development of the Post Office Film Unit, to the exclusion of the big commercial companies, is not now to be thought of."[10] This second set of planners conceded that film publicity was much more important and complicated than their predecessors had thought. They established a separate Film Sub-Committee, consisting of E. W. Langley, A. E. Watts, J. G. Hughes-Roberts (the Government Cinematograph Adviser), A. G. Highet (Controller of Publicity for the Post Office), S. J. Fletcher (Office Manager of the GPO Film Unit), and Gervas Huxley. The last three of these gentlemen had all been involved with the work of the documentary movement for several years. The Sub-Committee's terms of reference were to decide what arrangements ought to be effected now, and to make any necessary recommendations for the use of film for the purpose of steadying the national spirit during a state of emergency.[11]

This group of planners gave much more importance to the newsreels in their plans than the first group. This Sub-Committee was particularly impressed by the recent cooperation with the newsreel companies, which had resulted in the production of *British News,* then on display at the British Pavilion at the New York World's Fair. The Sub-Committee came to "regard it as essential that the work begun by the newsreels in collaboration should be continued until further notice."[12] The parent committee believed "it was possible that newsreels might perhaps be the most important medium of publicity, whether they were produced officially or (as would seem preferable) commercially." *British News* was considered "a particularly valuable prototype in this connection."[13]

The second set of publicity planners also had the opportunity to think in more detail about the type of films that any official film unit would be called upon to produce. They continued to believe that "the Post Office Film Unit will constitute a most important factor in the planning of film publicity."[14] In the year that had elapsed since the first group of planners had met, the GPO Film Unit had had an outstanding commercial and critical success with Harry Watt's *North Sea.* So Crutchley suggested that this indicated the area in which the GPO Film Unit should concentrate: "Its success has been considerable and warrants serious consideration of the story form in presenting government propaganda."[15] This anticipated one documentary genre in which the Post Office, and later, the Crown Film Unit, came to center its efforts during the war.

The Film Sub-Committee commissioned G. E. G. Forbes to write a report on the work produced for government departments by the various documentary and commercial film units during the previous five years.[16] He noted the existence of both Film Centre and the Strand Film Company, although not, surprisingly, the Realist Film Unit. The Sub-Committee recommended that the Strand Film Company, along with several commercial firms – Publicity Films, Gaumont–British Instructional, National Screen Services, and British Thomson Houston – should be earmarked to supplement the GPO Film Unit's production for official needs.[17] Significantly, the Committee chose not to include Realist, Film Centre, or Andrew Buchanan's company, British Films, in these plans. Realist and British Films were expected to do some work for the Joint Film Committee at the request of the Ministry of Information.[18] At no time were the documentarists brought in to discuss these arrangements. The planners expected the documentary units to execute, not decide, policy. Film Centre, the central policy-making organization of the documentary movement, was carefully excluded from the arrangements made for both the Ministry of Information and by the Joint Film Committee. The part played by Film Centre in undermining the official film display at the World's Fair, which was still in progress as these arrangements were being made, indicated the sort of problem they could expect if it was included in their plans.

This Sub-Committee did not anticipate official film production on a massive scale. Initially, it suggested the need for only three films in the event of war: a message from the King to the nation, a message from the Prime Minister and the leaders of the Opposition, and a film of detailed emergency instructions.[19] These films were expected to play an ancillary role to those made by the newsreel companies. As the Film Sub-Committee commented:

We regard news film as an essential and possibly the most important instrument for film propaganda and we urge that every effort should be made to ensure continuance of an efficient newsreel service. Consultation with the Newsreel Association should be undertaken without delay.[20]

The new Ministry of Information also intended to take over the Post Office's machinery for nontheatrical distribution, which would be used to reach evacuees in areas without cinemas and populations of towns where the cinemas had been closed down or destroyed.

Careful plans for cooperation with the film trade and a limited role for the documentary movement in official film production immediately went awry when the Ministry of Information was created. The Films Division suffered from the chaos that afflicted the new Ministry. The Ministry fell into a severe malaise that led it through six Director Generals and four Ministers in eighteen months. This procession of Ministers caused the film trade press to comment:

A prominent figure in the industry told me the other day there was a deep indentation in the pavement outside Senate House [the Ministry of Information building], where successive holders of the office have come out on their ear.[21]

The film trade press was very satisfied with the appointment of Sir Joseph Ball as the first Director of the Films Division of the Ministry of Information. Ball was thought "an outstanding example of the man who knows how to use the velvet glove."[22] From the documentarists' point of view, this was not such a good choice of candidate. Ball was openly hostile toward the documentary group. In particular, he had very little faith in Grierson personally. After listening to the advice of G. E. G. Forbes, the Assistant Director of the Division, who had been seconded from the Post Office Public Relations Department, Ball commented on Grierson's proposal to expand the nontheatrical distribution of British documentary films in the United States:

Experience of Mr Grierson during his connection with the [Post Office] Unit inspired in the officers of the Post Office closely concerned with the matter very little confidence either in his reliability as an adviser in the matters in question, or in his discretion as an executant of the extremely delicate mission which he has proposed himself.[23]

This mistrust of Grierson and his colleagues survived the departure of Ball and Forbes from the Division in December 1939. A. G. Highet took up the position of Assistant Director of the Films Division. He, too, had misgivings about Grierson and the documentary group after their dealings at the Post Office and from his membership of the Joint Film Committee. Highet had expected that the GPO Film Unit would produce films for the Ministry. He was therefore prepared to rely primarily upon the GPO Film Unit, with the independent units supplementing its output. But he was soon disillusioned. As he commented soon after leaving the Ministry:

I have had a good deal of experience in film production and control both at the Unit and at the Ministry and by the time the muddle at the latter place had been sorted out temporarily about the month of February this year I had acquired considerable knowledge of the practices, prices and qualifications of the production units which had always been attacked by the so-called documentary movement, led by Mr. John Grierson. I found myself being driven, somewhat unwillingly I admit, to the conclusion that a number of commercial producers could produce perfectly good films at prices strictly comparable with G.P.O. Film Unit costs and with very much less trouble and friction.[24]

Ball was succeeded by Sir Kenneth Clark in December 1939. In his autobiography, Clark claimed he was completely ignorant of film matters, so that when he was appointed, he did not even understand the difference between producers, exhibitors, and renters. The only thing he was certain about was that the Division should execute its work through the film industry.[25] It was not until Jack Beddington took over the Films Division in April 1940 that its work was put on a proper footing and that the documentarists had a much more active role there. Beddington and his chief adviser, Sidney Bernstein, were both known allies of the documentary group. Beddington was one of the representatives of the modern school of public relations upon which the growth of the sponsored documentary film depended. Bernstein, too, although principally associated with commercial exhibition, had been one of the documentarists' supporters. He had, for example, rescued their periodical, *World Film News,* when it was going through financial difficulties.[26] Bernstein engineered the agreement between the film trade and the Ministry that resulted in the "five minute film" scheme, whereby the trade agreed to devote a small portion of each cinema program to Ministry of Information films. Bernstein and Beddington also made it possible for the documentary group to slowly filter into the organization of the Ministry of Information.

The documentarists took charge of nontheatrical distribution at the Films Division before they became a major influence in film production policy. Nontheatrical distribution at the Ministry was initially built around the nucleus inherited from the Post Office and under the control of Joseph Reeves and Russell Furguson. Reeves had organized nontheatrical film displays before the war as Secretary-Manager of the Workers Film Association. Ferguson had been in charge of nontheatrical display at the Post Office. He was one of those members of the documentary movement, like Thomas Baird, who had been interested in film distribution and display rather than production. The immediate task for the Films Division's nontheatrical distribution section was to provide films for evacuees and to reach people in urban areas where the cinemas had been closed. The section utilized cinema vans that had been inherited from the Post Office. These vans gave displays in which entertainment films were mixed with propaganda films, just like the Conservative party's nontheatrical displays a decade earlier. Such displays were intended largely "to combat the loneliness and boredom of the women evacuated to remote Scottish areas and in an effort to avoid the women's return to crowded areas."[27]

Film exhibitors were as hostile to these proposals as they had always been to nontheatrical displays that threatened to compete with their own business.[28] They became extremely perturbed about the Ministry's plans to develop this nontheatrical distribution on an extensive and permanent footing. Under Beddington, Thomas Baird, the leading authority on nontheatrical distribution within the documentary movement, was brought in to reorganize the Ministry's distribution system. Baird proposed a scheme involving 115 mobile film display units and a free loan scheme to be administered by a Central Film Library.[29] During the autumn of 1940, the Cinematograph Exhibitors Association lobbied for the exclusion of entertainment films from this expanded distribution system. It was eventually satisfied by a promise from Beddington that "commercial entertainment films do not form any part of the displays now projected."[30]

The exhibitors and renters had been needlessly worried. Entertainment films were expected to play only a very minor role in this scheme for nontheatrical distribution, even though Baird did argue that "evacuees in the regions out of reach of cinema and therefore denied their normal recreation should have the cinema brought to them." This motive was very ancillary to the information and publicity role that he expected nontheatrical films to play when war brought "unavoidable deterioration in the public informational and educational services." Baird argued for an extensive nontheatrical distribution scheme because

the influence of the cinema, being a medium of information and propaganda, should be made effective over as wide an area and on as many levels as possible.[31]

This scheme was virtually the only aspect of the Ministry's early film activities that the documentary movement praised. The Select Committee on National Expenditure, which scrutinized the Films Division's work during 1940, opposed the distribution scheme, which it believed to be outside the province of the Ministry. It argued it should not be developed unless "the scheme is making a contribution to the war effort commensurate with the cost."[32] The documentarists believed that it was more necessary than ever for government departments to provide "means of general education" in wartime. In other words, they supported it for precisely those reasons that the Select Committee opposed it. It was also the first major project under the control of a member of the documentary movement outside the GPO Film Unit. The documentarists believed there was opposition to the proposed nontheatrical scheme on the following grounds:

It is big, bold and new; moreover, since it is not similar to anything being done by the feature film producers, the newsreel companies, the British Council and the Government Cinematograph Adviser, it cannot be handed over to any of them.[33]

Much to the chagrin of the film trade, Baird's plans for nontheatrical distribution went ahead. This caused considerable animosity, not least because the scheme was undertaken in complete disregard of the Select Committee's comments. As *Sight and Sound* commented:

Quite apart from the pros and cons of the scheme it is a disturbing thought that a Select Committee's suggestions can be thus set aside by those fledgling civil servants of Malet St. whose little spell of authority seems to have gone to their heads.[34]

The Ministry of Information's nontheatrical film distribution section remained a documentarists' enclave for the duration of the war. Production for this small audience, which the documentarists believed to be both substantial and important, became an important part of the documentary group's work for the Ministry during the war.

None of Grierson's inner circle – the principals being Basil Wright, Arthur Elton, and Edgar Anstey – or Paul Rotha found themselves recruited by the Ministry of Information during the first year of the war. Rotha's typically individualistic action was to temporarily stop filmmaking and work in a mobile canteen in the East End during the blitz.[35] The others set up *Documentary News Letter,* a small circulation journal much in the tradition of *World Film News.* Arthur Elton was the leading figure on the editorial board of the magazine. He provided the money for the journal, which was published by Film Centre and which he headed during Grierson's absence in Canada. This directed and purposeful publicity was intended to influence the Ministry of Information's film and information policies. The first issue was published in January 1940, and the journal was an outspoken advocate of documentary and information policy for the rest of the war.

The survivors of the documentary movement believed that their journal was very important. As Basil Wright maintained: "It had an enormous influence on government thinking in the information services."[36] Wright's statement is open to question, and Neville Kearney at the British Council Films Department, for example, condemned *Documentary News Letter* as an "absurd publication."[37] Any influence it had with him at least must have been largely negative. The newsletter advertised the documentarists' point of view before the Ministry of Information, but there is no real evidence that it influenced the senior policymakers there.

The documentarists' infiltration of film production at the Films Division began when the GPO Film Unit was handed over to the Ministry of Information when war was declared. In many ways, however, by 1939, the GPO Film Unit was on the periphery of the documentary movement. For example, none of the first generation of documentarists were still with the unit by that date. Under the control of Alberto Cavalcanti, the unit's films had come to diverge markedly from those made by the independent documentary units. It enjoyed official approval, unlike the other parts of the documentary movement. It pursued a policy that was different from that emanating from Film Centre. These differences increased when the GPO Film Unit was taken over to act as the Films Division's directly employed production unit, for it then became the only well-heeled production company making documentary films in Great Britain.

The GPO Film Unit, which became the Crown Film Unit early in 1941, produced films under quite different circumstances to those surrounding production at the independent units. In many ways, the unit had been heading toward the style of commercially produced films in the late 1930s. This trend continued when Ian Dalrymple replaced Cavalcanti as Director of Production in July 1940. Production was put on a proper commercial footing as a result of an officially commissioned report by H. G. Boxall, a production manager from Gaumont-British in November 1940. Boxall suggested that the unit should be divested of all duties apart from film production. The unit was, for example, still engaged in distribution and still photography and myriad other functions it had picked up over the course of a decade. In addition to streamlining production in this way, Boxall also suggested that the old division of the staff between the payrolls of the commercial contractor and the appropriate government department, which Grierson had found so useful, should be abolished. Most important was Boxall's suggestion that the unit be shifted out to new facilities to be requisitioned at Pinewood, one of the best-equipped studios in Britain.[38] The proposals were accepted. Many of the arbitrary arrangements that had come to surround the unit during the 1930s were dismantled. Production was modeled on that of the commercial film industry. Perhaps most significant was the movement of activities to Pinewood. There, the unit had facilities previously undreamt of by

Figure 28. *Target for Tonight* (Harry Watt, 1941): the most commercially success-ful documentary in World War II.

the documentarists and still unavailable to the independent documen-tary units. Equally significant, the unit was also geographically isolated from the other documentary units.

During the war, as Crutchley had anticipated, the story form documen-tary came to be an important part of official film propaganda. It also became the staple form of production for the unit he had once controlled at the Post Office. The unit spent most of its budget and much of its time upon the production of a small number of commercially oriented feature length story-documentaries, the first of these being Harry Watt's *Target for Tonight* (1941). The tradition that began with *The Saving of Bill Blewitt,* which was made cheaply and quickly in 1936, culminated in the production of *Western Approaches* (Pat Jackson, 1944), which was shot in Technicolor and took over two years to make. These films, with their big budgets, elaborate studio sets, and, most important, their use of conventional narrative forms, were completely distinct from the films produced by the other documentary units. Significantly, the Crown Film Unit was also the only documentary production company that made films that were regularly taken up for rental on commmercial terms. *Target for Tonight* alone, for example, made a profit of over £73,000 for the Ministry during the war.[39]

The Crown Film Unit also made one- and two-reel shorts, as well as a number of films for the five-minute film scheme introduced in August 1940, and the fifteen-minute film scheme that replaced it in August 1942.[40] The idea behind this type of programming was that short informational films could find their way into regular screenings in commercial theaters without too much trouble, although there has been some debate about the extent to which these were effective. Critical attention to wartime documentary filmmaking in Britain has always centered on a few major Crown Film Unit productions, and with much justification since these films – *Target for Tonight, Coastal Command* (1942), *Close Quarters* (1943), *Fires Were Started* (1943), and *Western Approaches* (1944) – were given a much wider distribution than any of the other films made by the documentary movement for the Films Division. This group of films was also fairly successful commercially and critically. These expensive and major productions were very different from the majority of the films made by the independent documentary units working on contract for the Ministry, which accounted for perhaps 90 percent of 726 documentary films that the Arts Enquiry estimated was made for the Ministry during the war.[41]

Arthur Elton was appointed Director of Production at the Films Division in January 1941. In many ways, Elton became the leader of the documentary movement in Grierson's absence. He had inherited control of Film Centre, and he and Basil Wright were the only two of the seniors of the movement who had remained continuously involved with documentary filmmaking in Britain. Edgar Anstey had spent several years with *The March of Time*, most recently having worked as a European editor for the series based in New York. Stuart Legg had joined Grierson in Canada, as did a number of his British protégés. It fell upon Elton and Wright to take charge of the documentary movement in wartime. Elton became the documentary movement's most authoritative representative within the Films Division. He was given responsibility for dealing with the established documentary units: Strand, Realist, Shell, and Spectator Films and also the new production units that came into existence during the war such as Paul Rotha Productions, Verity Films, Merton Park Films, Greenpark, and many others. Some of these production companies had only a fleeting existence, often being little more than temporary alliances between filmmakers and letterheaded stationery.

Elton's work at the Films Division quickly aroused the suspicions of those who saw a "Film Centre conspiracy" taking over production. M. Neville Kearney pointed out to the Foreign Office:

A number of the present staff of the Films Division of the Ministry of Information were formerly members of or associated with Film Centre and in addition the Ministry has, on its panel of Directors or Assistant Directors, which it allocates for the directing of the films it commissions, a number of gentlemen also directly or indirectly associated with Film Centre, although they are not . . . members of the Department's staff . . . the Film Centre attitude and atmosphere pervades the whole outfit.[42]

Kearney's position remained essentially unchanged throughout the war, and there was a lot of evidence to support his contentions.

The independent units undertook a diversity of documentary films for the Ministry of Information. The only films they made that received substantial theatrical distribution were those made for the five-minute and fifteen-minute film schemes. In addition, they made a great many newsreel "trailers." These were 200-foot instructional films that, beginning in June 1940, the Newsreel Association agreed to affix to all commercial newsreels. It was a condition of the agreement between the Ministry and the Cinematograph Exhibitors Association that five-minute films should have "entertainment value." The trailers, however, were straightforward instructional films made on behalf of the Ministry and other departments when "wide and speedy film publicity was required."[43]

Much of the documentary movement's work for the Ministry consisted of films destined for the growing nontheatrical film distribution system. They attached great significance to these films in their writing and publicizing at the time. Films were made for distribution in Britain through the system set up on the recommendations of Thomas Baird. Films were also made for distribution through the Ministry's nontheatrical distribution overseas. As during the years before the war, both the civil servants and the documentarists were particularly interested in reaching nontheatrical audiences in the United States. In the United States, as elsewhere during the war, the Ministry of Information came into conflict with the British Council over the division of responsibility for all types of publicity and information policy, including the use of motion pictures. M. Neville Kearney believed that the Films Division's policies were controlled by the documentary movement or its supporters. Kearney characterized the relationship between the Council and the Ministry on this matter as "those of the snake and the rabbit – we being the rabbit."[44]

The documentarists' consistent belief in the potency of their films demands an assessment of their impact during the war. In their writings both then and subsequently, the documentarists sought to impress with the sheer volume of nonfiction films that were produced for the Ministry and other government departments in wartime. *The Factual Film* suggested that annual production of nonfiction films of all types topped 500 films a year during the war.[45] The documentarists, using a very broad term of reference, claimed that this filmmaking war effort "represents the most spectacular use of films for a communal purpose ever achieved in the world."[46] The war created precisely the sort of demand for extensive public education and information services that the documentarists had been advocating for over a decade. During this time, they noted, they had been

working to a thesis of public enlightenment which now fits closely to official needs; so much is this so that many things which documentarists have urged long and vainly now look like being created as a result of the war.[47]

As the war progressed, many people and influential bodies came to share the views of the documentarists regarding the importance of public education and recognized that war made this need especially pressing. What was perhaps distinctive about the documentarists' films was their willingness to link public education in wartime issues, such as housing and employment, to a consideration of the prospects for these issues after the war. As *The Times* commented:

The keener popular interest, even at moments of spectacular military success, in domestic policies confirms the view that in the present war social reform stands in a closer and more direct relation to the national effort than government spokesmen and government propagandists have sometimes been prepared to admit.[48]

It is also true that the documentarists' films as well as their ideas had a wider currency during the war than had ever been the case in the 1930s.

Belief in the necessity of public education because of the massively increased extent of government departments' intervention into the lives of the general public had never been the documentarists' private property. The extent of the government's involvement in the economy and society because of the war, however, brought home to more people than ever before the necessity of government information services equipped to inform people about this involvement. By 1943, for example, there were over 200 full-time government public relations officers.[49] Their task was to provide the public education which the war demanded. This was just ten years after Tallents had set up the first public relations department. The documentary movement benefited greatly from this growing belief in the importance of public relations, and the willingness of public relations officers to sponsor documentary films as a means of public education.

Only in Canada, where Grierson was appointed General Manager of all propaganda services in February 1943, did the documentary movement succeed in becoming the leading directive influence upon official publicity and propaganda policy. In England, the documentarists proselytized for permanent and extensive systems of public education and information services, but they were never invited to participate in the planning of such arrangements. Their only direct entry into the creation of public information services was their control of the Ministry of Information's

Figure 29. *Listen to Britain* (Humphrey Jennings, 1942): the dance hall at Blackpool.

nontheatrical film distribution. This was one reason why the documentarists gave so much attention to nontheatrical distribution during the war. Subsequently, they hoped that it would be the basis for a permanent means of distribution for documentary films during peacetime.[50]

The documentarists constantly discussed the impact of their films during the war. Their very self-conscious discussions, stimulated by access to facilities and audiences they had never had in peacetime, focused heavily on the impact their films had upon the audiences their films reached. Subsequent critical attention has tended to concentrate upon the contribution of the wartime documentary film to the development of film art. A critical tradition grounded in the study of the commercial feature film and the "art" film has gravitated toward study of the feature length documentary films made during the war and the work of Humphrey Jennings in particular.[51] Both these aspects of wartime British documentary film are worthy of considerable attention. The feature length documentary films made by the Crown Film Unit were important for their unprecedented popular appeal. Jennings's work, which included shorts like *Listen to Britain* and feature length films such as *Fires Were Started* and *A Diary for Timothy,* was important as a major contribution to film art. His subtle cross structuring of sound and visual images instilled a uniquely poetic element in his films. Focusing of critical attention on these particular aspects of the Crown Film Unit, the work of Jennings and the feature length story-documentary films has been at the expense of neglecting the other films made by the independent units during the war. The Crown Film Unit's work was the most prestigious and glamorous of all the films produced by the documentarists; it was, however, only a part of their labors. There is also evidence that the documentarists were hostile to the work being produced by the Crown Film Unit. They found its interest in art films on the one hand and entertainment films on the other did not fall into line with using film as a means of public education.

The Crown Film Unit's feature length films had many of the production values of the commercial feature film. Two elements, however, served to keep them in the province of actuality and the documentary film, rather than that of the fictional story film. Initially, these films were constructed around reenactments of events. For example, Harry Watt has recounted how *Target for Tonight* was based on a script he produced after reading some two thousand pilots' raid reports.[52] Eventually, the Crown Film Unit abandoned even this tenuous manner of linking story-documentary films and actual events. Pat Jackson, for example, has noted how his own film, *Western Approaches* was based upon complete fabrication, not real-life events. The other vital element in Crown Film Unit films, and one that survived through the war, was the use of real people, or social actors, instead of professional actors to portray characters. It had become something of a gospel at the unit that social actors provided a necessary link between actuality and the story form. Great importance was attached by all Crown Film Unit directors to the careful selection of social actors. They became convinced that these people were capable of performances that were unattainable for professional actors. For example, Cavalcanti once cabled David MacDonald, a commercial director who had been brought in to direct *Men of the Lightship* (1940), to tell him to reshoot all the "totally unconvincing" footage where he had used professional actors, while the footage he had shot with real people was "splendid."[53]

Fifty million people flocked to see *Target for Tonight* in the United States.[54] In Great Britain, as Roger Manvell commented: "Exhibitors paid this film the supreme compliment of criticising the distribution agreement between the Ministry and the Exhibitors Association."[55] One of the reasons why this and some of the other major Crown Film Unit productions were so successful was their use of nonprofessional actors. The social actors provided an accessible and understated image of the British people at war. This was not a quality unique to Crown Film Unit films. For example, Thorold Dickinson's *Next of Kin* (1942), made for the Directorate of Army Kinematography, which received widespread popular acclaim, made equally successful use of nonprofessional actors and a similar realist approach to narrative.

The Crown Film Unit's predilection for feature length films portraying the heroic British people at war steered it away from films dealing with social issues and, particularly, specific problems caused directly by the war. This, and the willingness of the unit's masters to seek popular success largely on the terms of the commercial cinema, did not meet with the approval of the rest of the documentary movement. For example, when Ian Dalrymple left Crown in 1943, Alexander Shaw rejected the official invitation to take over control of the unit, giving as his reason that he disagreed with the production policies that prevailed there. Basil Wright similarly chose to turn down the opportunity to take over the most prestigious and best equipped of all British documentary units on this occasion.[56]

Basil Wright finally took over Crown in January 1945. In the interim between his arrival and Dalrymple's departure, the Crown Film Unit floundered. This was typified by the production difficulties that had beset *Western Approaches.* J. B. Holmes had taken charge of the unit after Dalrymple's resignation. That was actually the second time he had been given executive control there. The first time was in 1938 when he had been asked by his colleagues to stand down in favor of Cavalcanti. Sadly, it seems Holmes fared no better on this second occasion. Under his guidance, the unit sank into a malaise. Reporting to his Minister on the state of the unit during the last two years of the war, Cyril Radcliffe said it was "inadequately employed and a lack of leadership was getting business into some confusion and holding up production."[57]

The Crown Film Unit was often attacked for squandering resources. The leaders of the other documentary units thought its facilities would be better employed elsewhere, comparing the luxury of Pinewood with their own struggles to simply obtain film stock and personnel. Meanwhile, the Treasury had begun to ask why production at the Crown Film Unit was so much more expensive than at the independent documentary units working on contract for the Ministry.[58] The response to both these criticisms, echoing earlier defenses of the GPO Film Unit, was that the films made at Crown were fundamentally different from the films made by the other documentary units.

Until 1943, and the beginning of this decline, the MOI Films Division defended the Crown Film Unit fiercely. In 1941, for example, Jack Beddington had argued that it was impossible to compare the unit's work with the output of either the commercial industry or the independent documentary units on these grounds:

The truth is that there are no films such as the Crown Film Unit make with which to compare them. The smaller documentary companies do not do the rather elaborate reconstruction and dialogue work that the Crown Film Unit do. The big feature producers work almost entirely on fictional stories . . . The only fairly straightforward comparison that I can think of is *The Pilot is Safe* made by the Crown Film Unit compared with *The Royal Road* made by Movietone News. My view is that the quality of the former knocks *The Royal Road* into a cocked hat.[59]

The Films Division defended the Crown Film Unit before the Treasury as "a necessary instrument for the production of high-class propaganda films."[60] Qualitatively, the films made at the Crown Film Unit came to diverge markedly from the films made by the other documentary units. This Crown Film Unit style evolved directly from that which had emerged at the Post Office Film Unit. The bigger budgets, better facilities, and special status the war conferred upon the Crown Film Unit helped to accentuate the differences.

It is impossible to provide any quantitative measure of the impact of the feature length documentary films or of the work of Humphrey Jennings. Attempts to utilize scientific survey methods to gauge audience reactions to films, such as employed by Tom Harrisson's Mass-Observation organization, were only sporadic. In addition, since so many value judgments entered into these early and fairly primitive surveys, it would be wrong to ascribe too much importance to them. However, using box-office returns, the only criterion of the commercial cinema, it appears that many of the feature length documentary films were very successful. They generally received very wide theatrical distribution at home and overseas. For example, *Documentary News Letter* was elated at the manner in which these films were going through the American cinemas "with the rapidity of a dose of cascara and providing spitfires on their distribution proceeds."[61] The feature length story-documentary film was also a potent form of propaganda for foreign and domestic cinema audiences. The Films Division noted how difficult it had been attempting to influence the commercial film producers in its evidence for the Select Committee on National Expenditure in 1940.[62] It subsequently found that it was much better served in this respect by the Crown Film Unit.

Humphrey Jennings's films stand as a remarkable record of the British people at war. They were particularly popular with audiences abroad, especially in the United States, contrary to the expectations of the other documentarists.[63] There is little evidence, however, relating to the impact of these films upon cinema audiences in Britain. There was a considerable animosity toward "art" in the commercial cinema, and especially when it appeared in propaganda films. This almost certainly influenced the reception of Jennings's films in the cinemas:

It is no use playing Honegger and Stravinsky to a people whose musical appreciation does not go beyond "The Lambeth Walk" in the hope that they will eventually prefer those composers. Propaganda must be disseminated in the language most widely understood . . . Symbolism may make its appeal to the few cultured minds, but propaganda to have its widest and strongest appeal, must speak what a former generation called "the vulgar tongue."[64]

This was an accurate representation of the attitude of commercial exhibitors and their clientele. It seems likely that Jennings's complex and sensitive films did not have the impact upon wartime cinema audiences that they had upon critics and film students in later years.

The five-minute and fifteen-minute film schemes provided virtually the only opportunity the rest of the documentary movement had to reach audiences in the commercial cinemas. Again, the Ministry of Information undertook only occasional surveys to examine the response to these films. The film trade and the documentary movement, because of their vested interest in the reaction to these films, frequently examined how they were received by exhibitors and audiences. Some of the films, such as *Britain at Bay*, which was released at the time of the fall of France, were extremely popular. On the whole, however, judging by the extent to which Ministry of Information films were excluded from regular cinema programs, they were not generally well received by audiences. Exhibitors believed the usual reaction to the five-minute films was, at best, one of indifference. As one commented: "People just watch these films and don't seem much affected by them one way or another."[65]

The exhibitors' reaction to the Ministry of Information films was colored by their deeply felt belief that propaganda should not be mixed with entertainment. As R. S. Lambert noted:

The ordinary picture house is not a suitable place for direct propaganda. For each time the film-goer enters he pays for a ticket, entitling him to be entertained . . . anyone who has paid for his entertainment, and then finds himself subjected to propaganda, has reasonable grounds for complaint.[66]

This conviction that government propaganda films should be debarred from the cinemas had been one of the reasons for the failure of the documentary film in the cinema during the 1930s. Exhibitors regarded films made for government departments as akin to advertising films, which were shown after the exhibitor was paid a fee by the advertiser. In wartime, however, exhibitors could not resist all the efforts of the Ministry of Information to be given free screen time for fear of being regarded as unpatriotic. They viewed the agreement with the Ministry that introduced the five-minute film scheme as a great concession on their part. The *Daily Film Renter*, for example, believed that it gave the equivalent of £25,000 worth of free advertising to the Ministry every week.[67]

Audience indifference and sometimes downright hostility toward these Ministry of Information films combined with the exhibitor's own antagonism. It therefore became a common practice to exclude Ministry of Information films from regular evening performances. Many exhibitors chose to ignore the agreement between the Cinematograph Exhibitors Association and the Ministry. They chose not to show the films or used many of the tactics employed in the 1930s to exhibit quota quickies, showing films to empty cinemas and so on. For example, Donald Taylor wrote to *Kine Weekly* in 1941, outraged at the extent to which these evasive tactics were used by exhibitors. He cited cases of Ministry of Information films being shown at ten o'clock in the morning, of them being shown in the interval between programs when audiences were changing their seats, and of their being shown when the screen curtain was closed.[68] Another investigator revealed that during the week that the MOI film *Dover, Front Line* should have been playing in first-run houses, he had gone to fourteen cinemas before he found one where it was on display.[69]

Exhibitors were sometimes tempted to exclude the Ministry's films from their programs because of the reduced running times imposed by wartime regulations. Ministry of Information films could, however, be counted against American films for quota purposes. *Documentary News Letter* noted how this actually conspired against the exhibition of the Ministry's films. Exhibitors would count these films against American short films, and then if reduced running times compelled the exhibitor to shorten his program, very often, the Ministry of Information film, not the American film, would be dropped.[70] The antipathy toward official propaganda films intruding into the cinemas was so marked that it even extended to the 200-foot trailers attached to each newsreel. In 1942, for example, it was estimated that 30 percent of all cinemas regularly cut out the trailers before showing the newsreel.[71]

Exhibitors may have been ambivalent in their reaction to the five-minute and fifteen-minute film schemes, but the Ministry of Information valued them as their only regular and immediate access to commercial cinema audiences. These films were often geared to elaborate propaganda campaigns, which the Ministry believed to be effective. For example, in planning the fifteen-minute film program in 1943, the Crown Film Unit Board of Management mooted the possibility of making a film about the Red Cross Organisation. It was argued:

It is to be presumed that heavy casualties will be incurred in forthcoming operations and that the people would be greatly reassured by a sight of the comprehensive facilities provided by the Services and the British Red Cross Organisation.[72]

Even in wartime, exhibitors believed that politics and propaganda should have a small and strictly limited place in cinema programs. Writers returned to the "pill and jam" analogy, which they had used in the 1930s when excluding politics, official propaganda, and the documentarists' version of actuality film from the cinema screen. *Kine Weekly* stated the case for reserving commercial exhibition for fiction films:

In a time of crisis like the present we can put a few grains of powder in behind the jam, and if the medicine is not too unpalatable we shall excite little resentment. But at best it is a delicate balance we have to maintain . . . What is the real desire of the cinema patron? . . . to get away from the whole nasty business for a couple of hours – to live in another world and build up resistance to the wearying anxieties of the day by enjoying a spell of make-believe.[73]

The stress of wartime conditions drove people in far greater numbers than ever before to the cinema. Annual cinema admissions rose from 1,027 million in 1940 to 1,585 million in 1945.[74] These people went to be entertained. When exhibitors chose to exclude Ministry of Information films from their programs, they were reflecting the wishes of their patrons.

Because of the limited success of the documentary film in the cinema even in wartime, the documentarists chose to give even greater emphasis to the achievements of nontheatrical distribution of films than they had before the war. The war gave them an unprecedented budget for production for nontheatrical distribution and also the facilities for a large-scale nontheatrical distribution network in Britain. The documentarists believed that the cultivation of nontheatrical audiences was among the most important of their tasks for the Ministry. This was because films reaching their audiences outside the cinemas were believed to have a much greater impact than if they were directed toward audiences in the cinemas. Thomas Baird put it like this:

Two or three million people in the public cinema, who have come only to see the star of the featured film, are often unreceptive to the theme of a documentary film. But the same people in a different context may have a very real interest in the subject-matter of a film.[75]

Nontheatrical distribution undertaken for the Ministry of Information enabled the documentarists to experiment boldly with the use of documentary film as a means of public education. In films like *Tyneside Story* (1943), and many similar pieces specially made for nontheatrical distribution, the documentarists asked their audiences to think about the implications of "the peoples' war." They suggested to viewers what the permanent social changes might be as a result of the war. Documentarists thought these films brought alive contemporary social issues, and especially the "world revolution" that had been brought about by the war. Nontheatrical distribution was thought to be

creating again the market-place discussion; the public forum is returning to the village and the town alike with a new orator – film, to lead a lively and well-informed discussion of the country's wartime problems.[76]

William Farr, head of the Central Film Library, also believed that the documentarists' "celluloid circus" was an important development in public education. As he said before a conference arranged by the British Film Institute in 1943:

The Ministry of Information has established beyond all question that there is a unique job of work in the field of public information and education to be done by means of films. Twenty years of theory and discussion have been settled by three years of practical work.[77]

The writers of *The Factual Film,* who included Basil Wright, Edgar Anstey, and Paul Rotha, agreed with Farr. They believed that a means of public information had been created that would survive the demise of the Ministry of Information and the end of the war.[78]

The authors of *The Factual Film* were eager to maximize the effects they believed their nontheatrical film distribution had produced. They were very optimistic about the viewing figures for nontheatrical displays. Their figure for wartime nontheatrical audiences reaching a peak of 18,500,000 for the year of 1943–4, has often been cited. William Farr believed that figures were only relevant insofar as they related to regular viewers of films. He defined a regular viewer as someone who saw Ministry of Information displays at least three times a year. His figures are considerably less sanguine than those of *The Factual Film.* He suggested that in the year 1942–3, the Ministry's mobile film displays had reached only 2,250,000 regular viewers. In addition, another million regular viewers were reached by Farr's own Central Film Library. Finally, some 750,000 viewers had seen film displays at specially hired public cinemas. In that year, then, the total annual audience of regular viewers of nontheatrical films was some four million people.[79] It is improbable that the annual total for the following year, the wartime peak according to *The Factual Film,* was much higher than this figure.

Baird and his colleagues argued that the much smaller audiences for films in nontheatrical settings were subjected to a quite different experience from when they watched films in a regular commercial setting. The nontheatrical films were "directed to the great mass of the people, but along the lines of their special interests" and therefore had a much greater impact than if they were "broadcast indiscriminantly" in the cinemas. Baird also maintained that the audiences for nontheatrical films consisted in the main of "extra-mural education . . . the films are calculated to supply information and ideas to people who are already discussing or ready to discuss problems."[80] It was believed that such groups were social leaders and therefore had a social and political influence belied by their diminutive numbers.

During the war, nontheatrical distribution was not in fact directed primarily to social or political élites. The biggest group who regularly viewed MOI films consisted of factory workers, who attended displays staged by mobile film units in their works canteens at lunchtime or after work. Over one-third of all nontheatrical displays were given in factories or on construction sites. Such screenings were no doubt important and worthwhile, but this was hardly a case of films being directed to the nation's decisionmakers. The week ending March 6, 1943, was typical. During that week, a total of 1,298 displays were arranged. Of these, 475 were in factories or on construction sites. The next biggest category comprised the 244 shows given in villages and outlying areas that week.[81]

Baird argued for an extension of the nontheatrical distribution scheme in 1941. He demanded another fifty mobile cinema units, believing that "the demand for nontheatrical films was far greater than the Ministry could supply." He argued that the scheme was essential to the community for two reasons: In the first place, direct wartime instruction and propaganda could be put across in a palatable form, and second, the type of films shown led to informed thought and discussion among the audiences. There is a dearth of information about the impact of these nontheatrically distributed films. Little has survived of the information gathered through the distribution of questionnaires after displays. In addition, shortage of staff prevented "a detailed assessment of the two or three thousand films shown each week."[82] The influence of films that were "shown on hard-worn 16mm projectors in halls with bad acoustics or in factory canteens where the clatter of dishes would rival voices or sound effects," remains problematic.[83] For many people, Ministry of Information films were probably no more welcome when they intruded into lunchtime breaks or when they were screened at the factory after a hard day at work than when they appeared as part of an evening's entertainment at the local cinema. On the other hand, these films must have played some part in the general increase in political and social awareness that occurred among virtually all ordinary working men and women during the war.

Joseph Reeves left the Ministry of Information's nontheatrical distribution section in 1941. He left because of an agreement made between the Ministry and the Cinematograph Exhibitors Association that excluded entertainment films from nontheatrical displays. Reeves had been responsible for organizing many nontheatrical displays for working people in the 1930s, and it was this experience that had led to his own involvement with the Ministry. He was certainly much more in touch with audiences of this type than the middle-class intellectuals who staffed the Ministry of Information. He had little doubt about the impact of nontheatrical displays that consisted entirely of documentary films unleavened with entertainment films. He was convinced that the agreement with the Cinematograph Exhibitors Association had "ham-strung propaganda outside the commercial kinemas." People generally, he thought, were unwilling to accept programs that consisted completely of propaganda and documentary films:

People will tolerate, and even appreciate, propaganda in reasonable doses, but to offer the public whole programs of propaganda films lasting for over an hour, is more than human nature can stand.[84]

The documentary movement and the Ministry of Information were both very eager to develop nontheatrical distribution of a very different kind overseas. Both were particularly interested in the United States, and there was continued interest in reaching the extensive nontheatrical distribution system that had been such an inspiration to Grierson and his followers in the 1930s. A new development was an interest in reaching audiences composed of specialists and experts of high standing in the United States. This was in marked contrast to the popular nature of nontheatrical film distribution in Britain.

The Ministry of Information and the British Council both chose to concentrate their attempts to reach the general public in the United States in the commercial cinemas. As M. Neville Kearney stated for the British Council:

It would be quite wrong to suppose that any distribution we may contemplate will be mainly non-theatrical. We should naturally aim at theatrical circulation which is the only way of getting at a worthwhile audience.[85]

The Ministry of Information retained an interest in nontheatrical distribution in the United States. It too, however, thought that regular commercial distribution was the best way of reaching the American public. Throughout the war, the Ministry and the Council fought among themselves to become sole agents for the distribution of official films in the cinemas in the United States. Arthur Jarratt and Sidney Bernstein, the Ministry's top advisers on theatrical distribution, were both sent to the United States in 1941. Jarratt produced an abortive scheme for controlling official film distribution from Ministry of Information offices located in New York and Los Angeles.[86] Bernstein was more successful and when he went to the United States, he had *Target for Tonight* to offer to renters and was able to arrive at a very satisfactory arrangement for its commercial distribution by Warner Brothers.[87] Bernstein was subsequently appointed film liaison officer in Washington. There, he continued to develop an extensive commercial distribution for British official films during the war.

The Ministry of Information and the documentarists came to regard nontheatrical distribution as a means of reaching American élites since the general public in the United States were approached through the cinemas. Arthur Elton was responsible for the production of a number of "prestige propaganda" films that were intended for these special audiences in America. Outwardly instructional films on subjects such as medicine, personnel selection methods, and so on, were actually part of a sophisticated campaign to influence groups in the United States. Two such films were made on the personnel selection methods of the British army, *Personnel Selection: Recruits* (1945) and *Personnel Selection: Officers* (1945). Elton elaborated on the motives behind the production of these films when arranging the production of the film concerned with selection of officers. The film was

directed specifically to Army Officers and medical authorities in the United States and forms part of a series, the foreground intention of which is prestige propaganda. We are finding that this type of film, when well made, carries with it a very strong propaganda influence in our favour.[88]

Elsewhere, Elton elaborated on how these prestige propaganda films worked for his superior at the Films Division. He thought that such films helped to dispel ideas about British incompetence and showed sophistication in an area not generally associated with British expertise. As he noted:

There is a general opinion in America that we are inefficient and that we "muddle through." This is a deep-seated impression, and is being tackled at various film propaganda levels. One very important level is the specialist film for relatively specialist audiences.

The films on the selection of personnel were important for another reason too. In addition to demonstrating British efficiency in a particular area of expertise, they were also important for countering American misconceptions about the British class system. As Elton commented:

They show clearly that methods of selection for the Army are not based upon mere questions of class. This is a secondary, though very important, point, since another opinion which is common in the United States is that we still retain a strong measure of feudal society, and that our officers and men are graded, not according to intelligence and ability, but according to the social structure from which they originate.[89]

The documentarists considered their films for specialist audiences in the United States to be among the best of their work for the Ministry of Information. This use of film was far removed from their original intention of using documentary film as a means of reaching the ordinary people. Success in using films for specialist audiences was not, however, paralleled by success in reaching the general public.

The war provided many opportunities for the documentarists. They were given unprecedented budgets and facilities. The war gave them a plethora of film subjects. In addition, it provided the opportunity for more people to see their films than ever before. The agreement between the Ministry of Information and the Cinematograph Exhibitors Association guaranteed access for some of their films into the cinemas. In addition, they were also given the wherewithal for an extensive system of nontheatrical film distribution. Generally, however, documentary films were still not successful in the cinemas unless, as in the case of the major Crown Film Unit productions, they bore the trappings of commercial feature film. In wartime, cinema audiences wanted escapist entertainment even more than they did during the peace. They did not want actuality films intruding into their cinema programs. Nontheatrical distribution developed in a promising, but not very extensive manner, if William Farr's estimates are accepted rather than the somewhat misleading figures quoted by *The Factual Film.* The importance of films shown by this latter method is also open to question. Baird and his colleagues maintained that displays of this type were very effective. People with experience like Joseph Reeves were much more dubious. He was not alone in believing that programs consisting exclusively of documentary films were not especially palatable to mass audiences, even outside the context of the commercial cinema.

The documentarists had no greater impact upon the decisionmakers than they had upon the general public. Within the Ministry of Information, the documentarists were consumed by the Films Division; they did not take control of it, except in the area of nontheatrical distribution. Only in Canada, where Grierson built upon the achievements and mistakes of the British documentary movement, did documentarists come to control a government's information policies.

CHAPTER VIII
Conclusion

Writing a national cinema history for any country involves special difficulties for the historian. This is particularly true when dealing with an explicitly national school of film claiming responsibility for a whole genre of film, as seems to be the case with the British documentary film movement.

As Ed Buscombe has noted, relating a national cinema to Hollywood becomes an inevitable task.[1] There have been few other commodities or examples of cross-cultural exchange where the control exercised by one country and one outlook has been so predominant. From a very early point in the history of the form, Hollywood created and dominated the conventions of the narrative film to such an extent as to become synonymous with it.

Consequently, any attempt to develop or, indeed, to discuss a national cinema only makes sense in relation to the degree to which it was a reaction against or alternative to the American feature film. In a way, it is this relationship with Hollywood that *defines* a national cinema. Nowhere is this more true than in the case of a history of British cinema.

Until very recently, Britain and the British Empire were *the* major overseas market for Hollywood. This only ceased to be true with the withering away of the British cinema audience in the 1950s and 1960s. Given the commercial imperatives underlying virtually all aspects of film production, it was very hard to develop an indigenous tradition of film production or an approach, aesthetic, or philosophy toward film in Britain that was in any way truly national – as opposed to colonial and essentially derivative from the American example, in character. In the years between the two world wars, there were repeated demands from the political and cultural establishments in Britain for the self-conscious creation of such a national cinema. The British Film Institute, a large body of government legislation, ongoing public debate about the fate of the "British film" in the House of Commons and the correspondence pages of *The Times,* and, of course, the British documentary movement itself, were all part of this milieu.

174

Therefore, the rare successes experienced by filmmakers in Britain have seemed all the more spectacular and significant. Historians generally have been eager to identify an innately British tradition of film. The very term "British film" acquired a special significance in the 1930s. For the general film audience, the phrase was an oxymoron of sorts, since films made in Britain rarely had the properties they tended to associate with fiction films, so that for them at any rate, it was difficult for a film to be British and yet be something that they would pay to watch. On the other hand, the problem of the British film occupied many column inches in the newspapers and was of real concern to the country's political and cultural élites.

Britain was used to having most art forms and the mass media, particularly the press, controlled by a handful of powerful men. The feature film was different in that they did not control it, neither in a commercial nor in an ideological sense. Instead, motion pictures were controlled by another group of powerful men in the United States, and there were frequent attempts to wrest this control away from them. Often this campaign for the British film appears strongly idealistic. In 1922, William Friese-Greene, the father of British cinematography, died while speaking out against the perils of American domination of the film industry. Twenty-five years later, J. Arthur Rank wagered and lost much of his personal fortune challenging Hollywood. John Grierson and the British documentary movement were very much a part of this heroic tradition.

Conspicuous British achievements in virtually every other cultural domain tended to highlight the paucity of Britain's accomplishments in film. Perhaps the error has lain in trying to locate a tradition of *making* feature films. This has often taken the form of admiring the fairly small number of "quality" films produced in Britain and also in suggesting that there is some value in the much larger number of generally mediocre films made there.[2] In fact, it is easier to document strong traditions of film consumption and of film exhibition in Britain than filmmaking, although the temptation is strong to fix upon the work of the filmmaker rather than the film consumer.

This raises a second caveat. In their search for a national cinema the strategy of some historians has been to fix upon realism as being in some way a unique trait of British cinema. Such a position sees Ealing comedies, Grierson, Free Cinema, and British social realism essentially as parts of the same tradition, making it possible to identify a uniquely British realist tradition, quite distinct in aims, philosophy, and effects from the American feature film. A danger associated with this position is that it separates developments in Britain from those in other countries. Yet it is not really possible to discuss the British documentary movement without reference to actuality and avant-garde film in other countries or to talk about British Free Cinema without referring to the New Wave.

Another approach has attempted to rehabilitate many forms of marginalized filmmaking rarely taken seriously in studies fixed upon the fiction film, such as amateur, nontheatrical, and nonfiction film.[3] These forms warrant serious attention and should not be ignored simply because they were outside the brief of the feature film.

In the context of national cinema histories, John Grierson and the British documentary movement have a special appeal. The British documentary movement exemplified a very deliberate effort to remedy the inequities in the balance of cultural trade between Great Britain and the United States.

It was also an attempt to harness cinema to noncommercial and nonescapist ends. In other words, the type of film associated with Grierson and the British government was linked closely to the reaction against the type of film associated with the United States.

The Griersonian tradition is tied to a species of moral uplift to which the escapist feature film was anathema. Grierson often railed against the "scarlet ladies" of Hollywood. Many of Grierson's diatribes took the form of disparaging most films as wasted opportunities to elevate the emotions and consciousness of their audiences. This position is not without its contradictions, for Grierson the avowed critic of Hollywood, was himself a devotee of the American feature film. Grierson's calvinistic outlook was also not by any means wholly shared by all of his protégés. Documentary filmmakers like Cavalcanti, Harry Watt, and Ian Dalrymple leapt at the opportunity to direct feature films if it presented itself.

Grierson's own great personal charisma has also been very attractive to revisionist historians attempting romantic/heroic interpretations of the history of British cinema. Given this reading of events, Grierson's career as a producer is an example of the auteur theory of film production. Without particularly wishing to subscribe to this type of interpretation, it does appear that much of what was accomplished by the British documentary movement, and the form it assumed, in particular its apostolic nature, owed a great deal to Grierson.

Discussions of the British documentary movement must invariably proceed via a discussion of the role of the state in Britain's film history. There are few instances where the state has been more closely involved in virtually all aspects of the film industry. This extended beyond simpleminded protectionism. There was a great interest in using the film as a form of internal cultural projection and overseas publicity married to an acute belief in the unique persuasive properties of the new medium. The British example of state involvement in film production in a participatory democracy was an important model for other countries at the time, and continues as a significant factor in Britain's film industry.

John Grierson played a crucial role as producer, innovator, theorist, and civil servant, and it was largely through his work that the government came to have such a major role in the evolution of the sponsored film in Great Britain. It is important to keep things in proportion. In attempting to assess the impact of the work of the British documentary movement, it is helpful to discuss the number of films produced by the British documentary movement, and more importantly perhaps, the size of the audiences who viewed them. Even the most generous of assessments for either of these figures tends to chasten statements about the influence of the documentary movement's output.

The British documentary movement was part of a wide-ranging campaign to counter the American feature film. Countermeasures included the direct entry of government into film production and many other actions aimed equally at dealing with the "threat" posed by American films. At the same time, the campaign against the American feature film was part of a wider issue concerning the impact of American popular culture in Europe in general. The implications of the globalization of American popular culture were not fully felt until after World War II, but already in Britain in the 1920s and 1930s there was a widespread anxiety about the possible effects of "Americanization" that fueled the documentary movement's development.

The nature of the threat constituted by American feature films and other types of popular culture has its own history. Government memoranda tended to stress economic and commercial factors – but broader discussions of the "debasing effects" of the American film upon unsophisticated cinema audiences were never far from the surface.[4] This gave added fire to Grierson's early work, which promised an indigenous film tradition in Britain that would educate and elevate cinema audiences, not seduce them.

This is not intended to devalue the achievements of the British documentary movement in any way, but rather, not to succumb to the hyperbole often attached to statements made by members of the documentary movement about the impact of their work or about the extent to which what they were doing ran counter to the dominant ideology of the time. Although there were specific instances of friction between Grierson and his civil service bosses, in general, they worked well together toward largely common ends.

Grierson readily acknowledged his intellectual debts, particularly to his own Scots background and to the United States. In the United States he studied the social impact of mass communications, which in the 1920s was still in its infancy as an academic field, and specifically he learned about official and commercial public relations. In Britain, there were skilled practitioners of advertising and government propaganda, but this was quite a different thing from public relations and closely monitored public opinion – itself a term Britain appropriated from the United States. Perhaps Grierson's most important single contribution as a public servant was to act, along with a small cadre of others, as a bridge between the communications and public relations philosophies that emerged in the United States and a Britain that was a mass democratic society learning to operate on the basis of consensus.

It is ironic that the British documentary film of the 1930s and 1940s, which in so many ways is best understood as a reaction *against* the American feature film, was in the final analysis, deeply indebted in other ways to the United States. The emergence of the British documentary film was – and in many ways, with the recent advent of Channel Four in Britain still is – inextricably intertwined with aims and ends of American-style civics and corporate public relations.

After a phase of dramatic expansion during World War II, official public relations in Britain fell quickly from favor in the immediate postwar years and the documentary movement suffered a similar fate. The Labour party, for the first time in control of a majority government in Britain, was surprisingly inept in its information and public relations policies, and this proved very detrimental both to the official public relations system that had been built and to the documentary movement, which had played a key role in creating this system.[5]

The specter of Americanization provides the historical context for the British documentary film's evolution in the 1920s and 1930s. It does not, however, fully explain the shape assumed by British documentary. The Griersonian tradition became one of moralizing overtones and social, not socialist, commitment. Its basis primarily was middle-class nonconformism and the liberal and humane nature of most varieties of middle-class activism in Britain in the interwar years. This tradition accounts for the outlook common to most of the films made in the 1930s and 1940s, and also for the reception they were given. The Griersonian school was guilty of an élitism that was richly evidenced in its output and that was all too apparent to those who watched its films. This position was very much in contrast to the explicit populism of most American fiction films. Intellectually, most of Grierson's followers were tied to the idea of an information élite who would collect, collate, and represent those aspects of political and social life they felt the public ought to know. Toward the end of the 1930s, as we have seen, this approach was modified into a policy of aiming films at élites and decisionmakers, rather than broadcasting them to general audiences. This policy of using an innately mass medium to reach minority audiences is full of contradictions, and it might well be argued that the separation from mass audiences which it entailed, and the invariable objectification of film subjects adopted by these films were among the major flaws in the documentary film movement.

During World War II Grierson was given a chance to remedy these earlier problems. His creation of the National Film Board of Canada was a unique opportunity to meld together his Scots upbringing and his preoccupation with North America. Grierson created a very different model for state control of a national cinema, and one that succeeded in its efforts to reach and influence a large general public at home and overseas. Its success in part derived from the scale and funding of its operations, which were much more extensive than in Britain, but also from shedding much of the moralizing and condescension associated with the British documentary film.

Fifty years after the heyday of the British documentary movement and fifteen years after Grierson's death, it is hard to discern the lasting effects of their achievements. It is clear that in the 1930s and 1940s, they played a key role in encouraging the British government and big business to adopt what was widely perceived as the most effective and sophisticated form of mass persuasion as part of their general information policies. In a very real sense, it could be argued that even now government and commercial information policy in Britain and much of the West owe a lot to this experience.

The cinematic forms assumed by the British documentary film in the 1930s and 1940s are perhaps best considered as earlier stages in the evolution of contemporary forms of documentary. The approach and visual style of today's television documentary are most clearly indebted to the British model, although there are also slight vestiges of the British tradition in today's forms of direct cinema. The real debt of contemporary filmmakers to the Griersonian tradition is primarily an institutional one. The formulas for state involvement in the arts, for corporate media production, and for nontheatrical film distribution and exhibition are all part of the history of the British documentary movement. For all this, and for attempting to tie documentary film to socially committed, not frivolous ends, the British documentary deserves to be remembered.

British documentary films registered under the 1927 and 1938 Cinematograph Films Acts, 1930–1939

Table A.1. *Classification of films under the 1927 Cinematograph Films Act*

Year	Film	Registered by	Maker	Class
1930	*Drifters*	New Era	New Era	Br
1931	*Lumber*	New Era	New Era	Br
1934	*Cable Ship*	New Era	New Era	E
	Telephone Workers	New Era	New Era	E
	The Coming of the Dial	New Era	New Era	E
	Under the City	New Era	New Era	E
	Weather Forecast	New Era	New Era	E
	Granton Trawler	New Era	New Era	E
	Spring on the Farm	New Era	New Era	E
	6.30 Collection	New Era	New Era	E
	Windmill in Barbados	New Era	New Era	E
1935	*So This is Lancashire*	Zenifilms	New Era	E
	BBC: Droitwich	Zenifilms	New Era	E
	Taking the Plunge	Zenifilms	Strand	E
	Song of Ceylon	GPO Film Unit	New Era	Br
	BBC: The Voice of Britain	ABFD	New Era	Br
	Shipyard	GBD	GBI	E
	The Face of Britain	GBD	GBI	E
1936	*Heart of an Empire*	MGM	TIDA	E
	The Key to Scotland	Strand	TIDA	E
	Night Mail	ABFD	GPO	E
	Cover to Cover	ABFD	Strand	E
	Rooftops of London	MGM	Strand	E
1937	*Statue Parade*	MGM	Strand	Br
	Scratch Meal	ABFD	ARFP	E
	Enough to Eat	Kinograph	ARFP	E
	On the Way to Work	Ministry of Labour	Strand	Br
	The Future is in the Air	Strand	Strand	E

Table A.1. *(cont.)*

Year	Film	Registered by	Maker	Class
	Air Outpost	Strand	Strand	E
	Today We Live	ABFD	Strand	Br
1938	*Here Is the Land*	Film Centre	Strand	E
	Duchy of Cornwall	ABFD	Strand	E
	Five Faces	Strand	Strand	E
	The Smoke Menace	Film Centre	Realist	E

Note: Br, British film, eligible for renters' and exhibitors' quota; E, British film, eligible for exhibitors' quota.
Source: Compiled from *Kine Yearbook,* 1930–8.

Table A.2. *Classification of films under the 1938 Cinematograph Films Act, in effect from April 1, 1938*

Year	Film	Registered by	Maker	Class
1938	*Watch and Ward in the Air*	Technique	Strand	Br/R
	North Sea	ABFD	GPO	Br/R
	We Live in Two Worlds	Technique	GPO	Br/R
	London Wakes Up	Technique	Strand	Br/R
	Book Bargain	Technique	GPO	Br/R
	Of All the Gay Places	MGM	TIDA	Br/R
	Around the Village Green	MGM	TIDA	Br/R
	Dawn of Iran	United Artists	Strand	Br/R
1939	*London on Parade*	First National	TIDA	Br/R
	The Londoners	Technique	Realist	Br/E
	Wealth of a Nation	MGM	F. S. Legg	Br/R
	The Children's Story	MGM	Strand	Br/R
	The Face of Scotland	MGM	Realist	Br/R
	Speed the Plough	ABFD	Strand	Br/R
	Advance Democracy	Progressive Film Institute	Realist	Br/R
	Roads Across Britain	ABPC	Realist	Br/R
	Wings Over Empire	Anglo-American	Strand	Br/R
	Sidney Eastbound	Anglo-American	Strand	Br/R
	Do It Now	ABFD	GPO	Br/R
	The First Days	ABPC	GPO	Br/R
	The City	Anglo-American	GPO	Br/R

Note: Br/R, British film, eligible for renters' and exhibitors' quota; Br/E, British film, eligible only for exhibitors' quota.
Source: Compiled from *Kine Yearbook,* 1939–40.

Notes

I. Introduction: The British documentary film movement

1. R. Colls and P. Dodd, "Representing the Nation – British Documentary Film, 1930–1945," *Screen,* 26 (1) 1985, 21–33.

2. P. Swann, *The Hollywood Feature Film in Postwar Britain* (London, 1987).

3. S. Street and M. Dickinson, *Cinema and State; The Film Industry and the British Government, 1927–1984.* (London, 1985).

4. R. S. Lambert, *Propaganda* (London, 1938), pp. 101–2.

5. S. Tallents, *Post Office Publicity* (London, 1935), p. 6.

6. C. Stuart (ed.), *The Reith Diaries* (London, 1975), p. 31.

7. W. Crawford, *How to Succeed in Advertising* (London, 1931), foreword.

8. G. Huxley, *Both Hands* (London, 1970), p. 127.

9. E. L. Bernays, *Public Relations* (Norman, 1952), p. 71.

10. G. H. Saxon Mills, *There Is a Tide . . .* (London, 1954), p. 68.

11. D. Pope, *The Making of Modern Advertising* (New York, 1983), pp. 4–8 and passim.

12. R. Marchand, *Advertising the American Dream: Making Way for Modernity, 1920–1940* (California, 1985), p. 30.

13. J. Grierson, sermon, GA: 1: 5: 4, Grierson Archive, University of Sterling.

14. F. Hardy (ed.), *Grierson on Documentary,* rev. ed. (London, 1966), p. 14.

15. T. Baird, "The Cinema and the Information Services," Association of Special Libraries and Information Bureaux, 16th Annual Conference, October 1939.

16. F. Leavis, quoted in M. D. Biddiss, *The Age of the Masses: Ideas and Society in Europe Since 1870* (Humanities Press, Atlantic Highlands, 1977), p. 288.

17. G. M. Boltyanskii, *Lenin i Kino* (Moscow, 1925), quoted in R. Taylor, *Film Propaganda: Soviet Russia and Nazi Germany* (London, 1979), p. 44.

18. J. Grierson, "Film Propaganda," July 1930, PRO BT61/40/1 D.O.T. E12251 B. Paper no. 14.

19. J. Grierson, "What Makes a Special?" *Motion Picture News,* November 20, 1926, pp. 1933–4 (1933).

20. J. Grierson, "Summary and Survey: 1935," in *Grierson on Documentary,* pp. 169–86 (171).

21. J. Grierson, "The Product of Hollywood," *Motion Picture News,* November 6, 1926, pp. 1755–6.

22. J. Grierson, "The Seven Obstacles to Progress," *Motion Picture News,* December 11, 1926, pp. 2225–7 (2225).

23. J. Grierson, "Film Propaganda."
24. J. Grierson, "The Course of Realism," in C. Davy (ed.) *Footnotes to the Film* (London, 1937), reprinted in *Grierson on Documentary*, pp. 199–211 (203).
25. J. Grierson, "Putting Punch in a Picture," *Motion Picture News*, November 27, 1926, pp. 2025–6.
26. J. Grierson, "Film Propaganda."
27. M. D. Biddiss, *The Age of the Masses*, p. 287.
28. W. Albig, *Public Opinion* (New York, 1939), p. 375.
29. G. Atkinson, "Charwomen and Quota Films," *The Era*, July 10, 1935.
30. R. Nicols, *The Times*, August 27, 1925, p. 11. For an interesting American perspective, see E. G. Lowry, "Trade Follows the Film," *Saturday Evening Post*, November 7, 1925, p. 12.
31. E. Beddington Behrens, *The Times*, February 25, 1926, p. 12.
32. R. S. Lambert, *Propaganda*, p. 61.
33. *Kine Weekly*, January 22, 1931, p. 35.
34. "Political Propaganda Experiments," *The Times*, April 13, 1926, p. 12.
35. T. J. Hollins, "The Conservative Party and Film Propaganda between the Wars," *English Historical Review*, 96 (379) (1981), 359–69.
36. Brown to Messrs. Lawrence, Messer and Co., solicitors for I. Ostrer, July 29, 1931, PRO BT64/86 I.M.6267.
37. K. Kulik, *Alexander Korda* (London, 1975), pp. 254–6.
38. S. Tallents, *Post Office Publicity*, p. 4.
39. *Appendices to Summary of Proceedings, Imperial Conference*, 1926, Report of the General Economic Sub-Committee on Films, Cmd. 2769, p. 403.
40. P. Cunliffe Lister, *Hansard*, vol. 203, col. 2040, March 16, 1927.
41. Cunliffe-Lister to Amery, May 10, 1927, PRO BT64/86 I.M.5511.
42. Buchan to Tallents, June 8, 1927, PRO CO760/37 EMB/C/3.
43. A. Wilson, Proceedings, Moyne Committee, May 19, 1936, PRO BT55/4 CCF 2.
44. D. Milne-Watson, *The Times*, June 16, 1938, p. 12.
45. Grierson, foreword in A. Buchanan, *The Art of Film Production* (London, 1936), p. vi.
46. T. Fligelstone, Minutes of evidence, Moyne Committee, May 26, 1936, PRO BT55/4 CCF 2.
47. Draft Report of the Short Films Committee of the Cinematograph Films Council, July 1940, PRO BT64/4501 I.M. 1687 CFC (5) 14.
48. H. Bruce Woolfe, Memorandum of the British short film production industry, July 1943, PRO BT64/156 I.M.I. 4935.
49. J. Grierson, Minutes of evidence, Moyne Committee, June 30, 1936, PRO BT55/4 CCF 2.
50. T. Baird, "The Cinema and the Information Services," October 1939, Association of Special Libraries and Information Bureaux, 16th Annual Conference.
51. E. Barnouw, *Documentary* (New York, 1974), p. 100.
52. M. D. Biddiss, *Age of the Masses*, p. 299.
53. The Arts Enquiry, *The Factual Film* (London, 1947).
54. B. Wright, *The Long View* (London, 1974); P. Rotha, *Documentary Diary* (London, 1973); H. Watt, *Don't Look at the Camera* (London, 1974).
55. F. Hardy, "The British Documentary Film," in *Twenty Years of British Films: 1925–1945*, M. Balcon (ed.) (London, 1947), pp. 45–80 (47).

56. H. Watt, *Don't Look at the Camera*, p. 47.

57. E. Sussex, *The Rise and Fall of British Documentary* (London, 1975); E. Orbanz, *Journey to a Legend and Back: The British Realistic Film* (Berlin, 1977).

58. A. Lovell and J. Hillier, *Studies in Documentary* (London, 1972), p. 10.

59. A. Tudor, *Theories of Film* (London, 1974), pp. 59–76.

60. R. Low, *Films of Comment and Persuasion in the 1930s* (London, 1979); R. Low, *Documentary and Educational Films of the 1930s* (London, 1979).

II. The Empire Marketing Board Film Unit, 1926–1933

1. J. Grierson, "The EMB Film Unit," *Cinema Quarterly*, 1 (1933), 203–8 (203).

2. G. Huxley, *Both Hands* (London, 1970), p. 125; For a recent assessment of the EMB's publicity see S. Constantine, "Bringing the Empire Alive: The Empire Marketing Board and Imperial Propaganda, 1926–33," in J. M. Mackenzie (ed.), *Imperialism and Popular Culture* (London, 1986), pp. 192–231.

3. L. S. Amery, *My Political Life* (London, 1953), II, p. 348.

4. *Report of the Committee on National Expenditure*, July 1931, Cmd. 3920, 131–2.

5. Film Centre, memorandum for the Rockefeller Foundation, 1938, Grierson papers, Clevedon Court.

6. E. L. Bernays, *Propaganda* (New York, 1928), p. 156.

7. G. Huxley, *Both Hands*, p. 129.

8. L. S. Amery, *My Political Life*, p. 347.

9. G. H. Saxon Mills, *There is a Tide. . .* (London, 1954), p. 66. For Pick's concern with corporate publicity at the London Passenger Transport Board, see A. Forty, *Objects of Desire; Design and Society from Wedgwood to IBM* (London, 1986), pp. 222–38.

10. G. Huxley, *Both Hands*, p. 126.

11. Memorandum by the British Poster Advertising Association, December 9, 1929, PRO CO 760/22, EMB/PC/126.

12. Craig to Tallents, February 28, 1929, PRO CO 760/37 EMB/C/24.

13. EMB Publicity Committee minutes, June 27, 1927, PRO CO 760/22, EMB/PC/42.

14. Memorandum by the British Poster Advertising Association, December 9, 1929, PRO CO 760/22, EMB/PC/126.

15. "Propaganda by Cinema," *The Times*, April 8, 1926, p. 9.

16. *The Times*, May 24, 1926, p. 14.

17. S. Tallents, "Proposal for the preparation of a film under the auspices of the EMB," January 28, 1927, PRO CO 760/37, EMB/C/1.

18. EMB Film Committee minutes, February 1, 1927, PRO CO 760/37.

19. *Proceedings of the 1926 Imperial Conference*, November 1926. Cmd. 2768, p. 53.

20. "Thirteenth report of the General Economic Sub-Committee," *Appendices to the Summary of the Proceedings of the 1926 Imperial Conference*, November 1926, Cmd. 2769, p. 406.

21. W. Lippmann, *Public Opinion*, (New York, 1922), p. 92.

22. W. H. Hays, *Motion Pictures; An Outline of the History and Achievements of the Screen from its Earliest Beginnings to the Present Day* (New York, 1929), p. 322.
23. J. Grierson, "Notes for English Producers," April 29, 1927, PRO CO 760/37 EMB/C/2.
24. W. Lippmann, *Public Opinion,* pp. 166–7.
25. Buchan to Tallents, June 8, 1927, PRO CO 760/37, EMB/C/3.
26. J. Grierson, "Further notes on cinema production," July 28, 1927, PRO CO 760/37, EMB/C/4.
27. S. Tallents, "Exhibition of films at the Imperial Institute," September 12, 1927, PRO CO 760/37, EMB/C/5.
28. J. Grierson, "The EMB and the Cinema," March 1, 1928, PRO CO 760/37, EMB/C/9.
29. G. Huxley, *Both Hands,* p. 148.
30. S. Tallents, "The Birth of British Documentary," *Journal of the University Film Association* 20 (1968), 1, 2, 3, reprinted by Film Center, unpaged.
31. J. Grierson, "The EMB and the Cinema," March 1, 1928, PRO CO 760/37, EMB/C/9.
32. S. Tallents, *The Spectator,* November 19, 1937, cited in F. Hardy, *Grierson on Documentary,* 2nd ed. (London, 1966), p. 17.
33. F. C. Badgeley, "Report on the activities of the Canadian Motion Picture Bureau," August 24, 1928, PRO CO 760/37, EMB/C/14. For a recent account see P. Morris, *Embattled Shadows; A History of Canadian Cinema, 1895–1939* (Montreal, 1978).
34. *First and Second Reports of the Select Committee on Estimates,* April and July 1928, p. xviii.
35. EMB Film Committee minutes, November 13, 1928, PRO CO 760/37.
36. EMB Film Committee sub-committee report, December 4, 1928, PRO CO 760/37, EMB/C/22.
37. EMB Film Committee minutes, January 30, 1930, PRO CO 760/37.
38. *Report of the Controller and Auditor-General on Civil Appropriations Accounts for year ending 31 March 1930.*
39. Craig to Tallents, February 28, 1929, PRO CO 760/37 EMB/C/24.
40. *Kine Weekly,* November 14, 1929, p. 25.
41. Progress Report, September 18, 1930, PRO CO 760/37 EMB/C/49.
42. Progress Report, April 26, 1930, PRO CO 760/37 EMB/C/38.
43. *Manchester Guardian,* July 12, 1930.
44. Progress Report, September 18, 1930, PRO CO 760/37 EMB/C/49.
45. J. Grierson, "Creation of a small EMB producing and editing unit," April 28, 1930, PRO CO 760/37 EMB/C/39.
46. J. Leyda, *Films beget Films* (New York, 1964), pp. 20–1.
47. EMB Film Committee minutes, April 30, 1930, PRO CO 760/37.
48. P. Rotha, *Documentary Diary* (London, 1973), p. 45.
49. *Appendices to the Proceedings of the 1930 Imperial Conference;* Part 20, "Use of Kinematograph Films for the Education of Producers etc.," November 1930, Cmd. 3718, pp. 238–9.
50. *Proceedings of the 1930 Imperial Conference,* November 1930, Cmd. 3717, p. 52.

51. "Forthcoming film work," January 5, 1931, PRO CO 760/37 EMB/C/52.

52. "Forthcoming film work."

53. "Report by Mr. Grierson on his visit to America," May 9, 1931, PRO CO 760/37 EMB/C/57.

54. "Report by Mr. Grierson on his visit to America."

55. "Report by Mr. Grierson on his visit to America."

56. "Forthcoming film work."

57. Memorandum by J. Grierson, December 11, 1931, PRO CO 760/37 EMB/C/61.

58. EMB Film Committee minutes, December 15, 1931, PRO CO 760/37.

59. S. Tallents, "Note on formal agreement between the EMB and Ideal Films Ltd," January 25, 1933, PRO CO 760/37 EMB/C/83.

60. E. Betts, "On Being Bored with Films," *Close Up*, 3 (1928), 41–7.

61. "Report on non-theatrical distribution of films," March 19, 1932, PRO CO 760 EMB/C/71.

62. F. Evans, "Sight and Sound in a Modern School," *Sight and Sound*, 3 (1934), 19.

63. "Report on non-theatrical distribution of EMB films," October 1932, PRO CO 760/37 EMB/C/81.

64. Tallents to the Privy Council, December 12, 1932, PRO CO 760/37 EMB/C/82.

65. *Report of the Select Committee on National Expenditure*, July 1931, Cmd. 3920, p. 132.

66. J. Grierson, "The problem of the current year," December 12, 1931, PRO CO 760/37 EMB/C/68.

67. E. Sussex, *The Rise and Fall of British Documentary* (London, 1975), p. 8.

68. J. Grierson, "Progress Report," December 11, 1931, PRO CO 760/37 EMB/C/63.

69. J. M. Lee, "The Dissolution of the Empire Marketing Board, 1933," *Journal of Imperial and Commonwealth History*, 1 (1972), 49–57.

70. S. Constantine, "Bringing the Empire Alive," p. 222.

71. S. Tallents, *The Projection of England* (London, 1932), p. 32.

72. Tallents, *Projection of England*, p. 41.

73. Major Astor, M. P., *The Times*, June 21, 1935, p. 13.

74. J. Grierson, "Films of Substance," *The Times*, April 2, 1932, p. 8.

75. F. Pick, *The Times*, August 10, 1933, p. 11.

76. W. Crawford, *The Times*, July 12, 1933, p. 15.

77. R. J. Flaherty, *The Times*, September 1, 1933, p. 12.

III. The General Post Office Film Unit, 1933–1937

1. F. Pick, *The Times*, August 10, 1933, p. 11.

2. J. Grierson, "Cinema in the public service," an address before the Post Office Telephone and Telegraph Society, February 17, 1936.

3. Sir E. Parry, *The Times*, September 1, 1933, p. 12.

4. G. Huxley, *The Times*, July 14, 1933, p. 15.

5. *Kine Weekly*, September 28, 1933, p. 4.

6. *Kine Weekly,* November 2, 1933, p. 5.

7. "Government competing with the trade," *Kine Weekly,* November 23, 1933, p. 3.

8. M. N. Kearney to the Secretary, the Board of Trade, November 22, 1933, reprinted as Appendix 13, *Report of the Select Committee on Estimates,* July 1934, pp. 250–3 (251).

9. Editorial, *Sight and Sound,* 2 (1934), 117–18.

10. J. G. Hughes Roberts to F. P. Robinson, October 17, 1934, PRO T160/742 F13860/03/1.

11. E. J. Strohmenger to the Secretary, The Treasury, January 6, 1926, PRO T162/511 E17859/1.

12. Polden to Cuthbertson, July 21, 1934, T160/742 F13860/03/1.

13. "Public Relations: A New Art for New Needs," *The Times,* October 9, 1933, p. 5.

14. Appendices, *Report of the Select Committee on Estimates,* 1938, pp. 284–5.

15. Memorandum submitted by the Post Office, Appendix 12, *Report of the Select Committee on Estimates,* p. 240.

16. J. Grierson, memorandum, April 27, 1932, PRO CO 760/37 EMB/C/74.

17. Undated report, POST 33/4927 M19592/1935.

18. J. Grierson, "The GPO gets sound," *Cinema Quarterly,* 2 (1934), 215–21 (215).

19. Simon to Buckland, August 31, 1933, POST 33/4927 M19592/1935.

20. Robinson to Simon, September 14, 1933, POST 33/4927 M19592/1935.

21. Memorandum submitted by the Post Office, Appendix 12, *Report of the Select Committee on Estimates,* p. 241.

22. Kearney to the Secretary, The Board of Trade, November 22, 1933, reprinted as Appendix 13, *Report of the Select Committee on Estimates,* p. 252.

23. EMB Finance Branch to Accountant General's Department, Post Office, December 1933, POST 33/4927 M19592/1935.

24. Minutes of evidence, *Report of the Select Committee on Estimates,* p. 57.

25. Robinson, note on meeting with R. D. Fennelly, Board of Trade, June 27, 1934, PRO T160/742 E13860/03/1.

26. Memorandum submitted by the Post Office, Appendix 12, *Report of the Select Committee on Estimates,* p. 240.

27. S. Tallents, "The Birth of British Documentary," *Journal of the University Film Association* (1968), 1, 2, 3, reprinted by Film Center, unpaged.

28. P. Rotha, *Documentary Diary,* pp. 117–22.

29. Minutes of evidence, *Report of the Select Committee on Estimates,* p. 73.

30. Kearney to the Secretary, The Board of Trade, November 22, 1933, reprinted, Appendix 13, *Report of the Select Committee on Estimates,* p. 253.

31. *Report of the Select Committee on Estimates,* p. 10.

32. Minutes of evidence, *Report of the Select Committee on Estimates,* p. 45.

33. Robinson to Rae, August 17, 1934, PRO T160/742 F 13860/03/1.

34. Banks to Rae, October 24, 1934, POST 33/5099 M18036/1936.

35. Rae to Robinson, August 20, 1934, PRO T160/742 F13860/03/1.

36. Robinson to Rae, August 17, 1934, PRO T160/742 F13860/03/1.

37. Minutes of evidence, *Report of the Select Committee on Estimates,* pp. 88–94.
38. Robinson to Rae, August 17, 1934, PRO T160/742 F13860/03/1.
39. Robinson, note of meeting with R. S. Lambert, July 24, 1934, PRO T160/742 F13860/03/1.
40. Robinson to Rae, August 17, 1934, PRO T160/742 F13860/03/1.
41. Grierson to Tallents, November 30, 1934, POST 33/4951 M20552/1935.
42. Robinson, note of meeting with Gardiner, Tallents and Grierson, August 17, 1934, PRO T160/742 F13860/03/1.
43. Robinson to Tallents, January 21, 1935, PRO T160/742 F13860/03/2.
44. Draft Treasury minute, November 1934, PRO T160/742 F13860/03/1.
45. Robinson to Tallents, December 19, 1934, PRO T160/742 F13860/03/2.
46. Tallents to Robinson, January 8, 1935, PRO T160/742 F13860/03/2.
47. Watson to Bunbury, December 19, 1933, POST 33/4927 M19592/1935.
48. Robinson, note of meeting with R. D. Fennelly, Board of Trade, June 27, 1934, PRO T160/742 F13860/03/1.
49. Cuthbertson to Polden, July 24, 1934, PRO T160/742 F13860/03/1.
50. F. P. Robinson, "Government Propaganda Films," March 19, 1935, PRO T160/742 F13860/03/2.
51. Quigley to Tallents, March 9, 1934, PRO T160/742 F13860/03/1.
52. F. P. Robinson, "Government Propaganda Films."
53. J. Grierson, "Notes for English Producers," April 29, 1927, PRO CO760/37 EMB/C/2.
54. S. Tallents, "An analysis of the film needs which are common to more than one government department," May 24, 1934, PRO T160/742 F13860/03/1.
55. F. P. Robinson, "Government Propaganda Films."
56. Grierson to Jardine-Brown, June 27, 1934, POST 33/4927 M19592/1935.
57. Grierson to Tallents, November 30, 1934, POST 33/4951 M20552/1935.
58. F. P. Robinson, "Government Propaganda Films."
59. Chegwidden to Robinson, January 10, 1935, PRO T160/742 F13860/03/2.
60. Beddington to Kingsley Wood, July 20, 1934, PRO T160/742 F13860/03/1.
61. J. B. Priestley, *Rain Upon Godshill* (London, 1939), pp. 81–3.
62. T. Baird, "The Cinema and the Information Services," Address to the 16th Annual Conference of the Association of Special Libraries and Information Bureaux, 1939, p. 4.
63. The Arts Enquiry, *The Factual Film* (London, 1947).
64. Tallents, undated note of meeting with Board of Trade, POST 33/4927 M19592/1935.
65. H. Watt, *Don't Look at the Camera* (London, 1974), p. 80.
66. J. B. Priestley, *Rain upon Godshill,* p. 80.
67. Board of Trade memorandum for the Moyne Committee, April 1936, PRO BT55/3 CCF 1.
68. Introduction, *Kine Yearbook,* 1940; for a fascinating account of the British cinema audience in 1930s see J. Richards, *The Age of the Dream Palace; Cinema and Society in Britain, 1930–1939* (London, 1984).
69. J. Grierson, "Summary and Survey: 1935," in G. Grigson, *The Arts Today*

(London, 1935), reprinted in F. Hardy (ed.), *Grierson on Documentary* (London, 1966), pp. 169–86 (181).

70. Associated Realist Film Producers, Memorandum on documentary and cultural films and the quota regulations of the Cinematograph Films Act, 1927, May 12, 1936, PRO BT55/3 CCF 1.

71. G. Greene, *The Spectator,* August 2, 1935, reprinted in G. Greene, *The Pleasure Dome* (London, 1972), p. 10.

72. *National Savings,* 1 (1936), 9, 8.

73. "Films registered under the Cinematograph Films Act," *Kine Yearbook,* 1933, 1934, 1935, 1936, 1937.

74. Robinson to Tallents, November 27, 1935, PRO T160/742 F13860/03/3.

75. Tallents to Robinson, November 25, 1935, PRO T160/742 F13860/03/3.

76. Board of Trade memorandum for the Moyne Committee, April 1936, PRO BT55/3 CCF 1.

77. Draft Report, Short Films Committee of the Cinematograph Films Council, May 1940, PRO BT64/4501 IM1687 CFC[5]14.

78. Board of Trade memorandum for the Moyne Committee, April 1936, PRO BT55/3 CCF 1.

79. H. Bruce Woolfe, Memorandum on the British short film production industry, July 1943, BT64/156 IMI4935 33/1943.

80. Board of Trade memorandum for the Moyne Committee, April 1936, PRO BT55/3 CCF 1.

81. *Cinematograph Films Act, 1927,* Section 27 (1).

82. Board of Trade memorandum for the Moyne Committee, April 1936, PRO BT55/3 CCF 1.

83. ARFP, "Memorandum on documentary."

84. *Kine Weekly,* June 20, 1934, p. 4.

85. J. Grierson, "Is the Free Film Show a Menace?" *Kine Weekly,* October 17, 1935, p. 13.

86. *Report of the Select Committee on Estimates,* p. xi.

87. Robinson, note of meeting with Post Office representatives, August 17, 1934, PRO T160/742 F13860/03/1.

88. Tallents to Robinson, June 12, 1935, PRO T160/742 F13860/03/2.

89. Draft letter, Post Office to Lindsay, May 1935, PRO T160/742 F13860/03/2.

90. Lindsay to Crutchley, September 7, 1936, PRO T160/742 F13860/03/3.

91. Tallents to Robinson, August 17, 1934, PRO T160/742 F13860/031/1.

92. J. Grierson, "Four Million Audience for Propaganda Films," *The Commercial Film,* 1 (6) (July 1935), 3.

93. "People with Purposes," *World Film News,* 1 (9) (December 1936), 29.

94. Steward Committee report, April 12, 1937, POST 33/5089. M18036/1936.

95. Robinson to Tallents, November 25, 1935, PRO T160/742 F13860/03/3.

96. Post Office Film Program, 1938.

97. J. Grierson, "Four Million Audience for Propaganda Films," p. 3.

98. *World Film News,* 1 (2) (May 1936), 14.

99. *World Film News,* 1 (1) (April 1936), 19.

100. Jacobs to Warren Fisher, November 15, 1938, PRO T160/771 F15605/07/1.

101. Crutchley to Robinson, March 17, 1936, PRO T160/948 S46284.

102. Crutchley to Boyd, April 20, 1937, POST 33/5199 M16682/1937.

IV. The General Post Office Film Unit, 1937–1940

1. H. Watt, *Don't Look at the Camera* (London, 1974), p. 110.

2. Forbes to the Secretary, The Treasury, June 14, 1939, POST 33/5199 M16682/1937.

3. Post Office minute, undated, POST 33/5089 M18036/1936.

4. Stewart Committee Report, April 12, 1937, POST 33/5089 M18036/1936.

5. Post Office circular, August 1937, POST 33/5199 M16682/1937.

6. Fletcher to Highet, October 9, 1938, POST 33/5555 M11692/1940.

7. Highet to Fletcher, November 16, 1938, POST 33/5555 M11692/1940.

8. Minutes of evidence, *Report of the Select Committee on Estimates,* 1938, p. 111.

9. Crutchley to Banks, March 10, 1938, POST 33/5555 M11692/1940.

10. *Report of the Select Committee on Estimates,* p. xviii.

11. Crutchley to Trentham, May 18, 1938, POST 33/5555 M11692/1940.

12. Crutchley to Trentham, May 18, 1938, POST 33/5555 M11692/1940.

13. *Report of the Select Committee on Estimates,* p. 118.

14. Forbes to the Secretary, The Treasury, June 14, 1939, POST 33/5199 M 16682/1937.

15. Rowe-Dutton to Post Office, October 9, 1939, POST 33/5199 M16682/1937.

16. *Kine Weekly,* March 30, 1939, p. 5.

17. Primrose to Bridge, October 12, 1938, PRO BW 2/214 GB/30/1.

18. Guedalla to Bridge, October 13, 1938, PRO BW 2/214 GB/30/1.

19. H. Bruce Woolfe, Memorandum on the British short film production industry, July 1943, PRO BT64/156 IMI 4935 Series 33/1943.

20. R. Williams, "A Lecture on Realism," *Screen,* 18 (1) 1977.

21. H. Watt, *Don't Look At The Camera,* p. 113.

22. Forbes to the Secretary, The Treasury, June 14, 1939, POST 33/5199 M16682/1937.

23. Post Office memorandum, July 28, 1939, POST 33/5199 M16682/1937.

24. H. Watt, *Don't Look At The Camera,* p. 115.

25. E. Sussex, *The Rise and Fall of British Documentary* (London, 1975), p. 19.

26. *The Times,* April 20, 1939, p. 12.

27. Crutchley to Highet, June 26, 1938, POST 33/5555 M11692/1940.

28. Croom-Johnson, memorandum on G.P.O. films, May 3, 1938, PRO BW2/213 GB/30/1.

29. *The Times,* April 20, 1939, p. 12.

30. P. Rotha, *Documentary Diary* (London, 1974), pp. 220–1.

31. Crutchley, The General Post Office Film Unit, May 25, 1939, INF1/726 P1/30/2 HP (VII)47.

32. P. Rotha, *Documentary Diary,* p. 220.

V. The "independent" documentary film, 1932–1939

1. L. Hogben, "The New Visual Culture," *Sight and Sound,* 5 (1936), 6–9 (7).
2. P. Rotha, *Documentary Film,* 1st ed. (London, 1935), pp. 66–7.
3. D. Bower, "Film in the Social Scene," in *Cinema Survey,* R. Herring (ed.) (London, 1937), 23–31 (25).
4. S. Box, *Film Publicity* (London, 1937), p. 31.
5. P. B. Redmayne, "Cadbury Comedies," *The Commercial Film,* 1 (4) (May 1935), 5.
6. J. Grierson, "Further Notes on Cinema Production," July 28, 1927, PRO CO760/37 EMB/C/4.
7. "Making the Public Demand Advertising Films," *The Commercial Film,* 1 (1) (February 1935), 4.
8. E. L. Bernays, *Propaganda* (New York, 1928), pp. 37–8.
9. S. Tallents, *Post Office Publicity* (London, 1935), p. 3.
10. J. Grierson, "Film Propaganda," July 1930, PRO BT61/40 D.O.T. E12251 8 Paper 14.
11. *The Daily Film Renter,* June 10, 1930.
12. J. Grierson, "Film Propaganda."
13. P. Rotha, *Documentary Film,* p. 52.
14. J. Grierson, "Four Million Audience Claimed For Propaganda Films," *The Commercial Film,* 1 (6) (July 1935), 3.
15. P. Rotha, *Documentary Diary* (London, 1974), p. 143.
16. A. Calder-Marshall, *The Changing Scene* (London, 1937), p. 37.
17. "People with Purposes," *World Film News,* 1 (4) (July 1936), 25.
18. "People with Purposes," *World Film News,* 1 (3) (June 1936), 26.
19. S. Everard, *The History of the Gas, Light and Coke Company, 1912–1949* (London, 1949), pp. 346–7.
20. "Mr. Therm as Film Star," *Kine Weekly,* October 7, 1935, p. 55.
21. D. Milne-Watson, *The Times,* June 16, 1938, p. 12.
22. A. Calder-Marshall, *The Changing Scene,* p. 36.
23. "Mr. Therm as Film Star."
24. Quigley to Tallents, March 9, 1934, PRO T160/742 F13860/03/1.
25. S. Legg, "Shell Film Unit: Twenty-one years," *Sight and Sound,* 23 (1954), 209–11.
26. K. Clark, *Another Part of the Wood* (London, 1974), p. 253.
27. J. S. Mill, quoted in Tallents, *Post Office Publicity,* p. 7.
28. P. M. Taylor, *The Projection of Britain: British Overseas Publicity and Propaganda, 1919–1939* (Cambridge, 1981).
29. C. McArthur (ed.), *Scotch Reels: Scotland in Cinema and Television* (London, 1982), pp. 58–63.
30. National Advisory Council for Physical Training and Recreation, Propaganda Committee, Film Sub-Committee minutes, February 20, 1939, ED113/50 P(39) 2.
31. P. Rotha, *Documentary Diary;* E. Orbanz, *Journey to a Legend and Back: The British Realistic Film* (Berlin, 1977).
32. Beddington to Kingsley Wood, July 20, 1934, PRO T160/742 F13860/03/1.
33. J. B. Priestley, *English Journey* (London, 1934).

34. P. Rotha, *Documentary Diary*, pp. 72–74, pp. 96–8, p. 122.

35. P. Rotha, Moyne Committee minutes of evidence, May 19, 1936, PRO BT55/4 CCF 2.

36. *Kine Yearbook*, 1939.

37. P. Swann, "Rotha in New York," unpublished report for Master of Arts degree, University of California at Los Angeles, 1978.

38. P. Rotha, *Documentary Diary*, p. 111.

39. Annex I, Memorandum on documentary and cultural films and the quota regulations of the Cinematograph Films Act, 1927, May 12, 1936, PRO BT55/3 CCF 1.

40. A. Calder-Marshall, *The Changing Scene*, p. 36.

41. P. Rotha, *Documentary Diary*, pp. 156–7.

42. J. Grierson, "The documentary producer," *Cinema Quarterly*, 2 (1933) 7–9 (9).

43. P. Rotha, subtitle, *Documentary Film*.

44. J. Grierson, "Two paths to poetry," *Cinema Quarterly*, 3 (1935), 194–6.

45. The Arts Enquiry, *The Factual Film*, p. 12.

46. D. Bower, "Film in the Social Scene," p. 25.

47. See Appendix (this volume), "Documentary films registered for commercial distribution under the 1927 and 1938 Cinematograph Film Acts."

48. P. Rotha, Moyne Committee minutes of evidence, May 19, 1936, PRO BT55/4 CCF 2.

49. "Film without an audience, quota farce at the Adelphi," *The Era*, November 6, 1935.

50. Associated Realist Film Producers, "Memorandum on documentary and cultural films and the quota regulations of the Cinematograph Films Act, 1927," May 12, 1936, PRO BT55/3 CCF 1.

51. Film Producers Group, memorandum for the Moyne Committee, May 1936, PRO BT55/3 CCF 1.

52. A.C.T., memorandum for the Moyne Committee, May 13, 1936, PRO BT55/3 CCF1.

53. Evidence of the Cinematograph Exhibitors Association, May 1936, PRO BT55/3 CCF 1.

54. T. Fligelstone, Moyne Committee minutes of evidence, May 26, 1936, PRO BT55/4 CCF 2.

55. J. Grierson, "Why produce films by rule of thumb?" *Kine Weekly*, January 9, 1936, p. 35.

56. P. Rotha, Moyne Committee minutes of evidence, May 19, 1936, PRO BT55/4 CCF 2.

57. H. Bruce Woolfe, Moyne Committee minutes of evidence, June 30, 1936, PRO BT55/4 CCF 2.

58. T. Fligelstone, Moyne Committee minutes of evidence, May 26, 1936, PRO BT55/4 CCF 2.

59. "Two feature show kills shorts market," *Kine Weekly*, February 6, 1936, p. 5.

60. H. Bruce Woolfe, Moyne Committee minutes of evidence, June 30, 1936, PRO BT55/4 CCF 2.

61. *Kine Weekly*, May 27, 1937, p. 4.

62. J. Grierson, "Further Notes on Cinema Production," July 28, 1927, PRO CO760/37 EMB/C/4.

63. E. Sussex, *The Rise and Fall of British Documentary* (London, 1975), p. 64.

VI. The British documentary film, trade propaganda, and national projection, 1926–1939

1. J. Grierson, "One foot of film equals one dollar of trade," *Kine Weekly,* January 8, 1931.
2. P. Rotha, *Documentary Diary* (London, 1974), p. 234.
3. *Proceedings, 1926 Imperial Conference,* Cmd. 2768, p. 53; *Appendices, Proceedings, 1930 Imperial Conference,* Section 20, "use of kinematograph films for the education of producers, etc.," Cmd. 3718, pp. 238–40; *Appendices, Proceedings, 1932 Imperial Economic Conference,* Appendix 4, Committee on Methods of Economic Sub-Committee on Film and Radio, Cmd. 4175, pp. 50–3.
4. S. Tallents, *The Projection of England* (London, 1932), p. 39.
5. P. Cunliffe-Lister, introducing the second reading of the Cinematograph Films Bill, March 16, 1927, *Hansard,* vol. 203, column 2039.
6. *Kine Weekly,* June 12, 1930.
7. Association of Cinematograph Technicians memorandum for the Moyne Committee, May 13, 1936, PRO BT55/3 CCF 1.
8. R. Low, *The History Of The British Film, 1918–1929* (London, 1971), p. 75.
9. A. Wilson, Moyne Committee minutes of evidence, May 19, 1936, PRO BT55/4 CCF 2.
10. J. Grierson, "One Foot of Film Equals One Dollar of Trade," *Kine Weekly,* January 8, 1931.
11. J. Grierson, "Film Propaganda," July 1930, PRO BT61/40/1 D.O.T. E12251 B. Paper no. 14.
12. J. Grierson, "Film Propaganda."
13. J. Grierson, "Film Propaganda Technique," *Kine Weekly,* December 18, 1930, p. 35.
14. J. Grierson, "Film Propaganda Technique."
15. G. E. C. Hatton, Memorandum on industrial propaganda and interest films, May 14, 1928, PRO BT60/21/2 BWD 7084/28.
16. Inter-Departmental Committee on Trade Advertisement and Propaganda Film Sub-Committee minutes, December 11, 1930, PRO BT61/40/1 E12251.
17. Trade Propaganda Committee interim report, July 16, 1930, PRO BT61/40/1 E12251.
18. Enquiry into Non-theatrical Distribution of Industrial Documentary Films Abroad, July 1937, PRO BW2/35 GB/3/86.
19. Joint Film Committee minutes, October 24, 1939, PRO BW2/32 GB/3/83 (165).
20. Kearney to Campbell, July 21, 1941, PRO BW63/2 USA/1 (20540).
21. A. Elton, *World Film News,* 2 (5) (August 1937), 32.
22. Bridge to Leeper, August 11, 1937, PRO BW2/213, GB/30/1.
23. Croom-Johnson to Leeper, March 25, 1938, PRO BW2/213 GB/30/1.
24. T. Baird, Report on the distribution of British documentary films in the United States, August 1939, PRO INF1/628 F619/3.
25. For a full discussion of the work of the British Council, see P. M. Taylor, *The Projection of Britain* (London, 1981).
26. Percy to Tyrrell, December 5, 1935, PRO BW2/213 GB/30/1.

27. Joint Film Committee minutes, November 23, 1936, PRO BW2/35 GB/3/86.

28. Joint Film Committee minutes, February 24, 1939, PRO BW2/31 GB/3/83.

29. Joint Film Committee minutes, April 8, 1936, PRO BW2/35 GB/3/86.

30. "The Joint Film Committee and its work," November 1938, PRO BW2/214 GB/30/1.

31. Croom-Johnson to Bridge, November 15, 1937, PRO BW2/35 GB/3/86.

32. Croom-Johnson to Bridge, November 15, 1937, PRO BW2/35 GB/3/86.

33. Jennings to Croom-Johnson, January 14, 1938, PRO BW2/213 GB/30/1.

34. "The Joint Film Committee and its work," November 1938, PRO BW2/214 GB/30/1.

35. Joint Film Committee minutes, October 1, 1937, PRO BW2/35, GB/3/8.

36. "The Joint Film Committee and its work," November 1938, PRO BW2/214 GB/30/1.

37. Croom-Johnson to Johnstone, November 11, 1938, PRO BW2/214 GB/30/1.

38. Butler to Duff Cooper, May 23, 1940, PRO BW4/62 TGB16/12.

39. A. Elton, *World Film News,* 2 (5) (August 1937), p. 32.

40. J. Grierson, "Film-making in Scotland," March 31, 1938, G3A:4:1, Grierson Archive, University of Stirling.

41. J. Grierson, "A Scottish Experiment," *The Spectator,* May 6, 1938, reprinted in *Grierson on Documentary,* F. Hardy (ed.), pp. 212–4 (212).

42. J. Grierson, "Film-making in Scotland."

43. Bridge to Grierson, December 3, 1937, PRO BW2/213 GB/30/1.

44. Grierson to Bridge, December 6, 1937, PRO BW2/213 GB/30/1.

45. Memorandum from the producers and directors of the Films of Scotland, December 1938, PRO BW2/215 GB/30/1.

46. J. Grierson, "Film-making in Scotland," March 31, 1938, G3A:4:1, Grierson Archive, Stirling University.

47. Joint Film Committee minutes, October 10, 1938, PRO BW2/31 GB/3/83.

48. J. W. Jennings, memorandum, October 11, 1938, PRO BW2/214 GB/30/1.

49. Memorandum from the producers and directors of the Films of Scotland, December 1938, PRO BW2/215 GB/30/1.

50. Guedalla to Bridge, October 11, 1938 PRO BW2/214 GB/30/1.

51. Guedalla to Bridge, October 13, 1938, PRO BW2/214 GB/30/1.

52. R. Hurd, *The Times,* November 22, 1938, p. 10.

53. Memorandum from the producers and directors of the Films of Scotland, December 1938, PRO BW2/215 GB/30/1.

54. J. Grierson, *Kine Weekly,* February 23, 1939, p. 5.

55. Unsigned memorandum, January 3, 1939, PRO BW2/215 GB/30/1.

56. Johnstone to Bridge, January 13, 1939, PRO BW2/215 GB/30/1.

57. Bridge to Guedalla, October 11, 1938, PRO BW2/215 GB/30/1.

58. P. Guedalla, *The Times,* November 26, 1938, p. 10.

59. New York World's Fair Advisory Committee minutes, June 8, 1938, PRO BT60/52/3 D.O.T. 23198/339/1937.

60. *Today's Cinema,* October 27, 1938.

61. H. P. Croom-Johnson, "New York World's Fair: Films. Grierson, Guedalla, Rotha Situation," December 7, 1938, PRO BW2/214 GB/30/1.

62. D. Taylor, *The Times,* September 7, 1938, p. 8.

63. *News Review,* October 15, 1938.
64. J. Grierson, "Propaganda for Democracy," *The Spectator,* November 11, 1938.
65. J. Grierson, "Propaganda in its working clothes," *World Film News,* 3 (1938), pp. 254–5 (254).
66. J. Grierson, "Propaganda for Democracy."
67. *Evening Standard,* November 24, 1938.
68. "Films for New York," *The Times,* December 8, 1938, p. 17.
69. "Films of Great Britain," *The Times,* November 1, 1938, p. 12.
70. J. Grierson, "World's Fair and the Royal Visit are our greatest opportunities in 1939," *Kine Weekly,* January 12, 1939, p. 44.
71. *Daily Express,* November 23, 1938.
72. H. P. Croom-Johnson, "New York World's Fair: Films. Grierson, Guedalla, Rotha Situation." December 7, 1938, PRO BW2/214 GB/30/1.
73. H. P. Croom-Johnson, "New York World's Fair: Films. Grierson, Guedalla, Rotha Situation."
74. Lloyd to Grierson, January 1939, PRO BW2/215 GB/30/1.
75. McNicoll to Bridge, February 29, 1939, PRO BW2/215 GB/30/1.
76. Butler to Duff Cooper, May 23, 1940, PRO BW4/62 TGB/6/12.
77. Sir Louis Beale, British Pavilion progress report for the fortnight 12–26 June 1939, PRO BT60/52/4 D.O.T.23198/353/37.
78. Shakespeare to Guedalla, April 24, 1940, PRO BW2/33 GB/3/83.
79. Sir Louis Beale, British Pavilion progress report for the period 30 April to 12 June 1939, June 13, 1939, PRO BT60/52/4 D.O.T. 23198/353/37.
80. R. Griffith, *Films,* 1 (1940), reprinted in part, *Documentary News Letter,* 1 (2) (February 1940), 3.
81. Kearney to Lloyd, December 1939, PRO BW2/216 GB/30/1.
82. Kearney to Haigh, December 2, 1940, PRO BW63/2 USA/1.
83. Kearney to Guedalla, May 20, 1942, PRO BW4/21 TGB/6/22.
84. "Departure Platform," *Documentary News Letter,* 2 (10) (1941), 182.
85. J. Grierson, "Report on Canadian Government Film Activities," August 1938, Grierson papers, Clevedon Court.
86. J. Grierson, "World's Fair and Royal Visit are our greatest opportunities in 1939," *Kine Weekly,* January 12, 1939, p. 44.
87. T. Baird, "Report on the distribution of British documentary films in the United States," August 1939, PRO INF1/628 F619/3.
88. Grierson to Korda, September 19, 1939, PRO INF 1/628 F 619/3.
89. Grierson to Korda, September 20, 1939, PRO INF 1/628 F619/3.
90. J. Grierson, memorandum, September 20, 1939, PRO INF1/628 F619/3.
91. Ball to Hodson, October 1939, PRO INF1/628 F619/3.
92. Report from the British Embassy in Washington, October 9, 1939, PRO INF1/628 F619/3.
93. Ball to Whyte, October 1939, PRO INF1/628 F/619/3.
94. Agenda of meeting on films for overseas publicity, January 19, 1940, PRO INF1/628 F619/3.
95. Bell to Highet, November 26, 1939, PRO INF1/628 F619/3.
96. Ministry of Information to Treasury, draft letter, April 1940, INF1/629 F619/3.

97. F. Hardy, *John Grierson* (London, 1979), p. 121.

98. Joint Film Committee minutes, September 8, 1939, PRO BW2/32 GB/3/83.

VII. The documentary movement during the war, 1939–1945

1. Kearney to Haigh, December 2, 1940, PRO BW63/2 USA/1.

2. *The Times,* July 8, 1942, p. 5.

3. C. F. A. Warner, Overseas and Emergency Publicity Expenditure Committee (Henceforth; OEPEC) Paper No. 23, August 3, 1939, PRO T162/858 E399140/2.

4. E. Rowe-Dutton, note of meeting with Sir Michael Bruce, June 3, 1939, PRO T162/562 E19011/2.

5. P. Rotha, *Documentary Diary* (London, 1974), p. 233.

6. Ministry of Information Home Publicity Planning Sub-Committee minutes, July 12, 1938, PRO INF1/712 P1/3 C.I. P (H)I.

7. E. T. Crutchley, The Public Relations Department of the Post Office, July 20, 1938, PRO INF1/712 P1/3/2 C.I. P(H)6.

8. E. T. Crutchley, Films, September 1938, PRO INF1/712 P1/3/2 C.I. P(H)22.

9. Home Publicity Planning Sub-Committee final report, September 21, 1938, PRO INF1/713 P/1/3/3.

10. I. Macadam, memorandum, March 18, 1939, PRO INF1/711 P1/3/1.

11. International Propaganda and Broadcasting Enquiry Film Sub-Committee minutes, June 2, 1939, PRO INF1/726 P1/30/2 HP (VII)85.

12. Film Sub-Committee minutes, July 7, 1939, PRO INF1/726 P1/30/2 HP(VII)89.

13. International Propaganda and Broadcasting Enquiry minutes, June 8, 1939, PRO INF1/720 P1/30/1 HP(V)58.

14. International Propaganda and Broadcasting Enquiry minutes, April 27, 1939, PRO INF1/720 P1/30/1.

15. E. T. Crutchley, "The General Post Office Film Unit," May 25, 1939, PRO INF1/726 P1/30/2 HP (VII) 47.

16. Appendix "A," Film Sub-Committee interim report, July 7, 1939, PRO INF1/726 P1/30/2 HP(VII)89.

17. Film Sub-Committee interim report, July 7, 1939, PRO INF1/726 P1/30/2 HP(VII)89.

18. Joint Film Committee minutes, September 8, 1939, PRO BW2/32 GB/3/83.

19. Ministry of information memorandum, OEPEC Paper No. 5, May 1939, PRO T162/858 E39140/1.

20. Film Sub-Committee interim report, July 7, 1939, PRO INF1/726 P1/30/2 HP(VII)89.

21. *Kine Weekly,* May 16, 1940, p. 4.

22. *Kine Weekly,* September 14, 1939, p. 4.

23. Ball to Whyte, October 1939, PRO INF1/628 F619/3.

24. Highet to Braund, December 10, 1940, POST 33/5555 M11692/1940.

25. K. Clark, *The Other Half* (London, 1977), p. 11.

26. E. Sussex, *The Rise and Fall of British Documentary* (London, 1975), p. 103.

27. OEPEC Paper No. 80, September 23, 1939, PRO T162/858 E39140/4.

28. *Kine Weekly,* September 26, 1940, p. 3.

29. *Thirteenth Report of the Select Committee on National Expenditure,* August 21, 1940, pp. 9–10.

30. Beddington to Fuller, reprinted, *Kine Weekly,* November 21, 1940, p. 7.

31. T. Baird, "Memorandum on British non-theatrical film distribution," April 1, 1940, PRO INF1/30 A/108/7.

32. *Thirteenth Report of the Select Committee on National Expenditure,* p. 10.

33. *Documentary News Letter,* 1 (10) (1940), 4.

34. Editorial, *Sight and Sound,* 9 (1940), 38.

35. P. Rotha, "The British Case," in *Rotha on the Film* (London, 1958), pp. 217–20 (218).

36. E. Sussex, *The Rise and Fall of British Documentary,* p. 121.

37. M. Neville Kearney, marginal note on an issue of *Documentary News Letter,* 2 (10) (1941), PRO BW4/63 TGB/6/22.

38. "Reorganisation of the General Post Office Film Unit," OEPEC Paper No. 583, November 1940, PRO T162/858 E39140/9.

39. "Receipts from commercial distribution of films. Summary of Statement prepared for evidence to the Public Accounts Committee," May 1944, PRO INF1/199 F/228.

40. Five-minute films were distributed on a weekly basis to cinemas, 86 were made, 1940–1942; fifteen-minute films were distributed on a monthly basis, 37 were made, 1942–5.

41. The Arts Enquiry, *The Factual Film* (London, 1947), p. 66.

42. Kearney to Stuart, April 25, 1941, PRO BW4/62 TGB/6/12.

43. OEPEC Paper No. 399, June 27, 1940, PRO T162/858 E39140/8.

44. Kearney to Gurney, January 19, 1943, PRO BW63/3 USA/1.

45. The Arts Enquiry, *The Factual Film,* p. 74.

46. "Where do we stand?" *Documentary News Letter,* 2 (6) (1941), 103–5 (103).

47. "The Case for Documentary," *Documentary News Letter,* 2 (4) (1941), 64.

48. *The Times,* November 26, 1942, reprinted in *Documentary News Letter,* 3 (11) (November–December 1942), 145.

49. "Kicking Against the Pricks," *Documentary News Letter,* 4 (3) (1943), 185–6.

50. The Arts Enquiry, *The Factual Film,* p. 103.

51. For example, R. Armes, *A Critical History of the British Cinema* (London, 1978), pp. 145–58; A. Lovell and J. Hillier, *Studies in Documentary,* (London, 1972) M. Jennings (ed.), *Humphrey Jennings: filmmaker, painter, poet* (London, 1982), pp. 62–132.

52. H. Watt, *Don't Look at the Camera* (London, 1974), p. 146.

53. Cavalcanti to MacDonald, March 1, 1940, PRO INF5/66 F/2325.

54. "British Information Services Report," No. 178, August 3, 1942, PRO BW63/3 USA/1.

55. R. Manvell, *Film,* rev. ed. (London, 1950), p. 110.

56. Crown Film Unit Board of Management minutes, April 29, 1944, PRO INF1/58.

57. Radcliffe to Bracken, "Crown Film Unit," April 9, 1945, PRO INF1/56 A/426.

58. OEPEC minutes, Paper No. 983, October 8, 1941.

59. Beddington to Bamford, September 13, 1941, PRO INF1/81 A/529/4.

60. Bamford to Harvey, September 22, 1941, PRO INF1/81 A/529/4.

61. "Where do we stand?" *Documentary News Letter,* 2 (6) (1941), 103–5 (103).

62. *Thirteenth Report of the Select Committee on National Expenditure,* 1940, pp. 5–7.

63. E. Sussex, *The Rise and Fall of British Documentary,* p. 145.

64. *Kine Weekly,* 2 January 1941, p. 36. For audience viewing preferences in World War II, see J. Richards and D. Sheridan (eds.), *Mass-observation at the Movies* (London, 1987).

65. *Kine Weekly,* January 2, 1941, p. 36.

66. R. S. Lambert, *Propaganda* (London, 1938), p. 61.

67. *Daily Film Renter,* September 9, 1940.

68. *Kine Weekly,* July 17, 1941, p. 3.

69. *Documentary News Letter,* 1 (11) (1940), 2.

70. *Documentary News Letter,* 3 (3) (1942), 34.

71. *Documentary News Letter,* 3 (9) (1942), 122.

72. Crown Film Unit Board of Management minutes, May 27, 1943, PRO INF1/58.

73. *Kine Weekly,* September 18, 1941, p. 5.

74. P. Perilli, Appendix, "Statistical Survey of the British Film Industry," in J. Curran and V. Porter (eds.), *British Cinema History* (London, 1983), p. 372.

75. T. Baird, Report on the distribution of British documentary films in the United States, August 1939, PRO INF1/628 F619/3.

76. "Celluloid Circus," *Documentary News Letter,* 2 (9) (1941), 170–1 (170).

77. W. Farr, "Developments in Non-Theatrical Cinemas," *The Film in National Life* (Exeter, 1943).

78. The Arts Enquiry, *The Factual Film,* p. 103.

79. Farr, "Developments in non-theatrical cinemas."

80. T. Baird, Report on the distribution of British documentary films in the United States.

81. Farr, "Developments in non-theatrical cinemas."

82. OEPEC minutes, September 5, 1941, Paper No. 947, PRO T162/858 E39140/14.

83. R. Manvell, *Film* (London, 1950), p. 111.

84. *Kine Weekly,* July 24, 1941, p. 3.

85. Kearney to Guedalla, March 18, 1941, PRO BW4/63 TGB/6/22.

86. "Commercial distribution of films in the United States," May 5, 1941, OEPEC Paper No. 798, PRO T162/858 E39140/12.

87. *Kine Weekly,* September 18, 1941.

88. Elton to Anstey, August 20, 1942, PRO INF1/219 F256/689.

89. Elton to Mercier, June 5, 1943, PRO INF1/219 F256/689.

VIII. Conclusion

1. E. Buscombe, "Film History and the Idea of a National Cinema," *The Australian Journal of Screen Theory,* 9/10 (1981).

2. For example, T. Aldgate, "Comedy, Class and Containment: The British Domestic Cinema of the 1930s," in J. Curran and V. Porter (eds.), *British Cinema History* (London, 1983).

3. D. Macpherson (ed.), *Traditions of Independence* (London, 1981).

4. P. Swann, "Hollywood in Britain: The Postwar Embargo on American Feature

Films in Britain," in B. Austin (ed.), *Current Research in Film, III* (New Jersey, 1987).

5. A. A. Rogow, "The Public Relations Program of the Labor Government and British Industry," *Public Opinion Quarterly,* Summer 1952.

Bibliography

Unpublished document sources

Grierson Archive (University of Stirling).

General Post Office Records Department, St. Martins-le-Grand, London:
POST 33: Records of the Post Office Film Unit, correspondence and memoranda on Post Office film activities.

Public Records Office, Kew, London:
BT 55: Minutes and memoranda of the Moyne Committee.

BT 60: Department of Overseas Trade World's Fair Advisory Committee minutes and correspondence.

BT 61: Minutes and memoranda of the Inter-Departmental Committee on Trade Propaganda and Advertisement.

BT 64: Board of Trade Industries and Manufactures Department correspondence and memoranda on the British film industry; minutes and memoranda of the Cinematograph Films Council.

BW 2: British Council memoranda and correspondence on films; minutes, memoranda and correspondence of the Joint Film Committee.

BW 4: British Council correspondence with the Ministry of Information and the Foreign Office on films.

BW 63: British Council correspondence and memoranda on films for the United States.

CO 760/37: Minutes, memoranda and correspondence of the Empire Marketing Board Film Committee.

INF 1: Ministry of Information planning committee minutes, correspondence, and memoranda; correspondence and memoranda of the Ministry of Information Films Division.

INF 5: Correspondence and memoranda on production of films for the Ministry of Information Films Division.

T160: Treasury correspondence and memoranda on film activities of government departments.

T161: Treasury correspondence and memoranda on film propaganda for the Empire.

200

T162: Minutes, memoranda and correspondence of the Overseas and Emergency Publicity Expenditure Committee (OEPEC).

STAT 14/987: Correspondence and memoranda by the Government Cinematograph Advisor.

Printed documents

Parliamentary Debates (Hansard), 1926–1943.

Proceedings of the Imperial Conference, 1926, Cmd. 2768 (H.M.S.O., London, 1926).

Appendices to the Proceedings of the Imperial Conference, 1930 Cmd. 3718 (H.M.S.O., London, 1930).

Appendices to the Proceedings of the Imperial Economic Conference, Cmd. 4715 (H.M.S.O., London, 1932).

Report of the Moyne Committee, Cmd. 5320 (H.M.S.O., London, 1936).

Report of the Select Committee on Estimates, 1928 (H.M.S.O., London, 1928).

Report of the Select Committee on Estimates, 1934 (H.M.S.O., London, 1934).

Report of the Select Committee on Estimates, 1938 (H.M.S.O., London, 1938).

Thirteenth Report of the Select Committee on National Expenditure, 1940 (H.M.S.O., London, 1940).

Newspapers

Daily Express, 1938–9.

Daily Herald, 1936–9.

Manchester Guardian, 1936–9.

The Times, 1925–45.

Film trade daily and weekly newspapers

Daily Film Renter, 1933–6.

The Era, 1933–6.

Kinematograph Weekly, 1929–45.

Today's Cinema, 1933–6.

Memoirs and diaries

Amery, L. S., *My Political Life, 1914–1929* (Hutchinson, London, 1953).

Clark, Kenneth, *Another Part of the Wood* (John Murray, London, 1974).

—*The Other Half* (John Murray, London, 1974).

Huxley, Gervas, *Both Hands* (Chatto and Windus, London, 1970).

Ivens, Joris, *The Camera and I* (International Publishers, New York, 1969).

Priestley, J. B., *Rain Upon Godshill* (Heinemann, London, 1939).

Rotha, Paul, *Documentary Diary* (Secker and Warburg, London, 1973).

Stuart, Charles (ed.), *The Reith Diaries* (Collins, London, 1975).

Watt, Harry, *Don't Look at the Camera* (Elek, London, 1974).

Biographies

Barman, Christian, *The Man Who Built London Transport: A Biography of Frank Pick* (David and Charles, London, 1979).

Beveridge, James, *John Grierson: Film Master* (Macmillan, New York and London, 1979).

Calder-Marshall, Arthur, *The Innocent Eye: The Life of Robert J. Flaherty* (W. H. Allen, London, 1963).

Hardy, Forsyth, *John Grierson: A Documentary Biography* (Faber, London, 1979).

Kulik, Karol, *Alexander Korda: The Man Who Could Work Miracles* (W. H. Allen, London, 1975).

Rotha, Paul, *Robert J. Flaherty: A Biography;* ed. by J. Ruby (University of Pennsylvania Press, Philadelphia, 1983).

Saxon Mills, G. H., *There is a Tide . . . The Life and Work of Sir William Crawford* (Heinemann, London, 1954).

Secondary works

Books

Albig, William, *Public Opinion* (McGraw-Hill, New York and London, 1939).

Armes, Roy, *Film and Reality: An Historical Survey* (Penguin, London, 1974).

—*A Critical History of British Cinema* (Secker and Warburg, London, 1978).

Arts Enquiry, The, *The Factual Film* (Oxford University Press, London, 1947).

Austin, Bruce (ed.), *Current Research in Film*, Vol. III (Ablex, New Jersey, 1987).

Balcon, Michael (ed.), *Twenty Years of British Films, 1925–1945* (Falcon Press, London, 1947).

Barnouw, Erik, *Documentary: A History of the Non-fiction Film* (Oxford University Press, New York, 1974.)

Barr, Charles (ed.), *All Our Yesterdays: Ninety Years of British Cinema* (BFI, London, 1986).

Bernays, Edward L., *Crystallising Public Opinion* (Boni and Liveright, New York, 1923).

—*Propaganda* (Liveright, New York, 1928).

—*Public Relations* (University of Oklahoma Press, Norman, 1952).

Biddiss, Michael D., *The Age of the Masses: Ideas and Society in Europe since 1870* (Humanities Press, Atlantic Highlands, 1977).

Box, Sidney, *Film Publicity: A Handbook on the Production and Distribution of Propaganda Films* (Lovat Dickson, London, 1937).

British Film Institute, *The Film in National Life: Being the Proceedings of a*

Conference held by the British Film Institute in Exeter, April 1943 (British Film Institute, London, 1943).

Buchanan, Andrew, *The Art of Film Production* (Pitman, London, 1936).

Calder-Marshall, Arthur, *The Changing Scene* (Chapman and Hall, London, 1937).

Clockburn, Claud, *The Devil's Decade* (Sidgwick and Jackson, London, 1973).

Cooke, Alistair, *Garbo and the Night Watchmen,* rev. ed. (Secker and Warburg, London, 1972).

Crawford, William S., *How to Succeed in Advertising* (World's Press News, London, 1931).

Crutchley, Ernest Tristram, *G.P.O.* (Cambridge University Press, Cambridge, 1938).

Curran, James and Porter, Vincent (eds.), *British Cinema History* (Weidenfeld and Nicolson, London, 1983).

Davy, Charles (ed.), *Footnotes to the Film* (Lovat Dickson, London, 1937).

Dickinson, Margaret and Street, Sarah, *Cinema and State: The Film Industry and the British Government* (British Film Institute, London, 1985).

Dickinson, Thorold, *A Discovery of Cinema* (Oxford University Press, London, 1971).

Durden, J. V., Field, M., and Smith, F. P., *Cine-Biology* (Penguin, London, 1941).

Everard, Stirling, *The History of the Gas, Light and Coke Company, 1912–1949: Supplying Gas to London* (Ernest Benn, London, 1949).

Fielding, Raymond, *The March of Time, 1935–1951* (Oxford University Press, New York, 1978).

Forty, Adrian, *Objects of Desire; Design and Society from Wedgwood to IBM* (Thames and Hudson, London, 1986).

Goldman, Eric, *Two-way Street: The Emergence of the Public Relations Counsel* (Bellman, Boston, 1948).

Greene, Graham, *The Pleasure Dome: The Collected Film Criticism, 1935–1940,* edited by John Russell Taylor (Secker and Warburg, London 1972).

Hardy, Forsyth (ed.), *Grierson on Documentary,* rev. ed. (Faber, London, 1966).

Hays, Will H., *Motion Pictures: An Outline of the History and Achievements of the Screen from Its Earliest Beginnings to the Present Day* (Doubleday, Garden City, 1929).

Herring, Robert (ed.), *Cinema Survey* (Brendin, London, 1937).

Hillier, Jim and Lovell, Alan, *Studies in Documentary* (Secker and Warburg, London, 1972).

Jacobs, Lewis (ed), *The Documentary Tradition: From Nanook to Woodstock* (Hopkinson and Blake, New York, 1971).

Jones, Stephen G., *The British Labour Movement and Film, 1918–1939* (Routledge & Kegan Paul, London, 1987).

Kennedy, Joseph P. (ed.), *The Story of the Films* (A. W. Shaw, New York, 1927).

Klingender, F. D. and Legg, S., *Money Behind the Screen* (Lawrence and Wishart, London, 1937).

Lambert, R. S., *Propaganda* (Nelson and Sons, London, 1938).

Levin, G. Roy, *Documentary Explorations* (Doubleday, New York, 1971).

Leyda, Jay, *Films Beget Films* (Hill and Wang, New York, 1964).

Lippmann, Walter, *Public Opinion* (Allen and Unwin, London, 1922).

Low, Rachel, *The History of the British Film, 1918–1929* (Allen and Unwin, London 1971).

—*Documentary and Educational Films of the 1930s* (Allen & Unwin, London, 1979).

—*Films of Comment and Persuasion of the 1930s* (Allen & Unwin, London, 1979).

MacCann, Richard Dyer, *The People's Films* (Hastings, New York, 1973).

Mackenzie, A. J., *Propaganda Boom* (John Gifford, London, 1938).

Mackenzie, John M., *Propaganda and Empire: The Manipulation of British Public Opinion, 1880–1960* (Manchester University Press, Manchester, 1984).

—*Imperialism and Popular Culture* (Manchester University Press, Manchester, 1986).

MacPherson, Don (ed.), *Traditions of Independence: British Cinema in the Thirties* (British Film Institute, London, 1980).

McClaine, Ian, *Ministry of Morale: Home Front Morale and the Ministry of Information in World War II* (Allen and Unwin, London, 1979).

Manvell, Roger, *Film,* rev. ed. (Penguin, London, 1950).

—*Films and the Second World War* (Dent and Barnes, London, 1974).

Marwick, Arthur, *Britain in the Century of Total War* (Bodley Head, London, 1968).

Mayer, J. P., *British Cinemas and their Audiences* (Dobson, London, 1948).

—*Sociology of the Film* (Faber, London, 1947).

McArthur, Colin, *Scotch Reels: Scotland in Cinema and Television* (British Film Institute, London, 1982).

Meran Barsam, Richard, *Non-fiction Film: A Critical History* (Allen and Unwin, London, 1974).

Morris, Peter, *Embattled Shadows: A History of Canadian Cinema, 1895–1939* (McGill-Queens University Press, Montreal, 1978).

Muggeridge, Malcolm, *The Thirties* (Hamish Hamilton, London, 1940).

Orbanz, Eva, *Journey to a Legend and Back: The British Realistic Film* (Volker Speiss, Berlin, 1977).

Perry, George, *The Great British Picture Show* (Hart-Davis MacGibbon, London, 1974).

Priestley, J. B., *English Journey* (Heinemann, London, 1934).

Pronay, Nicholas and Thorpe, Francis, *British Official Films in the Second World War: A Descriptive Catalogue* (Clio Press, Santa Barbara, 1980).

Rhode, Eric, *A History of the Cinema from its Origins to 1970* (Allen Lane, London, 1976).

Richards, Jeffrey, *The Age of the Dream Palace: Cinema and Society in Britain 1930–1939* (Routledge & Kegan Paul, London, 1984).

Richards, Jeffrey and Sheridan, Dorothy (eds.), *Mass-Observation at the Movies* (Routledge & Kegan Paul, London, 1987).

Rotha, Paul, *Documentary Film,* 1st ed. (Faber, London, 1936), 3rd ed. (Faber, London, 1952).

—*Rotha on the Film* (Faber, London, 1958).

Smith, Paul (ed.), *The Historian and Film* (Cambridge University Press, Cambridge, 1976).

Spottiswood, Raymond, *A Grammar of the Film* (Faber, London, 1935).

Sussex, Elizabeth, *The Rise and Fall of British Documentary* (University of California Press, London, 1975).

Swann, Paul, *The Hollywood Feature Film in Postwar Britain* (Croom Helm, London, 1987).

Symons, Julian, *The Thirties: A Dream Revolved,* rev. ed. (Faber, London, 1975).

Tallents, Stephen G., *The Projection of England* (Faber, London, 1932).

—*The Birth of British Documentary* (Film Centre, London, 1968).

—*Post Office Publicity* (General Post Office, London, 1935).

Taylor, Philip M., *The Projection of Britain: British Overseas Publicity and Propaganda, 1919–1939* (Cambridge University Press, Cambridge, 1981).

Taylor, Richard, *Film Propaganda: Soviet Russia and Nazi Germany* (Croom Helm, London, 1979).

Thompson, Kristin, *Exporting Entertainment: America in the World Film Market, 1907–1934* (British Film Institute, London, 1985).

Tudor, Andrew, *Theories of Film* (Secker and Warburg, London, 1974).

—*The Uses of the Film* (Bodley Head, London, 1948).

Wright, Basil, *The Long View* (Secker and Warburg, London, 1974).

Articles

Baird, Thomas, "The Film and Civic Education," *Sight and Sound,* 5 (1936), 19.

Cavalcanti, Alberto, "Documents on Celluloid," *Life and Letters Today,* 19 (1938), 88–94.

Crawford, William S., "Publicity Films Reach Studio Quality," *The Commercial Film,* 1 (5) (May 1935), 4.

Colls, Robert and Dodd, Philip, "Representing the Nation – British Documentary Film, 1930–1945," *Screen,* 26 (1), 21–33.

Grierson, John, "The Product of Hollywood," *Motion Picture News,* 6 November 1926, pp. 1755–6.

—"The Documentary Producer," *Cinema Quarterly,* 2 (1933), 7–9.

—"The Industry at the parting of the ways," *Motion Picture News,* 13 November 1926, pp. 1842–3.

—"What Makes a Special?" *Motion Picture News,* 20 November 1926, pp. 1933–4.

—"Putting Punch in a Picture," *Motion Picture News,* 27 November 1926, pp. 2025–6.

—"The Seven Obstacles to Progress (part 1)," *Motion Picture News,* 11 December 1926, pp. 2225–6.

—"The Seven Obstacles to Progress (part 2)," *Motion Picture News,* 18 December 1926, pp. 2321–2.

—"Film Propaganda Technique," *Kine Weekly,* 18 December 1930, p. 35.

—"One Foot of Film Equals One Dollar of Trade," *Kine Weekly,* 8 January 1931, p. 87.

—"The Artist and the Teacher," *Sight and Sound,* 1 (1932), 45–6.

—"The EMB Film Unit," *Cinema Quarterly,* 1 (1933), 203–8.

—"Propaganda: A Problem for Educational Theory and for Cinema," *Sight and Sound,* 2 (1933), 119–21.

—"The GPO Gets Sound," *Cinema Quarterly,* 2 (1934), 215–21.

—"Introduction to a New Art," *Sight and Sound,* 3 (1934), 101–4.

—"Two Paths to Poetry," *Cinema Quarterly,* 3 (1935), 194–6.

—"Is the Free Film Show a Menace?" *Kine Weekly,* 17 October 1935, p. 13.

—"Why Produce Films by Rule of Thumb?" *Kine Weekly,* 9 January 1936, p. 35.

—"The Future of Documentary," *Cine-Technician,* 2 (1937), 215–21.

—"Propaganda In Its Working Clothes," *World Film News,* 3 (1938), 254–5.

—"World's Fair and Royal Visit are Our Greatest Opportunities in 1939," *Kine Weekly,* 12 January 1939, p. 44.

Hogben, Lancelot, "The New Visual Culture," *Sight and Sound,* 5 (1936), 6–9.

Lee, J. M., "The Dissolution of the EMB, 1933: Reflections on a Diary," *Journal of Imperial and Commonwealth History,* 1 (1972), 49–57.

Legg, Stuart, "Shell Film Unit: Twenty-one Years," *Sight and Sound,* 23 (1954), 209–11.

Luft, H. G., "Rotha and the World," *Quarterly of Film, Radio and Television,* 10 (1955), 89–99.

Pronay, Nicholas, "British Newsreels in the 1930s, 1: Audiences and Producers," *History,* 56 (1971), 411–18.

—"British Newsreels in the 1930s, 2: Their Policies and Impact," *History,* 57 (1972), 63–72.

Redmayne, P. B., "Cadbury Comedies," *The Commercial Film,* 1 (4) (May 1935), 5.

Stead, Peter, "Hollywood's Message for the World: The British Response in the Nineteen Thirties," *Historical Journal of Film, Radio and Television,* 1 (1) (1981), 19–32.

Swann, Paul, "John Grierson and the G.P.O. Film Unit, 1933–1939," *Historical Journal of Film, Radio and Television,* 3 (1983), 17–34.

—"The Selling of the Empire: The EMB Film Unit," *Studies in Visual Communication,* 9 (3) (1983), 15–24.

Taylor, Donald F., "In the Service of the Public," *Sight and Sound,* 2 (1934), 128–31.

Ward, Kenneth, "British Documentaries in the 1930s," *History,* 62 (1977), 426–31.

Willcox, Temple, "Projection or Publicity? Rival Concepts in the Pre-War Planning of the British Ministry of Information," *Journal of Contemporary History*, 18 (1) (1983), 97–116.

Woods, D. L., "John Grierson: Documentary Film Pioneer," *Quarterly Journal of Speech*, 57 (1971), 221–8.

Woolfe, Harry Bruce, "Producing an Educational Film," *Sight and Sound*, 1 (1932), 106–9.

Film periodicals

Cinema Quarterly, 1932–5.

Cine-Technician, 1936–9.

Close Up, 1927–33.

The Commercial Film, 1935–6.

Documentary News Letter, 1940–5.

Sight and Sound, 1932–45.

World Film News, 1936–8.

Press cuttings collections

Cuttings files, Clevedon Court.

Cuttings files, Rotha Collection (University of California at Los Angeles).

Lincoln Center for the Performing Arts, New York.

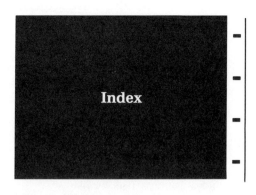

Index